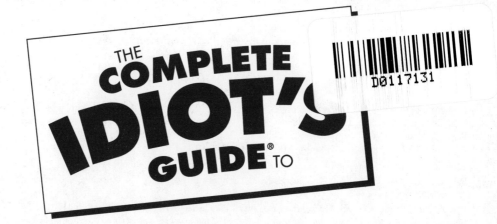

THE
COMPLETE
IDIOT'S
GUIDE® TO

Clear Thinking

by Joe LoCicero, Richard J. LoCicero, M.D.,
and Kenneth A. LoCicero, Ph.D.

ALPHA

A member of Penguin Group (USA) Inc.

With love to Pauline, whose clarity, simplicity, and creativity inspire us always.

ALPHA BOOKS

Published by the Penguin Group

Penguin Group (USA) Inc., 375 Hudson Street, New York, New York 10014, U.S.A.

Penguin Group (Canada), 10 Alcorn Avenue, Toronto, Ontario, Canada M4V 3B2 (a division of Pearson Penguin Canada Inc.)

Penguin Books Ltd, 80 Strand, London WC2R 0RL, England

Penguin Ireland, 25 St Stephen's Green, Dublin 2, Ireland (a division of Penguin Books Ltd)

Penguin Group (Australia), 250 Camberwell Road, Camberwell, Victoria 3124, Australia (a division of Pearson Australia Group Pty Ltd)

Penguin Books India Pvt Ltd, 11 Community Centre, Panchsheel Park, New Delhi—110 017, India

Penguin Group (NZ), cnr Airborne and Rosedale Roads, Albany, Auckland 1310, New Zealand (a division of Pearson New Zealand Ltd)

Penguin Books (South Africa) (Pty) Ltd, 24 Sturdee Avenue, Rosebank, Johannesburg 2196, South Africa

Penguin Books Ltd, Registered Offices: 80 Strand, London WC2R 0RL, England

International Standard Book Number: 1-59257-431-9
Library of Congress Catalog Card Number: 2005930985

07   06   8   7   6   5   4   3

Interpretation of the printing code: The rightmost number of the first series of numbers is the year of the book's printing; the rightmost number of the second series of numbers is the number of the book's printing. For example, a printing code of 05-1 shows that the first printing occurred in 2005.

Printed in the United States of America

Note: This publication contains the opinions and ideas of its authors. It is intended to provide helpful and informative material on the subject matter covered. It is sold with the understanding that the authors and publisher are not engaged in rendering professional services in the book. If the reader requires personal assistance or advice, a competent professional should be consulted.

The authors and publisher specifically disclaim any responsibility for any liability, loss, or risk, personal or otherwise, which is incurred as a consequence, directly or indirectly, of the use and application of any of the contents of this book.

Most Alpha books are available at special quantity discounts for bulk purchases for sales promotions, premiums, fund-raising, or educational use. Special books, or book excerpts, can also be created to fit specific needs.

For details, write: Special Markets, Alpha Books, 375 Hudson Street, New York, NY 10014.

Publisher: *Marie Butler-Knight*
Editorial Director: *Mike Sanders*
Senior Managing Editor: *Jennifer Bowles*
Senior Acquisitions Editor: *Randy Ladenheim-Gil*
Development Editor: *Lynn Northrup*
Production Editor: *Megan Douglass*
Copy Editor: *Keith Cline*

Cartoonist: *Richard King*
Cover/Book Designer: *Trina Wurst*
Indexer: *Angie Bess*
Layout: *Ayanna Lacey*
Proofreading: *John Etchison*

Contents at a Glance

Contents

Foreword

We have been told and readily observe that what separates us from the rest of the animal kingdom is our ability to think. "I think, therefore I am," exclaimed René Descartes in the seventeenth century. Whether you favor Darwin's evolutionary theory or Creationism, we are a unique species capable of generating thoughts and comprehending our emotions; a being that has the ability to remember the past and create our future. It is this very gift that over centuries has afforded mankind tremendous accomplishments. We have demonstrated over centuries our ability to establish civilizations, to travel into the depths of our oceans and into outer space, to combat disease, and to create works of art. Our ability to communicate an idea, an emotion, or a vision—through our voice, our writing, or our action—is our gift, and the tool we utilize to make our achievements possible.

We must understand, however, that every one of us encounters difficulties in our thinking process. From plumbers to prime ministers, janitors, teachers, and astronauts, we *are* all human, and yes, we *do* make mistakes. Poor perceptions, unrealistic goals, negative thoughts, and disruptive emotions can plague true abilities.

Each morning, my alarm goes off at 5:45 A.M. and I begin my day with myriad thoughts that will shape what I am able to accomplish, with whom I interact, where I travel, and what emotions I will experience that day. And these thoughts then lead to action that will affect the days and weeks to follow. I have many roles to fill in this life. I am a son, a brother, a husband, a father, a physician, a boss, a parishioner, a neighbor, a shareholder, a citizen, a voter, and a taxpayer. I am a traveler, a photographer, a skier, a diver, and a musician. I am a few of these things on my own, but mostly I play these roles in relation to someone else. It is primarily my relationships that shape me, and it is my ability to communicate clearly and effectively with others that bring me a sense of joy and accomplishment.

What the LoCicero brothers have cogently illustrated in *The Complete Idiot's Guide to Clear Thinking* is that we have the power to control our thoughts and to harness our emotions through proper mental exercise, enabling our daily works to be more productive. Imagine trying to watch twenty different television channels at once, or read ten different newspapers, or carry on five different conversations at the same time. It cannot be done, or at least it cannot be done effectively. Much of my daily sense of contentment rests on effective communication and my productivity. Clear thinking is required for me to communicate at home with my wife and my three children, at work with my staff and my patients, and in my community with my neighbors. This book offers everyone a guide to learning how the mind works, what factors distort your thinking process, and how to take back control of your thoughts. The LoCicero brothers help you understand how to be an effective receiver of information, how to process it effectively, and ultimately how to communicate it clearly.

Without a doubt, we are bombarded with a vast amount of data being thrown at us on a daily basis. *The Complete Idiot's Guide to Clear Thinking* provides you with many tools to take back control of your thoughts, to learn to think clearly, and to communicate effectively. And this process will lead to realizing your goals and improving your relationships at home, at school, or at the office, providing a sense of happiness and accomplishment for anyone who reads ahead.

Dr. Douglas Mathews

Dr. Douglas Mathews has been practicing neurosurgery for eight years in Nashville, Tennessee. He enjoys his general practice as a partner with Neurological Surgeons, P.C., treating adult intracranial, spinal, and peripheral nerve disorders. Originally from Los Angeles, both Dr. Mathews and his wife of 19 years graduated with honors from UCLA, completed their graduate degrees at Vanderbilt University, and raise their three children in their Nashville home.

Introduction

So you want be a clear thinker, do you? Who wouldn't, particularly because we all know that clear thinking is a boon to a more effective workplace, more productive learning, a thriving home environment, better relationships, less stress, and more thoughtful decision making. Let's face it: today's fast-and-faster-paced times are rife with problematic situations, thorny negotiations, and unclear communication. Now's your chance to blaze a streak through the clouds to successfully meet and conquer all the challenges that fly your way.

To dissect the thinking process, we literally thought a lot about what goes into thinking. Because you're seemingly always in the midst of it, you call on thinking to engage in reasoning, dream up ideas, size up problems, learn, listen, and understand.

But clear thinking faces many obstacles that come in many intrepid forms. There's the avalanche of information you must sift through each day. People you interact with who communicate differently from you. And an onslaught of misconceptions, fallacies, and often-misguided opinions.

Even so, never fear, because *The Complete Idiot's Guide to Clear Thinking* is right here. The enduring benefits of clarity are just pages away! In addition to serving up the ins and outs of thinking and knowing, you'll get the lowdown on logic and reasoning skills, and find great ways to improve your decision making, problem solving, and communication.

How to Use This Book

We organized this book by—in a sense—following how you think. First, we find it helpful to explain and understand the need for making your thinking the most productive it can be. Along with that, you should know how your brain parts work in concert to think, discern, organize, and create. Next, as you're faced with issues, situations, and decisions, you—coming from your own one-of-a-kind perspective—take in information from a variety of available sources. From there, you sift out facts and truths from fiction and opinions, and toss out sheer hokum. Then, you apply the context and concepts of logic and reason. Next, you spin out viable alternatives, put those under scrutiny, and formulate decisions. Finally, you take that thinking you've so expertly experienced and translate those clear thoughts into effective, cogent communication. And after you've mastered the skills, you determine the best ways to keep clear thinking sparked up.

Part 1, "Your Brain Trust," gives you the scoop on the attributes and benefits of clear thinking. We let you assess where you currently stand. And we survey great thinkers who provide windows into the value of knowledge, questioning, and reasoning, and tell you how to emulate them in your own thinking. We also take a tour of the left and right halves of the brain and tell you how to keep your thinking balanced.

Part 2, "The Invited Guests to Your Thoughts," shows you how to effectively gather information. In doing so, you'll discover how to astutely listen, actively learn, and adeptly understand. You'll realize the value of an open mind as you approach thinking and how to be attuned to the background you bring to it. Further, you'll canvass an array of areas offering facts and opinions for your thoughts—and learn how to discern between the two. And you'll become aware of information to avoid, which comes in such misleading forms as hoaxes and superstitions.

Part 3, "The Age of Reason," focuses on applying logic and reason to your critical thinking. We discuss concepts such as deduction, induction, fallacies, and common sense. And you'll discover the importance of and strategies behind generating alternatives. Then in considering those choices, you'll bone up on ways to make and evaluate decisions, form opinions, and shape judgments.

Part 4, "Resolve, Express, Engage!" shows you how to use clear thinking to define problems and the methods necessary to solve them. You'll also find tips, tools, and instructions to clearly state your case, message, or point of view. With this guidance, you can put your clear thoughts into wonderfully articulate spoken and written formats. And expressing clear thoughts also extends into creativity, and bringing them to fruition in sound ideas and innovations.

Part 5, "Head Coach," presents physiological ways to keep the flames of clear thinking stoked, including exercise, a healthful diet, and plenty of sleep. And as you continue your journey of clear thinking, you'll get a proper send-off brimming with strategies and wisdom.

Extras

Throughout these chapters, you'll also find six types of boxes that offer extra mental brain food to assist your clear thinking:

Cobweb Buster

Check out these boxes for fun facts, tips, and related information about clear thinking.

Mind Fogger

These boxes contain cautions to help prevent your clear thinking from turning cloudy.

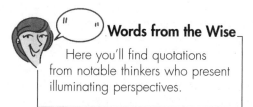

Words from the Wise

Here you'll find quotations from notable thinkers who present illuminating perspectives.

Think Tank

Check these boxes for definitions of words and terms that give more insights into the discussion.

Mind Games

Test your mental agility with these brain teasers, word problems, or perplexing puzzles. If necessary, use pen and paper—or this book's margins—to sketch out your thoughts as you work out these brain teasers.

Points to Ponder

These boxes present you with both age-old and freshly minted questions that we frequently face, either in individual pursuits, one-on-one conversations, or roundtable discussions.

Acknowledgments

We were fortunate to have been brought up by parents, Joe and Gloria, who prize clear thinking. We grew up in a robust, rousing household in which talents of all kinds were cultivated and cherished … which is how they ended up with a writer, an oncologist, a Ph.D., and an athletic guru as their kids. They imbued us with a sense that intellectual pursuits bring great rewards, and an open mind is a necessity. In that, they provided a vibrant, healthy foundation in which discussions and conversations were encouraged and enjoyed … and still continue to be. We'll always be so grateful. And, of course, in that household, our sister Suzanne was always quick to provide a dynamic female perspective; her insights into health and happiness particularly inspire us all.

Joe would also like to thank Jacky, an incredible agent who's got smarts, personality, good humor, and spot-on sensibilities … in spades. Gratitude also goes to Libby Gill for her generosity of spirit and her spirit of generosity. And deep, heartfelt appreciation to Ronda Rich, whose belief in him and Practical Whimsy set this era of authorship in motion. Plus, to Ron, thank you for your wisdom as a masterful mental architect.

Behind every good man is a better woman, and for Joe, that would be Lori. Her discerning eye, keen common sense, and inimitable wit allow creativity, ideas, and happiness to flourish, make every day an adventure, and light up their lives with grace and humor. And to the amazing Dalton and charming Garcy, daily reminders of all good things.

With the seriousness of his daily work, Ric appreciates the balance that his lively, beautiful family—wife, LeeAnn, and their children, Eli, Mary Elle, Tucker, and Paulina Jane—consistently offers.

Ken would like to thank his wife, Amie, his (better) partner in everyday clear thinking; and Ethan and Alex, who challenge and inspire him to be a clear thinker every day.

Trademarks

All terms mentioned in this book that are known to be or are suspected of being trademarks or service marks have been appropriately capitalized. Alpha Books and Penguin Group (USA) Inc. cannot attest to the accuracy of this information. Use of a term in this book should not be regarded as affecting the validity of any trademark or service mark.

Part 1

Your Brain Trust

How clear is your thinking? Is it usually sharp or continually fuzzy? You've got the goods; you've just got to make sure you're using them to maximum advantage. Let's analyze your thinking, and find out how the left and right sides of the brain work in tandem and influence how you think. Plus, we visit the domain of some great thinkers who—by providing excellent examples of powerful thinking—can help you unleash your own potential.

Let's Be Clear

In This Chapter

- ◆ Understand the need for clear thinking now more than ever
- ◆ Take inventory of possible obstacles to your own clear thinking
- ◆ Realize the advantages of clear thinking
- ◆ Find out how clear thinking can lead to more opportunities, increased productivity, less stress, and better decision making

Thinking: You're always in the midst of it—in the car, in your cubicle, or in the checkout line. Perhaps you recognize that you think not only in the classroom, but also on the ball field, at home, at the movies. There's just no escaping it! But that's not necessarily a bad thing.

Although today's challenging times may sometimes cloud our thinking, we can often crystallize our thoughts with just a moment of concentration. Beginning in this chapter, you learn how clear thinking can help you cope with trying times. (And you don't have to be in front of a chalkboard to "do it.")

Mind Games 1

A house has four walls; each wall faces south, and there's a window in each wall. A bear walks by one of the windows. What color is the bear?

(Turn to Appendix D for the answer.)

The Need for Clear Thinking Now More Than Ever

Notice your thinking patterns as you're in the midst of thoughts today. Are you fuzzy with repetitive or tangential thoughts, or do you generally stay focused?

Think Tank

Thinking involves using your mind to consider ideas, make judgments and choices, determine beliefs, imagine, understand, and focus on a subject. To be most effective, it requires precision, clarity, creativity, and balance. When you **understand,** you can effectively and definitively detail, explain, or express something.

Simply stated, *thinking* refers to the mental patterns and processes we use to arrive at decisions, make choices, believe, ponder, and imagine. Unfortunately, thoughts don't always follow a straight path to a logical destination. Sometimes the path may be quite crooked, and the destination can even seem less than logical.

You may believe your thinking is completely untamable, enveloped in fog or clogged with clutter and minutiae. You think, "Oh, if I could just have a few moments of calm, a chance to collect my thoughts, then ... I could have clear thoughts once again."

Here's the reality check: all that chaos is here to stay, but it doesn't have to roll over your thoughts. Whether you realize it or not, you have the power to get your wits about you, straighten them out, and keep them that way.

To begin, let's take a look at some of the factors prominent in all our lives that inhibit clear thinking.

Information Overload

According to a *Reuters Magazine* item nearly 10 years ago, in the past 30 years mankind has produced more information than in the previous 5,000 years. And nearly 20 years ago, a 1987 item concluded that a single issue of *The New York Times* contained more information than a seventeenth-century man or woman would have encountered in a lifetime.

Recently, have you been the victim of any of these "information ills"?

- Frustrated with figures out of Congress

- Confused by cultures with different agendas

- Baffled by too many choices

- Puzzled by nutrition labels

- Confounded by price structures

- Appalled by a company's ethics and policies

- Perturbed that you couldn't get your message across

In one way or another, all of these areas represent reasons why clear thinking is necessary, particularly today. Unfortunately, all of these things can also prompt immediate misunderstandings and inconsistencies that can muck up our thinking. We're living in a lightning-speed age that calls for us to process information quickly. If we want to keep on top of it all, we have to think—correctly and critically.

Advertising and Publicity

Information overload is magnified as companies collectively spend billions of dollars to get their message (that is, their product) across. Studies report that Americans are exposed to as many as 3,000 advertising messages a day!

Publicity machines churn out their own information with startling force. Publicity revolves around companies or personalities using the media—by planting a story or the seed for it—to disseminate a message. That method is even more confusing (and sometimes troubling) because the publicity can be dressed up as a news story when it's really just an advertisement.

Terror and Error

Although thinking has always been vital to survival, two events at the beginning of this millennium highlight a distinct and crucial need for clearer thinking: 9/11 and the 2004 U.S. presidential election.

The events of 9/11 caused many people to simply ask "Why?" and impelled them to spend a considerable amount of time thinking about their everyday lives and futures. Some aspects Americans have considered since the tragedy have involved the consequences of taking a flight, where they live, and how to survive a terrorist attack.

Unstable world events; elevated threat warnings; and random, horrifying terrorist attacks have seized our psyches, pushing panic buttons that cripple clear thinking.

And then, exacerbating this volatile atmosphere, we're not always given the straight "facts." Intelligence columnist Marilyn Vos Savant describes the era beginning in 1992 as "the reign of error." She believes that the presidential campaigns of Bill Clinton, George Bush, and Ross Perot inundated voters with mangled statistics and information that ushered in a new era of politics.

Many believe that the 2004 election continued this trend. Prime-time newscasts and news-channel programs devoted large chunks of telecasts to analyze statistics candidates cited during their stops and stumps. With seemingly gleeful abandon, each party tweaked figures to their advantage. Health care, the cost of the Iraq War, Social Security, energy plans … the avalanche of misinformation was staggering, no matter whom you voted for.

Cobweb Buster

Use your head; don't just take an election stat for granted. FactCheck.org, a website from the Annenberg Public Policy Center, is a nonpartisan, nonprofit entity that monitors factual accuracy of information disseminated—such as ads, speeches, and news releases—by major U.S. political players to determine the whole truth.

Even after John Kerry conceded defeat, the web, newspapers, and networks attempted to elaborate on or debunk myths regarding the roles of homophobia, the Christian right, young-voter apathy, and absent morality that had perhaps cost Democrats the election. So then, what's the best way to establish beliefs and form opinions?

External and Internal Factors

National politics don't have a monopoly on murky motives and questionable ethics that raise concerns and confound consumer thinking. You constantly have to keep in mind that, no matter what the situation, getting the facts straight may sometimes be a daunting task. You may feel you're gathering your information and facts from trustworthy sources, but those sources may be serving their own agendas. With the breadth of information overload, it follows that messages you're receiving could be at cross-purposes.

For example, the FDA is trusted with approving drugs for consumers. Recently, however, they have come under fire for being too cozy with the pharmaceutical firms they monitor. Unfortunately, accusations arose after two drugs proved to have fatal effects. The FDA previously had this information, but had failed to act on it. With this matter in mind, what questions should you ask the next time a drug is prescribed for you?

Beyond these "external" factors, your "internal" surroundings in the environmental, relationship, personal, and occupational realm can affect your thinking. For instance, time spent thinking about messy relationships or an energy-draining job can cause you to lose focus.

Maybe you've got an unproductive internal dialogue going on, perhaps flitting back and forth from subject to subject: the project you can't get off the ground, relationships, paying the bills. It's what yoga instructors call *monkey mind*, and it might be affecting you, rendering clear thinking impossible.

Think Tank

If you've got a **monkey mind,** your thoughts swing wildly, preventing you from concentrating on any single topic.

Take a moment now to answer these two questions, which suggest mental blockades that might be hampering your clear thinking:

♦ What's in your way, *externally*, from enjoying clear thinking?

♦ What's in your way, *internally*, from enjoying clear thinking?

A clouded mind is fertile ground for fear and panic, which limit your choices, affect your relationships, induce stress, and diminish happiness. Clearing out an overwhelmed mind might seem daunting, but don't lose hope. Help is on the way!

Where Are You on the "Clear Thinking" Scale?

Take stock of where you are on the "clear thinking" scale by completing the following quiz. This quiz explores five general areas, and the sections that follow the quiz offer some tips to improve your rating in each one. Think before you answer!

1. I see problems as opportunities.

    a. Never

    b. Sometimes

    ✓ c. Frequently

    d. Always

2. I'm open to others' views and opinions.

    a. Never

✓ b. Sometimes

    c. Frequently

    d. Always

3. I get my current events information from a newspaper.

    a. Never

✓ b. Sometimes

    c. Frequently

    d. Always

4. I jump to conclusions.

    a. Always

    b. Frequently

✓ c. Sometimes

    d. Never

5. During conversations, I've used stereotypes as a quick way to sum up a race, nationality, or group of people.

    a. Always

    b. Frequently

    c. Sometimes

✓ d. Never

6. Emotions factor heavily into my thoughts.

    a. Always

✓ b. Frequently

    c. Sometimes

    d. Never

7. I give my mind a workout with jigsaw puzzles, mind teasers, crossword puzzles, or Scrabble.

     a. Never

     b. Sometimes

  ✓ c. Frequently

     d. Always

8. I make lists that result in action.

     a. Never

  ✓ b. Sometimes

     c. Frequently

     d. Always

9. I meet goals.

     a. Never

  ✓ b. Sometimes

     c. Frequently

     d. Always

10. I'm an "idea" person.

     a. Always

  ✓ b. Frequently

     c. Sometimes

     d. Never

11. I'm gullible.

     a. Always

     b. Frequently

  ✓ c. Sometimes

     d. Never

12. I find it easy to understand others.

     a. Never

   ✓ b. Sometimes

     c. Frequently

     d. Always

13. My vocabulary is:

     a. Limited

   ✓ b. Good, but I don't use all I know

     c. Large, but I do mess up meanings sometimes

     d. Expansive, and I use it!

14. I'm typically afraid to ask questions.

     a. Always

   ✓ b. Frequently

     c. Sometimes

     d. Never

15. I'm not afraid to admit that I'm wrong.

   ✓ a. Never

     b. Sometimes

     c. Frequently

     d. Always

16. I proofread my e-mails before I send them.

     a. Never

     b. Sometimes

   ✓ c. Frequently

     d. Always

17. I engage in a relaxing (and commercial-free) activity (such as movies, reading, playing cards) at least twice a week.

    a. Never

    b. Sometimes

    ✓c. Frequently

    d. Always

18. I exercise 3 or 4 times a week, 30 minutes per session.

    a. Never

    b. Sometimes

    ✓ c. Frequently

    d. Always

19. I give in to irrational thoughts.

    a. Always

    b. Frequently

    ✓ c. Sometimes

    d. Never

20. I'm easily diverted from the task at hand.

    a. Always

    ✓ b. Frequently

    c. Sometimes

    d. Never

21. I tend to get stuck on small details.

    a. Always

    b. Frequently

    ✓ c. Sometimes

    d. Never

22. I can call on expert research techniques and sources to get information.

    a. Never

    ✓ b. Sometimes

    c. Frequently

    d. Always

23. My common-sense gauge is:

    a. Nonexistent

    b. Slow

    ✓ c. Steady

    d. Vroom-vroom!

24. I take on a problem without defining it.

    a. Always

    ✓ b. Frequently

    c. Sometimes

    d. Never

25. I take forever to make a decision.

    a. Always

    ✓ b. Frequently

    c. Sometimes

    d. Never

For each *a* answer, give yourself 0 points; for each *b*, 1 point; for each *c*, 2 points; and for each *d*, 4 points. Total your points, and then go back and review your answers. Do you notice any trends in specific areas—clutter, relationships, information sources, spare-time choices?

For a little extra credit, give yourself 1 point for each one of these statements that you agree with:

__1__ I know the difference between a subjective and objective view.

__1__ I'm a whiz with brain teasers.

_____ I know the difference between thinking and knowing.

_____ I know the limits of the Internet.

42

_____ I frequently ponder life's big questions.

How did you do?

76–105: Blue skies ahead. You're a clear thinker, looking for ways to maintain your clarity and extend your vision.

51–75: Partly sunny with scattered showers. You can improve the way you think in a few areas. Because more than a few questions gave you pause, you've got some work ahead.

Cobweb Buster _____

Were you born in September? If so, you may be predisposed to clear thinking. September's birthstone—the sapphire—has long been believed to be a symbol of clear thinking.

26–50: Thunderstorms. You're a prime candidate to consider and exercise the intricacies and processes of thinking in new ways. So, get ready to put your thinking cap on for the long haul; flashes of insight will soon be in your forecast.

0–25: Sound the alarm, it's a fog alert! Your thinking is completely clouded. It's time to hunker down and gird yourself for a clarity breakthrough.

This quiz focuses on five areas that clear thinking particularly benefits: options and opportunities, productivity, relationships, stress, and decisions. You'll see that some questions do overlap areas.

Realize More Options and Opportunities

Cloudy thinking inhibits choices, perhaps even obfuscating obvious options. Questions 1 through 6 delved into this area.

When you're open—to information, to ideas, to other people's views—the world opens up for you. You can more easily recognize and evaluate your "real" options. Further, being open means shedding prejudice, refusing stereotypes, and avoiding assumptions. To understand your real options and opportunities, follow these suggestions:

♦ Gather information from an array of sources. Start with a major newspaper, which can often offer opposing views, pros and cons, and just plain facts on a wealth of topics. Then consult magazines, attend lectures, and surf the web to extend your breadth.

◆ Engage in activities that require you to make choices. For example, Scrabble forces you to rearrange letters to form different words. Even a hand of poker offers options.

◆ The next time someone presents an opposing viewpoint to yours, don't immediately put your own opinion out there. Follow up their viewpoint with questions about where they're coming from. Then even try a little investigation on your own to see if you might come to their side of thinking.

Increase Your Productivity

When you think clearly, productivity follows. A clear mind means sizing up problems and obstacles, and gearing up for creative problem solving. Productivity was key to questions 7 through 11.

Productivity is the physical representation of clear thinking. Tasks that enhance clear thinking (and hence productivity) include making lists that prompt action, budgeting, and figuring out ways to make a profit. Here are a few tips for improving productivity:

◆ Determine when during the day you think most clearly. (Early morning, late at night?) Then work on your toughest tasks at this peak "thinking" time.

◆ Always have another task at hand in case your focus starts to wane on one particular task. Perhaps attention to the other task will clear your thinking and allow you to return to the original task with a fresh perspective.

Improve Your Relationships

Clear thinking leads to wonderful and articulate communication, which is key to successful relationships, the focus of questions 12 through 16. That's especially crucial in light of a 2004 Gallup poll that concluded that nearly 60 percent of all divorces result from poor communication, and the poor conflict-resolution skills that prompts. Fortunately, clear thinking in this area can help immensely.

How often are you in a conversation with someone and realize that you're not understanding each other? Often, we just can't convey our thoughts articulately. However, you'd be surprised how clear thinking on your part can create a domino effect. In other words, if you're exact in the information or feelings you present, you may find it easier to understand where someone else is coming from—and even help the other person to get a point across more cogently. Consider these avenues for tapping into clear thinking to improve your communication:

- Get away from the Internet if it's occupying a lot of your spare time (and thinking). If you're not interacting with others face to face, you're losing "practice" time in using your thinking to communicate with others. The web is a valuable tool, but don't let it atrophy your social skills. Studies show that the more someone has attached his or her social life to the Internet, the more it conflicts with "real life." And if you don't know real life, you can't think clearly about it.

- Increase your vocabulary. The more words you know, the greater your ability to articulate your thoughts to others.

- Check out your listening skills. Are you really hearing others? Are you listening without interrupting? The next conversation you have, try to summarize it in a line or so. What was discussed? Was it negative or positive? What views were expressed? Did the conversation have an outcome? If so, what was it?

> **Words from the Wise**
>
> The niftiest turn of phrase, the most elegant flight of rhetorical fancy, isn't worth beans next to a clear thought clearly expressed.
>
> —Jeff Greenfield, media analyst

Reduce Stress

Cloudy thinking fosters stress. When you're not thinking clearly, you open yourself up to the dastardly devices of fear, which can encroach on your clarity. And, of course, fear can produce such nasty byproducts as panic and stress. The preceding quiz tested this area in questions 17 through 19. Try these tips to combat stress:

- Don't give in to irrational thoughts. When panic ensues, step back for a reality check.

- Stay away from local news, particularly late newscasts before bedtime. "If it bleeds, it leads" is the editorial policy of many of these newscasts, and you want to avoid cluttering your mind (especially late at night) with the gruesome and sensational. Local news isn't the only source of such anxiety-inducing reporting. For example, although almost everyone gets a kick out of tabloid sensationalism (even if it's while standing in a checkout line), don't rely on those sources for your daily, weekly, or even monthly news doses.

◆ Don't let advertising be brain food; it's brain candy at best. Advertising might steer your thoughts into wayward, unproductive directions.

◆ Give your mind respite from the daily grind. If you're always focused on the kids, your career, or your partner, take time out for activities that refresh, but don't mute, the mind. Go to the movies. Read. Play cards with friends. That is, engage in activities that free up your thoughts.

◆ Get some exercise. Besides offering the obvious benefits, exercise inhibits stress. A freeing quality pervades not only your body, but also your mind when you engage in activities that promote cardiovascular health, flexibility, and strength. You just feel better! And let's face it, when you feel better, you think better.

Make Well-Reasoned Decisions

Thinking clearly involves concentration to navigate the many decisions you must make every day. And decisions include forming sound opinions, drawing definitive conclusions, and making fair judgments, components addressed in questions 20 through 25. Clear thinking enables you to avoid delays and confusion that can lead to indecision.

Clear thinking also enables you to weed out extraneous factors that you might have once thought relevant to a particular decision but now (with clear thinking) understand to be irrelevant to a specific decision you must make. Try these tips:

◆ Improve your logic and reasoning skills by trying out some brain puzzles and word problems. Is anything keeping you from getting the final answer?

◆ When making decisions, consider the big picture. Small things (that might not matter in the long run) often prevent clear thinking regarding bigger matters.

◆ Don't put off decisions because you're afraid you might make the wrong choice.

Enjoy Greater Happiness

The best reward from clear thinking? All of these areas—ample opportunities, buzzing productivity, fulfilling relationships, less stress, and sound decisions—can work in tandem to bring you greater happiness. Cloudy thinking can make everything look gray. Clear thinking, on the other hand, can brighten almost every aspect of your life. That's the goal of this book: to enhance clarity in all the diverse ways you think.

Next up, we examine specific attributes that can make your thinking powerful.

The Least You Need to Know

◆ Clear thinking enables you to cut through malarkey, bias, and clutter to get to facts, truth, and real information.

◆ External and internal factors may cloud thinking. Understand those factors, but don't let them trouble your thoughts.

◆ Take inventory of your clear thinking and pinpoint the areas that need a little help or complete restructuring. After you do, you can sharpen those fuzzy areas with exercises that foster improvement.

◆ As a clear thinker, you recognize more options, have higher productivity and better communication, and reduce your stress—all of which make decision making easier.

2

The Power of Clear Thinking

In This Chapter

- ◆ Get a working definition of thinking clearly
- ◆ Discover the attributes of great thinking
- ◆ Test-drive your thinking
- ◆ Learn about famous thinkers and what makes them stand out
- ◆ Apply famous thinkers' brainpower to your own thinking

This chapter takes clear thinking to the next level by pointing out some of the characteristics you can aspire to in forming your own thoughts.

By outlining the accomplishments of some of history's most famous thinkers, this chapter details the strengths they embraced that made their thinking so powerful. And from there, this chapter delineates how their ways of thinking can influence your own.

Mind Games 2

In an Atlanta bookstore, a copy of *Gone with the Wind* is rumored to have a $100,000 bill hidden in it. Although you'd have to canvass every bookstore in the area, you've been given the page numbers 341–342 in which to find the bill. So do you visit every bookstore in Atlanta, or write it off as an impossible task?

(Turn to Appendix D for the answer.)

Thinking Defined

"Beauty fades, but dumb is forever." As this old saying suggests, sound thinking is far more reliable—and age-proof—than good looks, making sharp thoughts the one constant you can depend on for success.

So what makes thinking so hot? As poet and philosopher George Matthew Adams said, "What you think means more than anything else in your life." That being the case, thinking—specifically, clear thinking—includes *critical thinking*, which refers to the disciplined skill, aptitude, and desire to assess information gathered, verify or deny it, and then make objective judgments based on it. Critical thinking requires sound reasoning to make those judgments that ultimately guide beliefs and action. Critical thinking requires conscious awareness, the practice known as *metacognition*. (In short, metacognition basically means you're thinking about your thinking.)

In 1909, philosopher John Dewey defined critical thinking as "active, persistent, and careful consideration of a belief or supposed form of knowledge in the light of the grounds which support it and the further conclusions to which it tends." Several philosophers and psychologists have weighed in since then. In 1997, thinking and education gurus Paul Fisher and Michael Scriven found it also required "skilled and active interpretation and evaluation of observations and communications, information, and argumentation."

Think Tank

Critical thinking refers to taking a disciplined approach to gathering information that you will determine is true or false, and then employing reason to make decisions based on your findings. **Metacognition** is thinking about your thinking.

Although critical thinking is essential to clear thinking, the latter goes "outside the box" to engage in other activities such as imagining, planning, problem solving, and communicating well. Before continuing, consider this: what does the term *clear thinking* mean to you?

Thinking Territories

Throughout this book, you will learn to master various techniques to focus your thinking. Therefore, a clear understanding of the terms employed herein is quite essential. The following terms are defined here so that you understand their meaning within the context of this book. To be a clear thinker, you have to master these areas. Consider this list your "clear thinking" mini-dictionary.

Brainstorming. The act of suggesting, devising, or generating creative ideas, techniques, or processes that promote new and effective directions

Communicating. The exchange and interchange of words, thoughts, messages, and opinions, either oral or written.

Discerning. To see, identify, and be aware of a difference or differences; to discriminate or distinguish.

Evaluating. Being able to rate or appraise, with tendencies geared toward determining whether collected information has met, fallen short of, or exceeded its expectations.

Learning. The process of gaining knowledge or information; ascertaining inquiry, study, or investigation; and acquiring the understanding of a skill, topic, or situation.

Listening. To give close attention with the purpose of hearing, and fully digesting what has been heard.

Logic. The science, and sometimes art, of exact reasoning or pure and formal thought, or of the laws according to which the processes of pure thinking should be conducted; the science and formation and applications of found notions.

Questioning. The act of asking and examining, allowing for more insights in the course of questions followed by answers.

Reasoning. Systemically combing through thoughts and considerations offered up that support the determination of an opinion, or present just grounds for a conclusion or action.

Research. Diligent inquiry or examination in seeking facts or principles; often the best research will also look for "two sides" to the story or problem being addressed.

Understanding. To "get it," such that you can take information and knowledge you've learned and expertly apply it to another situation, or to everyday living.

The Attributes of Clear Thinking

Now that you understand some prominent concepts regarding thought, let's see how you can enhance various attributes to attain a state of clear thinking.

In the course of a day, your thinking draws on a wide range of subject areas, including science, math, history, anthropology, economics, philosophy, and moral beliefs. A wandering mind, unsurprisingly, often results from the range of subjects dealt with daily.

However, the universal criteria for clear thinking are clarity, accuracy, precision, consistency, relevance, sound empirical evidence, good reasons, depth, breadth, and fairness. Those who can organize their ideas into sequences or chains of logic typically reason their way effectively through confused or complicated situations in everyday living. Let's attach some common adjectives to our own view of clear thinking:

Detailed	Intelligent
Articulate	Deep
Well organized	Lively
Illuminating	Enterprising
Direct	Successful

And while we're at it, let's also list the scourges of fuzzy thinking:

Ambiguous	Misleading
Chaotic	Anxiety-provoking
Dull	Lethargic
Cluttered	Superficial
Unfocused	Unproductive

It's pretty clear which qualities you want at your command. Understanding the difference between clear and cloudy thinking can help in your endeavors to …

◆ Gather your facts and conduct the necessary research.

◆ Dispel myths and superstitions.

◆ Employ apt logic and sound reasoning.

◆ Consider all your options.

◆ Make a decision.

◆ State your case, cogently and articulately, orally or in writing.

That's where this book comes in: you'll learn to extract the facts from the onslaught of information you face, employ reason and logic, and apply creative techniques for solutions.

Great Thinkers and What They Can Teach Us

Let's take a look at some of society's cherished thinkers—past and present—and how they attained that distinction. The tentacles of their unparalleled thoughts, findings, research, and knowledge have stretched far beyond their areas of discipline to pervade culture. Understanding where these thinkers were (and are) coming from, and their accomplishments, provides valuable insights into what we should prize—and strive for—in our own thought processes.

Socrates, 469–399 B.C.E.: Philosophy King

Considered the king of *philosophy* and *ethics*, Socrates was a great debater who advanced the idea that—in the pursuit of truth—questioning sets you free. Socrates became adept at questioning everything, setting the standard for all subsequent Western philosophy.

The Socratic method is posing a series of questions that—when successively answered—chip away to uncover a person or group's true beliefs about a topic. In his series *The Socratic Dialogues*, Plato communicates Socrates' ideas through the characters engaging in the Socratic method under the guidance of Socrates.

> **Think Tank**
>
> **Philosophy** is the branch of knowledge committed to understanding the tenets of truth, existence, and reality. **Ethics** is the branch of philosophy that examines what is "right" and "wrong," "good" and "bad."

An adequate inheritance from his sculptor father enabled Socrates to pursue his philosophical teachings with a legion of young men in Athens. The fact that he wouldn't accept payment for his instruction made him that much more popular. In the throes of these endeavors, he invented the practice of philosophical dialogue.

He regarded exercising mental power as a sacred duty and insisted that others rid themselves of ignorance and folly. His careful study of ethical problems in himself and others gave him remarkable tact in dealing with questions of morality. He is credited with founding the branch of philosophy known as ethics. Further, eager to banish vagueness in thought and laxity in speech, he advocated reason in all things— and fashioned himself to be a ready reasoner.

His wife, Xanthippe, was deemed a shrew by the day's cultural standards. But Socrates referred to the marriage as ideal training for dealing with all types of people, basically concluding that living with a difficult person makes you more of a "people person," enabling you to train your thoughts better to deal with any personality type.

He's particularly noted for his study and teachings about the five virtues: piety, wisdom, temperance, courage, and justice. He took his critics to task with a thorough examination of such topics. To their chagrin, Socrates pointed out their inconsistencies and inadequacies, raising questions that frustrated them.

Although Socrates wasn't directly prosecuted for political activities, he was found guilty of corrupting youth and interfering with the religion of the city and sentenced to death by drinking hemlock. Fittingly, his conviction prompted great debate.

Socrates often contended that his own wisdom was made up of the fact that "he knew that he knew nothing." Along those lines, he also taught that all wrongdoing by man could be attributed to that person's lack of knowledge.

Plato, 427–347 B.C.E.: Knowledge Rules

Plato began his philosophical career as a student of Socrates. He established the Academy, one of the earliest known schools of higher education, with studies including physical science, astronomy, mathematics, and philosophy. While at the Academy, he not only advanced Socratic thinking, but also guided his students to use math to achieve abstract philosophical truths.

Cobweb Buster

Plato's views rejected sensory experiences in trying to find the truth. He believed that, because they change from person to person, they were too unreliable to be regarded as dependable. Plato's protégé Aristotle would later make exceptional points that experiences and observations give your arguments more credence and your thoughts more heft.

Many records suggest that Socrates' trial moved Plato to present his master's philosophical teachings to prevent similar injustices from occurring in society.

Plato's early Socratic dialogues delved into a single issue, such as *Laches* (courage), *Euthryphro* (piety), and *Charmides* (temperance). One of Plato's masterpieces is *The Republic*, which begins with a Socratic conversation about the nature of justice and segues to an extended discussion of the virtues as they appear both to individuals and society as a whole. The work suggests a utopian society in which each individual contributes his best talents to benefit the whole.

At the heart of Plato's philosophy is his theory of forms or ideas. Plato was convinced that knowledge is attainable and has two essential characteristics. First, knowledge must be certain and infallible. Second, knowledge must have as its object that which is genuinely real as contrasted with that which is an appearance only. For instance, the theory therefore holds that there is the definition or idea of a dog. While the "idea" of a dog would be considered perfect, the physical manifestations of dogs—the actual poodle on the street or the terrier in the backyard—can never measure up to the idea. The theory of forms was not restricted to material objects; it could also extend to concepts of beauty, justice, truth, and even math. The theory of forms would even eventually have an effect on Christian ideology, in the belief that man is made in the image of God.

Aristotle, 384–322 B.C.E.: Logic Pioneer

Aristotle initially took his lead from Plato, who schooled him for 20 years at the Academy. When Plato died, Aristotle returned to his native Macedonia, and reportedly began the education of Alexander (eventually the Great). With Alexander's blessing, Aristotle returned to Athens and opened his own school at the Lyceum.

Aristotle is recognized as one of history's few figures who studied practically every subject possible during his time, including anatomy, astronomy, embryology, geology, geography, meteorology, physics, and zoology. In philosophy, he wrote on aesthetics, economics, ethics, government, metaphysics, politics, psychology, rhetoric, and theology.

Words from the Wise

It is the mark of an educated mind to be able to entertain a thought without accepting it.
—Aristotle

In his logical treatises—known collectively as the *Organon*—Aristotle sought to develop a universal method of reasoning so that you could learn everything there is to know about reality. Recognized as the inventor of formal logic, Aristotle devised a litany of reasoning concepts, creating new truths from established principles.

Unlike Plato and others before him, Aristotle was a huge proponent of observation. He believed that investigating an issue involved considering opinions of experts and laypersons before detailing your own arguments. For this reason, he is often considered the father of *empiricism* and scientific method.

Aristotle proposed that man's primary function is to reason, and to reason well, you must do so with virtue.

Sigmund Freud, 1856–1939: A Boon to Self-Discovery

Viennese neurologist Sigmund Freud is the founder of modern-day psychoanalysis, a term he coined in 1896. One of the most significant scientists of the twentieth century, Freud influenced the professional practices of psychology (the study of the mind) and psychiatry (medical treatment pertaining to the mind), and arguably changed the way people in Western cultures think about themselves and their lives.

The crux of Freud's movement pertained to *unconscious* motives controlling much of a person's behavior. (Unconscious is also described as subconscious, although that is technically not a psychological term.)

Opening a private practice in 1886, Freud initially sought to treat nervous and brain disorders. But his practice evolved as he realized that he could get patients to talk by putting them in a relaxing position on, say, a couch. When he did, he encouraged them to engage in free association, and they would say whatever came to mind. From there, he could analyze their memories or expressions and determine past traumatic events that were prompting current suffering.

With his treatment, Freud contended that patients weren't always driven by conscious thoughts and that a person's awareness occurred in layers. He also proposed a structure for the unconscious: *id, ego,* and *superego*. Id represents gratifying basic needs, superego counteracts the id with moral and ethical thoughts, and ego serves as the balance. Overall, the goal of Freudian therapy was to bring repressed thoughts and feelings to the forefront so that a patient could develop a stronger ego. Now psychoanalysis isn't considered so much a cure for mental illness as a part of the process of self-discovery, a chance for clearing out thoughts so that clear thinking can ensue.

Albert Einstein, 1879–1955: Sheer Genius

So there's genius, and then there's sheer genius. Albert Einstein—and even just his last name—has become synonymous with concepts of extreme brilliance, amazing discoveries, and boundless intelligence. In addition to his work as a theoretical physicist, he made contributions in the fields of quantum mechanics, statistical mechanics, and cosmology.

The German-born Einstein devised theories for relativity, Brownian motion, and the photoelectric effect. Einstein's achievements are particularly impressive because he boldly took an idea in theoretical physics, devised logical consequences for it, and then lucidly explained experimental results. Previously, each case had baffled other scientists for decades.

Einstein won the Nobel Prize in Physics in 1921 for his work on the photoelectric effect. However, his theory of relativity has served as a linchpin for both his notoriety and his most important work. The central aspect of Einstein's works is that the speed of light is constant. For starters, that notion fuels the famous equation $E = mc^2$; E is energy, m is mass, and c is the speed of light. This equation rules out the possibility that two events can be observed as simultaneous, and promotes the principle that space and time are not independent dimensions. In layman's terms, the theory of relativity brings new meaning to a full complement of topics once regarded as sci-fi hooey, such as time travel, the time continuum, and even between cause and effect. (Just think about those *Back to the Future* movies, and you get the idea.)

Einstein was a professor at the University of Prague in 1911, and—from 1914 through 1933—served as director of the Kaiser Wilhelm Institute for Physics in Berlin. Afterward, he segued to be a professor of theoretical physics at Princeton, retiring from the post in 1945.

Cobweb Buster

Einstein's theory of Brownian motion dealt with random, vibrating movement. His work on the photoelectric effect explained that light striking metal could release energy in particles rather than waves.

Although his research is well chronicled, his more important works include *Special Theory of Relativity* (1905), *Relativity* (1920 and 1950), *General Theory of Relativity* (1916), *Investigations on Theory of Brownian Movement* (1926), and *The Evolution of Physics* (1938). His nonscientific works include *About Zionism* (1930), *Why War?* (1933), *My Philosophy* (1934), and *Out of My Later Years* (1950). He was named "Person of the Century" by *Time* magazine in 1999.

Stephen Hawking, 1942– : The Mind Trumps All

Stephen Hawking is one of the world's leading theoretical physicists, taking over the mantle of Einstein. Since 1979, he has been a Lucasian professor of mathematics at the University of Cambridge in a post endowed since 1679, and once held by Isaac Newton. His principal fields of research are theoretical cosmology and quantum gravity. His major contributions to research include papers on the relationship between black holes and thermodynamics. He has a knack for explaining his complex findings to physicists and the general public alike.

Delving into the basic laws that govern the universe, Hawking was part of the team that showed that Einstein's theory of relativity implied that space and time could have a beginning in the Big Bang and an end in black holes.

His most famous publication—the bestseller *A Brief History of Time* (1988)—describes the origin and future of the universe. In 2002, another plain-speaking book, *The Universe in a Nutshell*, was published.

Despite being disabled by amyotrophic lateral sclerosis (also known as Lou Gehrig's disease) since being diagnosed with it at age 21, Hawking has outlasted the three-year "death sentence" initially given to him. His brilliance has demonstrated that physical challenges don't have to limit the mind's potential.

Marilyn Vos Savant, 1946– : IQ Maven

No discussion of thinkers would be complete without *The Guinness Book of World Records* Hall of Famer for highest IQ, a distinction that goes to Marilyn Vos Savant with a score of 228.

Since 1986, Vos Savant has written the hugely popular "Ask Marilyn" column for the weekly *Parade* magazine, dealing with mathematical and logical puzzles, and even applying those principles to some traditional self-help.

One of her most popular problems was "The Monty Hall Dilemma," which prompted outrageous reader reaction from an array of scholars, professors, mathematicians, and statisticians. That conundrum deals with a contestant facing three doors on a game show, behind one of which stands a grand prize. The dilemma: After picking door 1 and then shown by the host that door 3 has a goat behind it, should the contestant stick with the door he's already chosen or now select door 2 instead? (Vos Savant determined that switching to 2 raised the probability for winning the grand prize because the host's interference had changed the odds). Despite an avalanche of testy reader mail that disputed her answer, Vos Savant held firm. She devoted additional columns to the problem, and calmly offered ways to test her theory, delighting math and science classrooms across the country. Eventually, most of her detractors admitted she was right.

Her books include *The Power of Logical Reasoning* (see Appendix A) and *Brain Building in Just 12 Weeks.* Currently, she also works with her husband, Robert Jarvik, the inventor of the Jarvik-7 and Jarvik 2000 artificial hearts.

What You Can Learn from the Greats

The legacy of each of these thinkers is a call to use your mind to its greatest potential. Let these seven thinkers be your muses as you embrace new ways to think clearly:

1. **Socrates:** "How often do you question?" Socrates teaches us that to examine an issue or an idea to the fullest, we have to use our mind to ask questions about it. Not doing so is a disservice to our reasoning and lulls us into a false sense of security. Never assume that you know something to the full extent; there's always room for another question. So many people too readily accept information as is, without considering that they might not have the whole story.

2. **Plato:** "How important do you think it is to know?" Plato stressed that knowledge supercedes all else. How much do you prize knowledge? Do you regard knowledge as power? With so much information spinning around so forcefully, you owe it to yourself—and your mind—to know as much as possible.

3. **Aristotle:** "Do you take experience and observations for granted?" Aristotle encourages us to explore and experience. Gather knowledge from a range of subjects. Then live! Use your experiences in any of those subjects to help gauge and evaluate.

4. **Freud:** "How deep does your thinking go?" Freud presents a call to delve deeper into your thoughts. Don't consider the surface issue the only one to solve or learn more about. Use it as a springboard to dive into more issues, increasing your awareness and providing you with more insights.

5. **Einstein:** "How well do you communicate?" Einstein was able to put into thoughts and words what so many before had tried but failed to do. You don't have to be talking or writing about universe-changing theories to cogently state your point.

6. **Hawking:** "Do you allow challenges to create obstacles to your thinking?" Taking a cue from Einstein, Hawking has shown ways to make complex principles even clearer. And he hasn't allowed physical challenges to constrain his thinking. Don't let life and conditions get in the way of clarity and growth.

7. **Vos Savant:** "Are you using reasoning and logic to their full extent?" Vos Savant provides a window into how a calm, logical approach avoids fallacies to draw sound conclusions. Take her cue: see what stands to reason and then find a way to figure it out.

Your Clear-Thinking Arsenal

Being a clear thinker comes at the confluence of many factors. To be a clear thinker, you must draw on all of these thinkers' best attributes:

- Appreciating the learning process

- Knowing what it means to understand

- Asking great questions

- Employing logic and reasoning

- Communicating effectively

- Gathering information

- Observing

- Experiencing

- Challenging yourself to know—and think—more

> **Points to Ponder**
>
> Is there someone in your life who you regard as a "great thinker"? Why? What qualities or attributes does that person have that you wish you had?

But before we begin to examine all of these areas more deeply, we need to look more closely at where your thoughts originate: the brain. Optimal clear thinking is only possible when you understand what is happening side by side "upstairs." So next up, an overview of the brain's physiology and, more specifically, the left and right way to think.

The Least You Need to Know

- Thinking draws its power from mastering brainstorming, communicating, discerning, learning, logic, reasoning, and understanding, among other territories.

- Take an honest look at your thinking: in what areas could you use more work?

- Great thinkers such as Socrates, Plato, Aristotle, Freud, Einstein, Hawking, and Vos Savant all present prime examples of clarity through their legacies and approaches.

- Clear thinking requires such practices as asking great questions, gathering information and observing, and appreciating the learning process.

Head Games: Left Brain vs. Right Brain

In This Chapter

◆ Refresh your knowledge of the brain

◆ Recognize the roles and responsibilities of the brain's left and right hemispheres

◆ Determine whether you're a "lefty" or a "righty"

◆ Understand how the other half lives

◆ Learn how two halves can make a more productive and powerful whole

How do you view the world? Through an intuitive and artistic prism or through a logical and scientific looking glass?

This chapter examines some brain physiology—particularly your left and right brain—and their roles in your thinking processes. We review some of the theories behind how your approaches and attitudes can break down into left- and right-brain sensibilities. Getting a handle on your own left and right sides will help you balance your thinking. It'll give you new insights into problem solving and decision making, and help you recognize, deal with, and work with the approaches of others, all in the name of clear thinking.

A Thinker's Best Friend

Meet your brain: the central command center for your body. It's where thinking, remembering, problem solving—and even your personality cues—originate. With rapid-fire speed and impulses, the brain quickly assesses—with help from your five senses—information inside and outside your body that is being thrown at you from all directions. Analyzing this information, the brain transmits messages that control your body's functions and actions.

Although you certainly realize that the gray matter really matters, understanding the specifics on the brain's composition and operations will generate optimal perform-ance. If you can grasp a few simple anatomical notions and primary responsibilities, you can put your noggin to work for you that much more efficiently.

On the thinking front, the brain's interconnected cells allow you to speak, decipher, describe, argue, create, articulate, organize, decide, and dream. That maze of power-ful circuitry can lead you (and maybe has led you) to tackle an algebra equation, plot a marketing plan, strategize a football game, paint a masterpiece, launch a political campaign, or compose a symphony. You can take a stand, share thoughts and ideas, make critical decisions, and develop crucial insights. As it gains and organizes new information, the brain synthesizes current data to influence our present. And previ-ously, it has accumulated information from past experiences to remember tomorrow, help learn today, and shape your future.

As you may remember from high school biology, the brain is composed of three parts:

- **The cerebrum.** The main part of the brain where thinking, feeling, and remembering take place; speaking, your intellect, personality, sensory interpre-tations, motor functions, and the ability to plan and organize are all housed here

- **The cerebellum.** Lying below the back part of the cerebrum, this part of the brain controls balance, posture, and coordination of movement

- **The brain stem.** The part of the brain located at the bottom of the brain; the brain stem controls automatic body functions, such as breathing, heartbeat, and regulation of body temperature

In simplistic terms, your brain actually presents two personalities, a yin and yang combination that—optimally—can provide your thinking with a one-two punch that's knockout-worthy. You might have heard about the left-brain versus right-brain quandary, and maybe even speculated which side you're on. So you may be wondering, "Is it more sane to be guided by the left or more hip to be dictated by the right? And if we all have a dominant half, do I get a say in which half is the stronger one?"

Think Tank

The **corpus callosum** is a thick band of fibers bridging the right and left hemispheres of the brain, allowing the two sides to communicate with each other.

Anatomically speaking, the brain is split into two halves or—more technically—hemispheres. The halves are separated by a deep groove called the *corpus callosum*. This bridge keeps the two halves in touch, swapping information back and forth. Fortunately, that connection keeps the left and right brains working in concert, or you might never get anything done, said, or written.

Each hemisphere seems like it should be completely identical to the other, but they're not, really. The left side of your brain actually controls the actions of your right side and vice versa. The nerves from each side cross over at the top of the spinal cord. However, that doesn't mean that being right-handed makes you "right brain" or vice versa.

Are You a Lefty or a Righty?

Is it better to be right-brained than left-brained? Certainly not! In life, each hemisphere is totally even-Steven. Simply realizing your natural preferences makes you open to try new approaches in thinking, deciding, and problem solving.

Take the following quiz to recognize your "allegiance." After you do, you'll be able to bridge the gap, veering toward "other-side" endeavors that will balance your thoughts regarding problem solving and decision making.

1. How often do you make a decision based on a hunch?

   ✓ a. Often

       b. Rarely

2. Is your work area …

    a. Neat and organized?

✓ b. Chaotic, although you know where most things are?

3. How often are you late for a meeting, appointment, or date?

    a. Very rarely

✓ b. All the time

4. Do you have your best ideas when you're …

    a. Lying down?

✓ b. Sitting up?

5. Do you work on …

✓ a. Several projects at once, in various stages?

    b. One project until it's finished, and only then do you start another one?

6. Would you prefer an art piece to be an …

    a. Ansel Adams?

✓ b. Picasso?

7. When attempting a skill for the first time, do you …

    a. Conduct research through reference books or observation?

✓ b. Jump straight in and see what happens?

8. Is it easier for you to remember someone's …

✓ a. Name?

    b. Face?

9. Do you judge a person's comment by …

✓ a. Its content?

    b. Its pitch or intent?

10. When you start to work on a project, do you have …

✓ a. An overall idea of what the project will entail and look like?

    b. A step-by-step plan of how it will develop?

11. Do you use your hands when you talk?

    a. Hardly ever

    ✔ b. Frequently

12. Do you like to have music playing when you work?

    ✔ a. Yes

    b. No

13. Do you prefer …

    ✔ a. Group activities where you all collaborate and work together?

    b. Working individually, against yourself?

14. When you're working, does time seem to …

    a. Pass by quickly, almost unnoticed?

    ✔ b. Tick-tock, slowly—you're aware of the time you've spent working?

15. When someone asks for input on his work, do you …

    ✔ a. Think carefully before you answer so you don't hurt feelings?

    b. Impulsively say exactly what's on your mind (although you may add comforting comments to soften the blow)?

16. When you want to buy a new (pair of shoes, briefcase, watch), do you …

    ✔ a. Buy it only if you have the money?

    b. Charge it to your credit card regardless?

17. Are you more likely to approach a how-to book by …

    ✔ a. Starting with the table of contents and reading the book in order?

    b. Diving in and reading whatever catches your eye?

18. When you hang a piece of art or photo on a wall, do you …

    ✔ a. Put it up where you think it'll look right and, if necessary, move it until it does?

    b. Use pencil, ruler, and string (or some combination thereof) to ensure it'll be in the right position after it's hung?

19. For you pet people, do you prefer …

    ✓ a. Dogs, who tend to obey what their owner says?

    b. Cats, who tend to retain their independence?

20. Would you be into answering another 10 questions about the left and right brain?

    ✓ a. Totally

    b. No way

Now assess your score by adding up your responses for each brain hemisphere:

Left brain: 1-b, 2-a, 3-a, 4-b, 5-a, 6-a, 7-a, 8-a, 9-a, 10-b, 11-a, 12-b, 13-b, 14-b, 15-a, 16-a, 17-a, 18-b, 19-a, 20-a

Right brain: 1-a, 2-b, 3-b, 4-a, 5-b, 6-b, 7-b, 8-b, 9-b, 10-a, 11-b, 12-a, 13-a, 14-a, 15-b, 16-b, 17-b, 18-a, 19-b, 20-b

You will most likely find a (probably fairly high) number signaling left or right. Don't panic if you thought you're a creative type and tallied up mostly left responses. That just means you might have your two halves more in concert than you thought.

Cobweb Buster _____

This whole concept of right- and left-brain thinking was borne out of research conducted by American Nobel Prize Winner Roger Wolcott Sperry (1913–1994). His research at the California Institute of Technology in the late 1960s separated and identified different functions originating from the left and right hemispheres. Determining where mental processes occurred in the brain, he developed surgical and experimental techniques to study them. With Canadian-born David H. Hubel and Sweden's Torsten N. Wiesel, Sperry was honored with the 1981 Nobel Prize for physiology or medicine for his study of brain functions. Subsequent research has revealed that their groundbreaking studies aren't as conclusive or simple as once thought.

Left Strengths, Right Strengths

In most people, the left side seems to be the "words" side, controlling speech, understanding language, and reasoning things out. You can also attribute such logical tasks as language and math to that side. The right side seems to be the "picture" side, specializing in visual tasks, giving you a sense of where things are, and responding to intuition. The right brain also is touted as the "emotional" one, responding to sensory perception, faces, and music. Basically, the left-right phenomenon boils down to administration on the left, and creativity on the right. What's more, one half of your brain is usually your dominant one and takes charge.

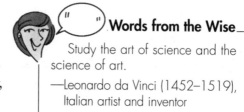

Words from the Wise

Study the art of science and the science of art.

—Leonardo da Vinci (1452–1519), Italian artist and inventor

We're not so much concerned with laying out the intense research that has been (and continues to be) conducted regarding the two hemispheres. However, we do think much can be gleaned from these two schools (left and right) of thought. And, more importantly, when you realize where you fit in on the left to right spectrum, you can also learn about ratcheting up your own clear thinking in new ways. In other words, if you're favoring left-brain tendencies, some right-brain techniques could give you some appreciative balance.

Further, assessing these dichotomies will offer valuable insights into others. If you can size up where someone else is coming from—say, an analytical or creative stance—you can foster easier communication and effective problem solving with that person.

Which Is It? Left or Right?

Before we give the brain halves a closer inspection, which of the following would you classify as left- or right-brain activities?

1. Composing a concerto   R
2. Giving oral directions using your hands   R
3. Color-coding a filing system   L R
4. Dreaming of being the winning quarterback in the Super Bowl   R
5. Recognizing a Marimekko print   R
6. Balancing a checkbook   L
7. Making a cheese soufflé by following a recipe   L
8. Conducting a PowerPoint presentation with a bulleted outline   L

Now, let's see how correct you were with this snapshot of each side:

The left brain ...

- Controls the right side of the body.

- Is analytical and sequential.

- Looks at the parts and then pieces them together.

- Is concerned with speaking, reading, and understanding speech.

- Is preoccupied with writing and using language.

- Understands numbers and quantities, and performing calculations.

- Solves problems with logical thinking.

The right brain ...

- Controls the left side of the body.

- Processes information intuitively and simultaneously.

- Gets the whole picture, and then sorts out the details.

- Likes painting, playing music, and other creative activities.

- Recognizes expressions, faces, shapes, and patterns.

- Judges size, distance, and position of objects.

- Is given more to emotions, imaginative ideas, and insights.

The answers to the questions on the previous page are: 1–5 are right brain; 6–8 are left brain.

Cobweb Buster _____

In a few left-handers, word control switches to the right side of the brain, and visual images to the left. However, in some left-handers, the right side of the brain—their dominant side—remains the picture projector. Some scientists believe this theory accounts for many of history's greatest artists being left-handed. Writing from left to right can be awkward for left-handers; Leonardo da Vinci was left-handed but wrote all his notes backwards, from right to left. You need to look at a mirror to read them. Experts wonder: was he trying to keep secrets, or just tired of writing left to right?

How the Other Half Thinks

The left- and right-brain modes also bring us the different types of cognitive processing. The left brain uses linear, sequential, symbolic, logical, verbal, and reality-based thinking; the right brain works with holistic, random, concrete, intuitive, nonverbal, and fantasy-oriented approaches.

As we move into a more in-depth discussion of the left and right halves, here are some terms that will come in handy:

Analysis. The tracing of things to their source, and the resolving of knowledge into its original principles.

Intuition. Immediate knowledge as in perception or consciousness; following hunches.

Rational. Reasonable, grounded, and sensible; the antithesis to foolish or absurd.

Synthesis. The combination of separate elements of thought into a whole, such as simple components into complex conceptions, specifics into generalities, and individual propositions into systems; the opposite of analysis.

Sure, you probably have a natural tendency toward either the left-brain or right-brain way of thinking. But the two really do work together in our everyday lives. The left brain concentrates on the verbal, processing information in a sequential and analytical way, looking first at the pieces and then putting them together to form the whole. Conversely, the right brain focuses on the individual, processing information in an intuitive and simultaneous way, looking first at the whole picture, and then the details. Let's jump into each hemisphere for a side-by-side examination.

The Left Brain's Role

For a broad look at the left brain, we turn to Andy the Administrator. Andy is a whiz with numbers, crunching them, analyzing them, churning out reams of reports on cost-effective measures, employee efficiency, and profit suggestions. Always punctual, Andy keeps a very organized day, breaking down his hours into precise time blocks and assigned tasks. And when the execs are stuck on a problem, they call in Andy.

He tackles any crisis with verve and ferocity, specifically and intelligently breaking down each one with a series of exact steps that can each be thoughtfully worked out for a completely solved whole. Plus, he's a master of understanding cause and effect.

To that end, he knows you can't take on any project without first analyzing previous experiences and transactions, laying those out and then—and only then—predicting consequences. For all of Andy's staunch efficiency and effectiveness, he has also been warned that his laser-sharp focus and intensity make him a little dry, a bit distant, and even perhaps somewhat staid.

Logic's Home

For the left brain, common sense, a planned and structured approach, and predictable scenarios are the norm. Valid, sound reasoning is non-negotiable for producing pre-scribed outcomes and consequences. To that end, information is gathered piece by piece—usually in sequence—for exacting solutions. In other words, certain effects can be reasonably deduced from certain causes; if A is proposed, then B and C follow. (We discuss the principles of logic in much more detail in Chapter 9.)

Analyzing the Action

When you process on the left side, you line up the data, arrange it in sequence, and draw conclusions. Along these lines, outcomes and consequences can be predeter-mined. Putting that linear, sequential, and logical thinking to work makes analysis especially a snap for the left brain—as long as words, symbols, and numbers are involved. Established and certain information is preferred to grapple with problems and make decisions. Veering off the hard and fast brings in unknown factors, a way-ward deterrent for the left brain. Preferred modes of information include master schedules, daily to-do lists, goal sheets, instruction manuals, and scorecards.

A Rational Place

For the left brain, reality rules! No need in dabbling in fantasy when you've got enough cold hard truths, numbers, figures, and symbols to deal with. The beauty of this stance is taking situations, events, and scenarios as they are, accurately assessing and presenting a picture-perfect snapshot. Basically, left-brainers want to know the rules from the outset, and strive to follow them. This representation also allows for rooted-in-reality starting points that don't bog down problem solving in fantastical or tangential experiences.

The Right Brain's Role

As a way of initially explaining the right brain, we're going to rely on an exaggerated portrait of a right-brainer called Arlene the Artist. Very talented and naturally creative, Arlene has really had to hunker down so that she can earn a living from her craft. Her work area is continually a mess, though she can readily find her paints and supplies. Warm, effusive, and lively, she's also habitually late, and more than a little impulsive. That's a little dangerous when she has to meet a gallery owner, because she may be spontaneously sidetracked to pick up some flashy new jewelry along the way.

When a client hires her for a piece, she tends to picture the client's needs in her mind, and sketches it out from there. No step-by-step outline in her thoughts guides her. And although more than one person has considered Arlene to be pretty emotional, she also taps into that trait, even suggesting that it influences greatness in her work. Although she gets that work done, she tends to take a freewheeling approach to her daily schedule, letting a creative muse structure her day. In other words, a nine-to-five job? No way! For her, that's a confining racket that gets bogged down in too many restrictions and constraints for her style.

Cobweb Buster

Betty Edwards's *Drawing on the Right Side of the Brain* (1979) applies the concepts of left- and right-brain learning to drawing. (A twentieth-anniversary edition was published in 1999 by Putnam.) Techniques encourage readers to access the right side of their brain for successful drawing. Part skill-building exercises, part brain science lessons, Edwards lays out an approach for never-beens and experienced ones alike.

Intuition Reigns

Ever get a hunch about something? That's your right brain talking. A launching pad for intuition, the right brain thrives on emotion, going with gut feelings as a guide.

The right brain kicks in when you just know you know an answer but aren't sure how you got it. It's a creative approach that focuses less on rules and regulations and more on innate sensibilities. Think about one of those contestants on the *Who Wants to Be a Millionaire?* game show. He's stuck on a question and out of lifelines, but, for some reason, feels like he should go with the answer D … which turns out to be the right one.

Words from the Wise

I feel there are two people inside me—me and my intuition. If I go against her, she'll screw me every time, and if I follow her, we get along quite nicely.

—Kim Basinger, Oscar-winning actress

Sizing Up Synthesizing

This right-brain role refers to processing information holistically, which means going from the big picture to itty-bitty parts. More concerned with the overall vision than the details, the right brain wants an idea of where something—a plan, an idea, a person—is headed before it gets there.

That vision includes the motto "pictures over words." If you're a right-brainer, you'd rather take a mental snapshot than remember a string of words to describe something.

Synthesizing also extends to analyzing information using sensory perception. Rather than hearing about an object, you want to take it in using your senses. Instead of reading how a carburetor operates, you want a demonstration of how it works. Your right brain prefers illustrations over descriptions, action over words.

That's So Random!

In this realm, spontaneity is supreme, and *free association* rocks. The right-brain person wants lots of projects going at the same time, segueing from one task to another. In that aspect, you can get just as much done as a left-brain person, but you're not into prioritizing.

Think Tank

Free association is the ability to spontaneously relate subjects, even if they don't seem to share anything in common.

Still, the right brain likes finding a connectedness amid the random. Right-brainers enjoy seeing patterns form and looking for that angle. They prefer clustered images and drawing correlations, taking in resemblances and similarities. In that vein, the dreamweaver also prevails in the right-brainer. If you're a righty, reality checks may be important, but fantasy thinking is a boon to your creative problem solving.

Where Do I Go from Here?

Okay, so you understand that the left and right hemispheres of your brain process information in different ways, and that you tend to use a dominant side in that. Being aware of your place on the left-to-right scale will almost automatically make you open to thinking from the "other" way.

You can devote some thought to bringing the two sides into alignment. Follow these tips for drawing the left or right side in:

◆ If you're a lefty, use your analytical and organizational skills, your keen observation, and your matter-of-fact approach to your best advantage. For example, meet a perceived problem head-on by articulating the pros and cons of possible solutions. Then assess the best solutions by further delineating the ramifications of time, budget, and goals.

◆ If you're a righty, consider using your creativity, intuition, and knack for pictures and images in inventive ways for thinking. For example, if you're entrusted with divvying up a budget, use a pie chart to illustrate distributing the monies instead of listing line items. If you're in a brainstorming session, don't squelch your intuition; let your gut guide you in the suggestions you make. Don't know what to make for dinner? Try "creative cooking" using whatever ingredients you have on hand.

◆ Talk with friends whose thinking is on the opposite side of the tracks from yours. What makes them tick? Ask them questions regarding their problem-solving capabilities. How do they tackle challenges or answer questions?

◆ Try some activities that are decidedly not on your brain's wavelength. For a left-brainer, draw a map rather than write out directions. For a right-brainer, make and follow a to-do list for a day.

◆ Try combining traditional right and left activities. Listen to music while writing out personal goals or your company's monthly projections. Scan the business section for a story about a foundering company and create solutions for their crisis.

Whether you are a lefty or a righty, there is no better or winning side to be on; you use what you've got and go from there. But your thinking will benefit from identifying your preference, and then expanding on it by giving consideration to the other half. These are two halves that make a much better whole.

Next up, we use both left and right sensibilities to approach learning, listening, and understanding, and demonstrate how you can make them a crucial component of your clear thinking.

Points to Ponder
If you could choose to be left brain or right brain, which side would you select?

The Least You Need to Know

- ◆ Both left-brain and right-brain characteristics offer illuminating windows into thought processes.

- ◆ The left-brain approach is more logical, analytical, and linguistic in nature.

- ◆ The right-brain approach is more holistic, random, and creative in nature.

- ◆ After you determine which side you're more aligned with, you can work toward incorporating more of the aspects of the opposite side for a more balanced way of thinking.

Part 2

The Invited Guests to Your Thoughts

With the onslaught of information presented daily, it's up to you to ferret out fact from faction and truth from opinion. Each of us works from our own base—that is, background—as a launching pad to assess the information flow. We take a look at the benefits—and drawbacks—of your current state. And you learn all about the richest resources to take in, and the nuisances to avoid in the information-gathering process.

Chapter 4

Learn, Listen, and Understand

In This Chapter

- ◆ Use learning to think better
- ◆ Determine how good a listener you are
- ◆ Glean tips to understand ideas, concepts, and topics more fully
- ◆ Find ways to tackle esoteric topics

Assimilate and assess. Clear thinking demands these two qualities, which wouldn't be possible without learning, listening, and understanding. They present key tenets for your thought processes to flourish. The better you can learn about and understand something, the clearer your thinking will be about it. So give that concept some thought: are you learning, listening, and understanding in ways that help—or hinder—your thinking?

This trio of abilities (learning, listening, and understanding) has applications throughout everyday living, getting our minds to, for instance, churn up thoughts to have conversations with others, try out a recipe, or start up a new laptop. This chapter shares tips and know-how on being a "thought-full" student, to make your mind broaden your skills and deepen your capacity for listening, learning, and understanding.

Mind Games 4

Three tourists check into a hotel, paying $30 to the manager before heading to their room. The manager realizes he's overcharged them; the room rate is actually $25. He gives $5 to the bellboy to return to them. On the way to the room, the bellboy reasons that $5 would be difficult to share among three people, so he pockets two bucks and gives $1 back to each person. Now each person has paid $10 and received $1 back, meaning they paid $9 each, which totals $27. Add that to the bellboy's take of $2, and that totals $29. Where's the missing buck?

(Turn to Appendix D for the answer.)

Learning to Think

In your clear-thinking arsenal, learning gives you access to many obvious areas, such as understanding and gathering information, as well as such realms as reasoning and problem solving (when you want to *learn* from your mistakes and find new options). In fact, without learning, clear thinking would be a bust.

So to prime your learning potential, first think about what kind of learner you are. Each of us has our own learning style. In school, you may have preferred studying alone, or you might have favored working with others. You may have loved taking copious notes, or you may have preferred using a tape recorder in class. You may rely on intuition over logic, practical experience rather than reflection. Being in touch with your learning style allows you a better channel to the thinking you'll need to make it most effective.

Consider this: chemistry may be a breeze for a guy who can't swim the butterfly stroke, and vice versa for his next-door neighbor. We all learn some topics and skills more easily than others.

Recall the left-brain, right-brain information we covered in Chapter 3, and take a minute to reflect: what kind of thinker are you? How'd you score on the left-brain, right-brain quiz in that chapter? As you're giving yourself a one-minute analysis, consider these aspects:

- What subjects are you a natural in?

- Do you process information better visually or written?

- Is studying an adventure or a chore?

Now that you have a perspective on where you're coming from, realize that whatever you learn, and whatever your aptitude, learning is enhanced by embracing …

- Reading.

- The advantages of technology.

- A good memory.

- The ability to summarize easily.

- Access to information from a variety of sources.

- A commitment to time, whether it be hunkering down in spread-out sessions, or just one long one.

Breaking down the best way for you to learn depends on four aspects:

- Knowing yourself and your approaches

- Your capacity to learn

- What processes have worked, and not worked, for you in the past

- Your aptitude for the subject you're taking on

And finally, to take on a topic/subject/issue, etc., answer for yourself the following:

- How interested am I in it?

- How much time do I want to spend learning it?

- What competes for my attention to it?

- Do I have a plan to learn it? (Hint: great learning requires understanding, and we delve into techniques for that in just a little bit.)

Now let's take a step back to bring in some information on listening, which isn't only a service to learning, but to understanding, too.

Cobweb Buster

In 1957, Ralph Nichols and L. A. Stevens published *Are You Listening?*, which featured a list of poor listening habits, many of which are still around today. They included faking attention, creating distractions, and tuning out difficult materials. The authors also suggested that people talk at an average speed of 125 words per minute. They claimed that evidence shows that—if thoughts were measured in words per minute—you could think at about 4 times that rate. The point? You normally have about 400 words of thinking time to spare during every minute a person talks. That surplus gives the listener way too much time for thoughts to dart around in the interim. In light of that realization, focus on becoming a more intent listener. If necessary, take that extra time to mentally sum up points, or become proficient at mental note-taking for the subject at hand.

The Importance of a Good Listen

Listening is a critical component of learning and understanding to think well. But listening—believe it or not—is hard work, requiring constant and conscious effort. In fact, studies show we only "get" about 25 percent of what we're listening to, leaving 75 percent ignored or distorted.

When you don't listen carefully, the monstrous five M's can result:

Think Tank

Listening is the ability to receive, interpret, and respond to verbal messages and other clues such as body language.

- Mangled messages

- Misunderstandings

- Misinterpretations

- Missed information

- Missed opportunities

What's Your LQ?

So let's find out how good a listener you are. The following questions test your LQ— your listening quotient. Answer the following questions yes or no:

1. I take calls while someone else is talking to me.

2. The majority of the time, I focus on what the other person is telling me.

Y 3. I ask questions about what the other person is saying if I don't understand.

Y 4. I sometimes interrupt when another person is talking.

Y 5. If the other person is having trouble articulating a thought or comment, I help him out.

N 6. If I'm talking to someone at a party, I flit my eyes around the room to see if someone more interesting is around.

N 7. I wait until the other person has finished speaking before I comment or state an opinion.

Y 8. I can usually restate with accuracy what someone else has told me.

Y 9. When I'm listening, my eyes are focused on the other person's, I'm concentrating on the topic at hand, and, if we're sitting down, I may even be learning forward.

N 10. When I'm listening, I watch for body language from the other person.

Y 11. I know that how someone is saying something could be as important as what they're saying.

N 12. I believe you can do two things at once, so I might be working on something else while someone is talking to me.

If you're an "all-ears" listener, you answered yes to 2, 3, 5, 7, 8, 9, 10, and 11; and no to 1, 4, 6, and 12.

How did you rate? Are you looking for some better ways to listen? Usually, the worst listeners are the ones who have no idea how much room there is for improvement. We'll be getting into some helpful hints here, but you can begin to assess your listening skills by being "present" during your next conversations, and asking yourself—and, if appropriate, the other conversant—a couple of questions after a talk:

- How often did I interrupt the other person?

- How accurately can I summarize our conversation?

Tactics to Try Out

For effective listening, try these tactics:

- Look at the person speaking to you.

- Listen to content and intent.

◆ Ask questions for clarification when you don't understand.

◆ Really care about the speaker's opinions and beliefs.

◆ Don't interrupt.

◆ Don't change the subject.

◆ Watch for body language, including facial expressions and gestures, and be mindful of your own. Sometimes body language is conveying a different message.

◆ Discern the tone of voice; that can also be inconsistent with the message.

◆ Evaluate what you're hearing in the message. Don't jump to conclusions. Weigh and analyze information before responding.

◆ Look, act, and be interested; empathize if appropriate.

◆ Respond verbally and nonverbally.

◆ Repeat information for clarity. Let the speaker know you heard and understood.

The Bridge from Learning and Listening to Understanding

Now that you've got a handle on the basics of learning and being a good listener, let's move into a tougher territory: understanding. For clear thinking, you should only be interested in *active* (or *deep*) *learning*, which means learning something with a commitment to understanding it, and gauging it with insight. On the contrary, *surface learning* concentrates on words rather than meanings in what is being studied.

> **Think Tank**
>
> When you engage in **active learning,** you are insightfully seeking and acquiring knowledge or skills with the intent to understand and apply them. **Surface learning** is only scratching the surface, collecting words rather than uncovering meanings.

A surface learner takes a superficial approach to learning, regurgitating material and relying on rote memorization. That learning is pretty much restricted to what's presently needed and doesn't look for relationships between ideas or draw links between subject areas.

To *remember* is great, but it's not the same as active learning. You either remember something or you don't. However, you can *understand* something on many levels. That deeper understanding may come from seeking meaning and forming your own ideas and opinions on topics, especially when you're really interested in them.

Active Learning, in Theory

Theoretically speaking, active learning works best for you if you're up for these challenges:

- ◆ Consciously looking for meaning in learning

- ◆ Examining evidence critically

- ◆ Actively relating new information to previous knowledge

- ◆ Wanting to know the underlying principles of what's being learned

- ◆ Being interested in what's being learned for its overall sake; that is, its place in the "big picture"

Active Learning, in Practice

The practice of active learning succeeds when you incorporate several elements into your endeavors. First, you concentrate on what you need to know, and cut away peripheral information that doesn't relate to the topic at hand. For instance, to learn more about organic gardening, you'd want to find out the best plants to grow without pesticides in your area and the intricacies of natural pest control, but probably wouldn't be so concerned with the latest advancements in cool patio furniture.

Second, you engage in observations. You can learn much from watching others, whether they're playing a sport you're mastering or handling a customer complaint calmly and efficiently. Observing what others do allows your mind to process how you can perform a task or skill, too.

Active learning also insists that you gather data on what you're studying, and research what others have found and said. (We delve into some research tips in Chapter 6.) In the course of accumulating information, you immediately look up words and concepts you don't understand, and find out more about experts you don't recognize who are cited. Whereas knowledge begets knowledge, gaps in research always come back to haunt you. And here's another tip: if you're feeling particularly adventurous, you even look up a word's etymology—the word's origin and history—to give you an even deeper understanding and feel for the word.

CAUTION

Mind Fogger

In this day of information overload, active learning can be a challenge. With so much data, there is a tendency for each piece of information to mean less. Therefore, you must evaluate the importance of each piece, and organize it—mentally, or sometimes even on paper—so that you can readily find it again, if necessary.

Active learning thrives on making comparisons and looking for patterns in the information you collect. You know how reading a really great metaphor can be gratifying, when you can make a correlation between two disparate entities? That's how active learning works, too: making a connection with the information you're studying and your ability to relate it to your current topic. For instance, Shakespeare's use of the iambic pentameter in his sonnets has been applied in math courses to teach metrics. (Iambic pentameter is a common meter of poetry with lines that are 10 syllables long (with an accent on every other one), and is analogous to the metric ruler, which is divided into tenths.)

In addition, try showcasing ideas you glean in as many relevant applications as possible. For instance, if you're learning about product packaging for your brand of gel soap, consider how other beauty items are marketed.

Also in the active learning process, spin out a series of questions to fine-tune and elucidate. (We elaborate on asking great questions in Chapter 7.) For instance, you're learning about putting items up for sale online on eBay. Beyond initially asking about which products sell well, the length of time for auctions, the resolution required for your scanned photos on the site, and shipping requirements, you would look into the eBay listing options that improve sales and how can you organize sales to efficiently manage your time and bring in the maximum profit.

And finally, watch out for falsehoods, the pieces of information that steer you down the wrong path. They can create and perpetuate misunderstandings. (We look at a host of falsehoods in Chapters 8 and 9.)

Some Ways to Say "I Get It!"

Don't you love when somebody "gets" it? Getting it means you truly understand something without having to be told.

Understanding extends to concepts, subjects, and even other people. Often it can be a lot like detective work, as you're solving the mystery of a subject you've taken on. And approaches to understanding can encompass visual aids, discussions, and role playing.

Mind Mapping

A relatively recent thinking and learning tool, mind maps refer to a concept that takes a cue from outlining. But instead of a written, verbal representation to organize ideas, mind maps allow a freer rein. Key words, symbols, and charts supplant the ideas and words of outlines and sentences. Developed by Tony Buzac, he has described this method in many books; one of his most popular is *The Mind Map Book* (Plume, 1996). The concept of mind mapping utilizes visual images. Starting with a center word, theme, or image, and thinking in 3D, you build out from your center, creating branches if you like. From there, you print words that conjure up subthemes, and use color for associations, as well as arrows, icons, and other visual aids to link elements.

> **Cobweb Buster**
>
> The early English thought that really knowing what you were talking about was kind of like standing beneath—or under—it. You could almost compare it to understanding being so weighty and important, it was like a burden on your shoulders.

By focusing on key ideas written down in your own words, and looking for connections between ideas, key words, or symbols that represent ideas, you're mapping knowledge in a manner that helps you understand and remember new information. Personalizing the map and constructing relationships therein also assists you in recall and understanding.

Role Playing

Role playing offers great rewards in understanding, and has become a staple in settings from high school classrooms to corporate retreats. By engaging in role playing, you get a hands-on understanding of two or more sides to an issue.

Two popular role-playing games—and there are several—include "Barnga," in which participants are in teams for a card game where the rules keep changing, and "The Owl," in which a group of reporters are assigned to interview members of another country to gain access to a mysterious cultural event. Each of these games allows the participants a deeper understanding for how people, situations, and even cultures can be perceived differently.

Case Studies

With case studies, you can gain a better understanding of a topic or issue—particularly a complex one—by examining cases that illustrate real-life examples, and learning from others' experiences. For instance, suppose you're interested in getting a deeper understanding of how a company builds their brand. In a 2002 article, the magazine *Fast Company* listed three companies worthy of study as great cases in brand building: the gift website Red Envelope, detailing how it increased its emotional pull with customers; Chicago design firm Archeworks, showing off its initiatives in companies using them to create branded environments; and Yahoo!, outlining its success in launching global recognition.

Understanding how others "get it" brings clarity to your own initiatives. In that spirit, applying case studies to your understanding also reaches into the questioning in learning that we discussed earlier. In a best-case scenario, case studies fire up questions in you for a deeper understanding. That said, your inquiries may require doing further fact finding and investigation, perhaps taking a class or interviewing experts.

Pair-Share-Compare

Higher levels of understanding can often be achieved by working with others, sharing your knowledge and experience, and gleaning the same from others. Understanding benefits from different perspectives. So by working with just one other person, or several, you can positively impact your understanding, and consequently, your thinking.

" " Words from the Wise

The improvement of understanding is for two ends: first, our own increase of knowledge; secondly, to enable us to deliver that knowledge to others.

—John Locke, seventeenth-century English philosopher

Another variation of this method works like a jigsaw puzzle. Members of a team each learn about individual parts of a subject, and then bring their information together for a round-table discussion. Here again, you're getting exposure to other people's interpretation of a topic or situation, which invariably gives you a better understanding of it, too.

Understanding: A Practical Application

Here's a practical application for understanding that really resonates. In this example, the topic is wine. The Culinary Institute of America's Karen MacNeil suggests four ways to understand wine, but interestingly, her take can be applied to many of life's challenges.

First, she urges paying attention. With wine, you'd notice a vintage's flavor, aroma, and personality. Next, she suggests creating tastings to learn by, sampling and comparing different wines. We like this step because it gives us an analogy for making comparisons and noticing patterns in life. Then she adds getting a group together—a variation on the pair-share-compare—so that wine tasters can bounce ideas off one another to see how their comprehension of the topic can affect yours. Because others may like different wines than you do, and detect different flavors, trying wines out with others broadens your knowledge. And finally, as questions

Words from the Wise

Knowing is not understanding. There is a great difference between knowing and understanding: You can know a lot about something and not really understand it.

—Charles F. Kettering, prolific American inventor

inevitably arise through the process (and they certainly should as your knowledge increases in whatever area you're tackling), seek out experts, books, or classes for further investigation.

Trying to Understand Esoteric Topics

No matter how hard you try to think about some things, they may escape your understanding. Although you should always try to understand the motives at work in any given situation, you still have a right to be flabbergasted sometimes. Clear thinking allows you to realize that although you should do all your homework to grasp a topic, issue, or situation, you may not always understand it.

Indeed, some things aren't *meant* to be understood ... at least not right away. In fact, studies of the brain show that scientists have little idea how we can grasp such esoteric subjects as religion and philosophy and their inherent concepts. And wouldn't you know it? These are some of the very topics that can have profound effects on our thinking.

You'd probably agree that at least a few of the following topics could make your head spin, subjects such as alchemy, the Kabbalah, Christianity and Catholicism, gnosticism, quantum physics, the Paleozoic era ... heck, even the *Matrix* films have entered the fray as worthy of esoteric study.

To channel such heady topics into your thoughts, here are some guidelines:

◆ As always, gather up your relative information.

◆ Scan subject matter first to get a general idea of the information you're facing.

◆ Prepare questions that arise—and don't be afraid to have questions!

♦ Determine if the questions can be investigated further on your own with more reading and research, or if you'll need to consult an expert.

♦ For the information you've collected, make a commitment to studying it.

♦ Instead of highlighting the pertinent information or passages you deem important, consider pausing to organize your thoughts and write down comments and questions in the margins. Sure it'll slow down your reading, but you're going for understanding here. Allow a little patience!

♦ As you're reading, force yourself to periodically ask yourself, "Could I quickly, accurately summarize what I just read?"

♦ Consider reading books on the subject in a different order than you normally would. Check out the table of contents, the introduction, and conclusion (if there is one) before diving in. An appraisal of those elements will give you a point of reference for the work.

♦ Get together with others to talk about the material and ask questions. Many esoteric subjects must be discussed and debated to be clearly understood.

Points to Ponder

Even if you've been "in someone else's shoes," can you ever truly understand another person's point of view?

Now that you've got this trio of learning, listening, and understanding under control, let's use them! Next up you learn about how your belief system can influence clear thinking.

The Least You Need to Know

♦ For clear thinking, the desire to learn, the skill to listen, and the will to understand are vital.

♦ Listening is a challenge, but with conscious effort you can become a better listener.

♦ Clear thinking subsists on active learning, the process of taking on a subject, topic, or idea with the intent to truly understand it.

♦ Understanding can evolve from active learning and applying such strategies as mind mapping, role playing, case studies, and exchanging information and ideas with others.

♦ Esoteric topics can be understood, but they require more effort, more questions, and frequent discussion.

Chapter 5

Factoring In Your Existing Belief System

In This Chapter

- Recognize that your background influences your thoughts
- Determine if you easily make assumptions or jump to conclusions
- Learn about the harmful affects stereotypes and prejudice can have on your thinking
- Take steps to banish those scourges from your thoughts
- Regard the value of an open mind

You just can't help it: you have a treasure chest of a background that infiltrates your thoughts at every turn—for better or worse. Although some of those chest's components can be precious, some of them are fool's gold. Some will add incredible value to your mind, and some will taint your bounty, like jewels that have lost their luster.

In this chapter, you examine what's packed in your mind's treasure chest and figure out what to toss and what to keep, what can muddy your thoughts, and what can enhance your focus.

Mind Games 5

The man who invented it doesn't want it. The man who bought it doesn't need it. The man who needs it doesn't know it. What is it?

(Turn to Appendix D for the answer.)

Your Background in the Equation

Your background—the combination of your heritage, your *beliefs* and *values*, your siblings, your childhood friends, your favorite subjects, your hobbies, your romantic relationships—is unique to you and only you. In concert, they've woven the multi-textured tapestry that represents the place you're coming from right now to think, reflect, give opinions, and make decisions. All these aspects also link together to build a platform for your thoughts.

Think Tank

A **belief** can refer to your acceptance of a fact, opinion, or assertion as real or true, without immediate personal knowledge; your beliefs can also involve the faith or religion you ascribe to and follow. **Values** are virtues and principles that you hold in high esteem.

For instance, consider who is the better candidate for an auto company that wants to recruit some interviewees for a focus group they're conducting. The company is considering making numerous changes to make an SUV model more family-friendly for running errands, driving to practices, and recreational outings. Who would be a better choice to glean practical information for the best changes to make: a working mother with four children living in suburban St. Louis, who was raised in a family with six kids; or a single metropolitan guy in Manhattan who was an only child? (Hint: who is more apt to drive a car daily rather than take a subway or taxi?)

Additionally, we can enhance our own thinking when we take into account the background of others. Because we are all different, you would be shortsighted if you considered everyone else to be like-minded … even if others seem just like you.

Take a moment to reflect on how each of the following aspects of your life can influence your thinking—and how they are unique to you—by answering these questions:

◆ **Your grandparents.** What values do/did they seem to prize? Is/was English their first or second language? Did they emigrate from another country?

- **Your parents' jobs.** What were they when you were growing up? Were they traditionally "white collar" or "blue collar"? Did their jobs take them out of the home environment often?

- **Your siblings (if applicable).** How close in age are you? Do you share common interests and career paths?

- **The town/borough/village/city you grew up in.** Was it rural, urban, or suburban? Did most people stay there after graduating high school? What's the main source of income for the town?

- **Your summer jobs.** Did they expose you to many other people? Did you learn about the "real world" from them?

- **The high school you attended.** Was it diverse? Was it public or private? What subjects were important to you?

- **Your beliefs.** Does religion play a role in your life? Are you guided by certain ethics and morals?

- **Your values.** Do you prize family? Are you driven by money?

- **Your college major (if applicable).** What drew you to it? Did you enjoy it, or skip around to other majors? Do you use the one you graduated with?

Take Your Emotional Temperature

So how do you feel right now? Are you in a good mood or a bad one? Are you cheerful, forlorn, upset, calm, peaceful, or contemplative? Our emotional reactions during situations can hinder or enhance clear thinking.

Has a situation similar to this one happened to you? You've just waited 45 minutes for a table at a bustling restaurant. You're finally seated, but no server arrives to take your order, give you some water, or reel off the evening's specials. A couple of minutes pass … 10 minutes pass … you're ready to walk out, but you're thirsty and hungry. When the server finally arrives, he's flippant and rude. You're ready to talk to the restaurant's general manager, dash off an e-mail to corporate, report the whole operation to the Better Business Bureau.

Well, you could do that—or you could take a step back. Sure, it could be a restaurant mishandling their business, but other factors could be in play that you're not aware of: perhaps the restaurant is shorthanded, and the server is having a stressful day trying to cover more than his usual workload. Although bad service rarely merits excuse, thinking through a calm approach to management is probably more apt to bring quicker service (and maybe even a couple of freebies). In an instance such as this one—even if you think you're "in the right"—you're better off taking a moment to ask, "Would emotions affect my clear thinking and resultant actions just now?" If so, quiet them down before proceeding.

Several emotions can really tamper with clear thoughts: anger, fear, disgust, depression, anxiety, hurt, frustration, hopelessness, and overconfidence. Although we'd typically associate all of these emotions with a "bad" label, some positive ones can muck up clear thinking, too. For instance, how many times have you heard about the head-over-heels couple who—seemingly madly in love—were consumed by their euphoric emotions and rushed into plans? They plotted their whole life together, merged bank accounts, planned the wedding … and the whole affair fell apart in a broken engagement or divorce. Because euphoria took over their thoughts, they didn't take the time they should have to calmly and rationally think through the situation and their motives.

> **Words from the Wise**
>
> Anger blows out the lamp of the mind. In the examination of a great and important question, everyone should be serene, slow-pulsed, and calm.
>
> —Robert Green Ingersoll, nineteenth-century American orator and lawyer

If you accept and acknowledge that you're experiencing those feelings right now, you'll be much better off in addressing the matter at hand. Co-author Dr. Ken always offers this bit of advice when clients are overwhelmed with problems, worries, or concerns. If you're overwhelmed, you might be in the midst of several emotions, such as anger or fear—admittedly not a great place to tackle the obstacle you're trying to commit to clear thoughts. So take a breather before you engage the thinking again.

As a guide when facing a situation that emotions may be adversely influencing, ask yourself these questions:

♦ Using three adjectives, how am I feeling right now?

♦ Are one or more of those words describing an emotion that could have a negative impact on my thinking?

If so, wait a bit, rather than regretting your actions.

Adjust Your Attitude

Just like out-of-whack emotions can tamper with clear thinking, negative attitudes—that is, your feeling toward a topic, subject, concept, other person, etc.—can mar it, too. We'll let motivational speakers, life coaches, and inspirational authors give you the lowdown on perking up your attitude: that's their domain. We just want you to be cognizant that it can affect your thinking.

Aside from a negative attitude, be aware of your attitude toward a topic at hand. Like your background, your attitude may be guided by preconceived notions that prevent open-mindedness.

Trouble at Assumption Junction

Although you wouldn't be making *assumptions* maliciously, we often make them—sometimes influenced by our background, our emotions, our attitude—without even realizing it. In a worst-case scenario, you might make an assumption that leads to a faulty conclusion, which may even result in some prejudicial thinking.

You're making assumptions when you ...

> **Think Tank**
>
> When you make an **assumption,** you take something for granted, or suppose something without proof or warrantable claim. A **paradox** is a situation or phrase that seems too absurdly incompatible to be true.

- ◆ Categorically believe things will remain the same about certain situations and people.

- ◆ Are close-minded, believing that possibilities don't exist and that matters, situations, and people only go one way.

Assumptions can bring these consequences:

- ◆ Cause you to make negative judgments (about a situation, problem, person, project concept)

- ◆ Neglect to determine if change has occurred from similar situations in the past

- ◆ Make rash decisions (and jump to conclusions)

- ◆ Prompt stereotypes

- ◆ End in prejudice

Here are some "don'ts" to avoid making assumptions:

- Don't take a phrase or comment for granted; ask for a clarification.

- Don't live with blinders on; be open-minded toward people and groups of people.

- Don't expect people to act according to stereotypes.

- Don't act in a stereotypical ways toward others.

- Don't speak before you think.

- Don't work from negative assumptions rather than from reality.

- Don't ignore the *paradoxes* in life. (An example of a paradox is the story of the tortoise and the hare; you can't always assume that the fastest will win).

Words from the Wise

If we all worked on the assumption that what is accepted as true is really true, there would be little hope of advance.

—Orville Wright, American airplane inventor

Here's a riddle that preys on an assumption you might make:

> Mr. Smith and his son, Tony, were driving home from work. They got into a car accident. Mr. Smith died immediately. Tony was rushed to a hospital unconscious and he was taken to surgery. When the surgeon saw Tony, the doctor said, "I cannot operate on this man because he is my son." Who was the doctor?

Answer: His mother. Did you naturally assume that an implausibility was at work because the doctor was a man?

Jumping to Conclusions

Here's a popular test we love giving (and taking) that preys on people's rush to judgments. We've found that pretty much everyone—no matter the age—gets something out of it. Kids delight in learning the right answers, and adults wonder how they could have gotten any of them wrong.

1. Do they have a 4th of July in England?

2. How many birthdays does the average man have?

3. Some months have 31 days; how many have 28?

4. A woman gives a beggar 50 cents; the woman is the beggar's sister, but the beggar is not the woman's brother. How come?

5. Why can't a man living in the United States be buried in Canada?

6. How many outs are there in an inning?

7. Is it legal for a man in California to marry his widow's sister? Why?

8. Two men play five games of checkers. Each man wins the same number of games. There are no ties. Explain this.

9. Divide 30 by ½ and add 10. What is the answer?

10. How far can a dog run into the woods?

11. A farmer has 17 sheep, and all but 9 die. How many are left?

12. How many animals of each sex did Moses take on the ark?

13. A clerk in the butcher shop is 5'10" tall. What does he weigh?

14. How many two-cent stamps are there in a dozen?

15. What was the president's name in 1950?

Answers:

1. Yep, and so do Canada, France, Australia ... and a July 2nd And July 3rd, etc.

2. One a year.

3. Wouldn't you know it? All months have 28 days.

4. The beggar is a woman: the woman's sister.

5. Because he's living, so he shouldn't be buried.

6. Six, that's three outs per inning for each team.

7. No; the man has left a widow behind ... so he's dead.

8. No crazy games or split wins here; the players just aren't playing each other.

9. Seventy (30 divided by ½—not in half—is 60).

10. Halfway (and then he would be running out).

11. Nine (all *but* nine die).

12. None. (Moses wasn't on the ark; that was Noah.)

13. No math skills necessary for this answer: he weighs meat.

14. It doesn't matter the stamp's denomination; a dozen is always 12.

15. George W. Bush; he was born in 1946.

After learning the answers, were you surprised how assumptions may have caused you to jump to a conclusion for a wrong answer? How often do you rush into a situation, a conversation, a label, or a judgment, without thinking? Because haste can produce unexpected—and sometimes ugly—results, you're smart to adopt an adage that's a favorite for clear thinkers: Look before you leap.

Make Common Stereotypes Uncommon in Your Thoughts

Your background may have also led you to stereotypes—a generalized, oversimplified image or idea of a group of people—which are obvious, huge impediments to clear thinking. They've been described as "mental cookie cutters" that force a simple description onto—often—a complex mass.

The term *stereotype* initially referred to a printing stamp that was used to make multiple copies from a single model or mold. The great journalist and commentator Walter Lippmann adopted the term in his book *Public Opinion* (1922) as a means of describing the way society categorizes people, "stamping" them with a set of characteristics. In his work, he identified four aspects of stereotypes, arguing that they are always 1) a simple assessment, 2) acquired secondhand, 3) erroneous with varying degrees of falsehood, and 4) resistant to change.

Does your thinking give way to stereotypes, convenient labels slapped on people (and even places and objects)?

Avoid Labels That You Can't Read

What thoughts arise as you look at each one of these groups? Do you immediately notice any labels you're associating with them:

Alaskans	Building contractors	Exotic dancers
Arabs	Casino owners	Lawyers
Bartenders	Catholic priests	Native Americans

Now let's look at stereotypes another way. Look at the following list of "characteristics." Have you stereotyped someone and assumed certain personality traits about the person by readily associating that person (or a group of people) with one of these descriptions?

- Loves show tunes

- Is an only child

- Likes spicy food

- Is overweight

- Is male with long hair

- Has been divorced

- Has been convicted of a white-collar crime

- Smokes cigarettes

- Dates much younger women

- Is on welfare

Mind Fogger

All stereotypes are false. Some may be less false than others, but the inherent nature of them is false. If we know that all individuals are different, then stereotypes are a logical impossibility.

Stereotypes are always wrong, and they're sometimes harmful. Here are a few you may have heard: welfare recipients don't want to find work, the English can't cook, teachers are awful dressers, restaurateurs work too hard.

So why do we stereotype? With so much information out there, sometimes you may think stereotyping is a time-saver, an easy way for our minds to quickly sift through the essentials. But don't be fooled: stereotyping is always a sloppy, ineffective route.

A Stereotype Exercise

Here's a true-life example: a new home-furnishings company was founded by a stockbroker (with the last name Fumad) and a lawyer (last name Hirsch) who left their high-profile jobs. To get the goods for their company to start, they went on a lengthy worldwide shopping spree, on the hunt for great dishes.

Have certain words triggered you to believe that the company was founded by men or women? What words did the deed? If you found out the owners are men, did you assume any specifics about them or their lifestyles? If you found out they're women, did the description seem congruent with your thoughts? What about the owners' last names? Did they strike up a religious or ethnic impression? Did that cause you to put any labels on each of the pair?

Think about your thinking. Does it frequently include stereotypes? Try to catch yourself conjuring up verbal shorthand to describe a person, place, or thing, and ban stereotypes from your thoughts.

Think you're completely immune from stereotyping? Harvard has an "implicit association test" (IAT) that indicates unconscious/conscious preferences in your minds. Taking the test could reveal long-held stereotypes you might not even realize you have about age, race, sexuality, religion, disability, skin tone, and even gender's link between liberal arts and females and science and males, and family and females and career and males. You can take the IAT test at https://implicit.harvard.edu/implicit/demo.

There's No Pride in Prejudice

Stereotypes can form the basis for prejudice: unfounded, unfavorable views or opinions that could lead to fear or mistrust of a person or group (and particularly involving religion, ethnicity, nationality, social status, or sexual orientation). Prejudice can be an uncomfortable topic for many of us, for many reasons. But no matter how uncomfortable to you, it's important to recognize and to confront it. Your clear thinking depends on it.

Often when you assume that a person or group of people will always act the same way, you react to them in a negative way. This reaction is not only unfair to the individual or group, but also creates distance, detracting from honest discussions and assessments. And although you may have had little choice in the home or surroundings you were brought up in—or your ancestry—you do have the opportunity, right now, to shed elements that may be clogging up your mind.

Everyone raised in the same suburban neighborhood or the same big city high-rise didn't all have the same life experiences. Neither did everyone who is of African American descent, or Latino, or Caucasian. Not all plumbers are the same, nor are advertising executives, or department store managers. Therefore, it's unfair to make sweeping generalizations that all plumbers overcharge, all advertising executives are slick hucksters, and department store managers never believe the customer is right.

Have You Been a Victim of That Thinking?

In his monumental book *The Nature of Prejudice* (1954), psychologist Gordon Allport suggested the five escalating degrees of acting out prejudice, as follows: antilocution, or a verbal expression of negative attitudes; avoidance; discrimination, or excluding others in hiring, housing, or membership; physical attacks of violence against the person or group; or the worst, extermination, which would be execution.

Our family background is Cuban and Italian. Since some of our ancestors are from Sicily, we've been asked countless times if we have Mafia connections. This type of comment would be the stereotype gone wrong into prejudicial thinking: all Italians are mobsters and should be avoided by law-abiding citizens. Have you ever been the victim of a prejudice or a prejudicial comment? What were the circumstances of the situation? How did it feel? Did you find yourself wanting to lash out with a comment that "turned the tables"?

Cobweb Buster

American psychologist Gordon Allport (1897–1967) was one of the first to study personality, researching human attitudes, prejudices, and religious beliefs. As a social theorist, much of his research has become ingrained in our study of human nature. He stressed the uniqueness of the individual, treating problems in terms of present conditions as opposed to childhood experiences. In addition to *The Nature of Prejudice*, he wrote *Personality* (1937), and *The Individual and His Religion* (1950).

Get Rid of Prejudicial Thinking

It looks like we all could use a little counsel on prejudice. Although surveys show that more than 75 percent of the U.S. population do not consider themselves to be racist, additional research exposes that those who identify themselves as low in prejudicial beliefs still discriminate.

How can you take the thorn of prejudice out of your thinking cap?

♦ Acknowledge that you may have learned prejudicial information about other people.

♦ Confront the prejudices you've learned.

♦ Commit to change.

◆ Beware of your own self-talk about other groups of people, and eliminate it.

◆ Challenge the irrationality of prejudicial thoughts by getting information to disprove each prejudicial thought. (Look more closely at general statements about a population of people, and you'll see how statements fall apart under examination.)

◆ Increase your exposure to or contact with those who belong to the groups toward which you have learned some prejudices.

◆ Learn how others see your "group."

◆ Develop listening skills so that you can really hear other people (see Chapter 4).

◆ Learn about other groups; that's an important way to develop understanding.

Your Perception vs. Reality

Emotional flare-ups, assumptions, hasty conclusions, and painful prejudices are all detriments that can shade your thinking to create a perception that might not be commensurate with reality.

In the swirl of real life, your thoughts can be overtaken with all that has to be done, should be done, hasn't been done. During conversations, rather than being present in the now and having a cup of coffee with your boss, your thoughts can become littered with "What is she thinking about me now?" "Did I just say the right thing?" "What if I messed up on that expense report?" You may have suddenly turned a casual office break into a setting for a demotion, when she just thinks she's treating a valued employee to an iced latte.

Because perception is not always reality, consider these guidelines:

◆ Apply the brakes to a racing mind.

◆ List your assumptions.

◆ Eliminate stereotypes and prejudices.

◆ Label facts and fabrications.

◆ Ask yourself, "What am I perceiving to be going on here?" and "What's *really* going on here?"

CAUTION

Mind Fogger

Let's face it: we all have different perceptions of reality. They may be somewhat similar, but they'll still be different.

Do yourself a favor. Untangle your perception from the actual reality. Ask yourself those preceding questions. If you find yourself in the land of outlandish meanderings, draw yourself back in.

The Importance of an Open Mind

Having an open mind brings you the greatest, most appealing opportunities for clear thinking. But having an open mind also requires hard work to mold, craft, tend to, and sustain. We've tried to make a little mincemeat of that work to give you some insights into the challenges you might face in getting that mind open for business—and the immense payoff when you do. Because although you'll see the obstacles to having an open mind that can pervade at every turn, you'll also be amazed at the advantages to be gained.

> **Words from the Wise**
>
> A mind is like a parachute. It's only good when it's open.
> —Anonymous

In many ways, an open mind is really the crux of clear thinking. An open mind allows for a clean slate for ideas to marinate, thoughts to brew, opinions to be formed, solutions to be evaluated, and others' notions to be accepted. You'd be pretty hard-pressed to come up with benefits or advantages to living in the thought bubble of a closed mind and still consider yourself fair, just, and worldly. An open mind is rational, impartial, nonjudgmental, insightful, and absorbent. A closed mind tends to be opinionated, judgmental, defensive, accusatory, and provincial.

> **Points to Ponder**
>
> Without religious texts—such as the Bible or the Koran—would humans still be able to know right from wrong?

Try this exercise. Peruse the following list of past and present prominent figures. Do you think their public persona was indicative of having an open mind or closed mind?

- Fidel Castro
- The pope
- Mr. Rogers
- Howard Stern
- Bill Gates
- Malcolm X
- Oprah Winfrey
- Mahatma Ghandi
- Saddam Hussein
- Jefferson Davis

What made you decide one way or the other in each case? And did you answer with an open mind or a closed one?

The Least You Need to Know

◆ Assumptions are a bane to your thinking and can lead to hasty or wrongful conclusions.

◆ Don't infiltrate your thoughts with stereotypes; they're always wrong.

◆ At their worst, stereotypes can lead to prejudicial thinking, which can harmfully and improperly shade opinions, beliefs, and knowledge.

◆ An open mind is the crux of clear thinking.

Chapter 6

Facts-travaganza

In This Chapter

- ◆ Understand what a fact is
- ◆ Learn about the avenues of research available
- ◆ Cultivate new areas of research
- ◆ Organize and pare down your findings

Thinking thrives on information. You can always think more clearly if you've effectively assembled an array of information to consider. Whether you're making decisions, solving problems, or just collecting information, you'll be more effective and well rounded in your approach if you take in as much knowledge as possible about a subject.

Information is readily available through a variety of sources. So where are they, and how do you access them? This chapter teaches you how to find and organize facts.

Mind Games 6

What is familiar about this string of numbers: 1, 4, 1, 5, 9, 2, 6, 5?
(Turn to Appendix D for the answer.)

Is That a Fact?

Today more than ever, lots of information is parading around out there, often masquerading as fact. Sometimes it's actually someone's opinion, or another's misconception, or even a flat-out superstition. And sometimes it truly is a fact.

Although facts are obviously your most reliable resources, much can be gleaned from opinions, critiques, experiences, and observations, too. For the purposes of this chapter, however, we concentrate on the great fact-gathering mission and inventory the whole kit and caboodle, including the web, books, personal experiences, and interviews. We cover sorting out what's right and wrong in the next two chapters. We put the "facts" to more stringent tests then.

Collecting Information and Gathering Facts

When you decide to get your facts together, you need to take a no-holds-barred approach to find out every aspect, element, and facet you possibly can about a topic. Stay on course, but don't limit yourself; explore as many information "storage facilities" as possible—in the time you have—to become subject savvy.

Today, information abounds: on the net; in books, magazines, the newspaper, the classroom; on the evening news, television newsmagazines, entertainment newsmagazines, the morning shows, talk shows, interviews … even at your neighbor's house, at the cinema, and through the grapevine down at your local coffee house. And sometimes your own personal experiences provide you with the most valuable information of all.

Gathering that information can seem like an insurmountable task. But fear not, we've got the rules and tools right here.

Fact Attack

As you proceed, keep in mind these basic fact guidelines. (These rules will also help in the next two chapters when we distinguish between objective and subjective, rational and irrational, and point out "wayward" facts such as urban legends, frauds, and myths.)

Facts come in the following forms:

- *Hard facts*, which often include names, numbers, and the like, and also characteristics and details of specific people, items, and places. Examples: There are 50 U.S. states; your home address; the number of cousins you have; a 14 oz. can of cannelini beans is $1.39 at the supermarket today; Paul Newman has blue eyes. (Statistics also fall into this area, but they can be manipulated. We talk about those in more detail in Chapter 10.)

- *Personal observations*, which are firsthand accounts of sights, sounds, and smells. Examples: Cows moo; lemons are sour; those sweaters are selling briskly; she is a warm hostess.

- *Definitions*, which provide common descriptions. Example: In this case, the definition of the word "definition" is the meaning of a word or phrase.

- *Accepted general descriptions*, which time and reason have borne out as accurate. Examples: Apartments in Manhattan are expensive; Christmas presents are wrapped in holiday paper; Iowa has many cornfields; Williamsburg, Virginia, is rich in American history. (Descriptions that stray toward stereotypes are problematic to clear thinking, as discussed in Chapter 4.)

Get Ready to Gather

After the following review of numerous information outlets, you must decide which ones best serve your purposes. So before you begin this survey, make sure you can answer these questions:

- What am I looking for? *or* What specifically am I trying to think more about?

- Do I need a variety of "for" and "against" viewpoints or just general information?

- What are 10 words that relate to my subject matter? (This answer will be particularly helpful with Internet and article searches.)

Be Resourceful with Your Sources

Although you want to make the best use of your time and venture into the information arenas that will be most helpful, also realize that the more pertinent information you take in, the more you'll benefit. We believe in the saying "The more you know, the better you can think."

The Internet

We begin with the Internet because this has steadily—and vastly—become the most accessible vehicle for information, some of it wildly disparate. For better or worse, the Internet is widely available, bringing thousands of bastions of information right into your own home, office, school, library, or wi-fi location (wireless high-speed locations where you can access the Internet). At last count, Google was combing through more than eight *billion* web pages covering every conceivable topic. On those sites, you can access details about corporate figures, political scandals, the daily news, TV stars' favorite foods, sex studies, historic timelines … the information is seemingly infinite.

Those websites are created, produced, and maintained by various sources: individuals, companies, not-for-profit and for-profit organizations, community groups, schools, churches, and government entities. Although some of them have purely noble motives, others may be driven by their own agendas.

Those billions of web pages contain an array of free or low-cost databases, journals, books and other publications, reports, and high-profile blogs. Because of those extensive offerings, some people use the web as their primary source of information, relying on it almost exclusively. In addition, the web often represents the quickest way to answer a query. But be warned: although some websites may be simply presenting what they know, what they know might not be right. We'll help you put them to the test with questions to sort out which ones are true-blue and which are harum-scarum in the next chapter. For now, let's just take a look at how to accumulate the information you're seeking.

Cobweb Buster

The search engine Google has become so popular as an information vehicle that it's also become a slang verb, as in "I Googled you before this interview."

To begin a search for web pages that relate to a topic you want to research, enter some key words into a web search engine, such as Google, Yahoo!, or Dogpile. Perhaps you're preparing for an interview at a company and really want to wow them. Check out their corporate website, but look at their competitors' sites, too. The person you're meeting with may have a bio on the company's website, and you may notice some commonalities in your career paths.

Start your Internet search with a word or simple phrase, but don't stop there. A search for synonyms, related topics, and even opposite subjects will greatly enhance and expand the amount of information you can peruse, research, and analyze. In addition, try to be as exact as possible in the words or phrase you select; you can also rearrange word order in your search to yield other results.

Regardless of which search key words you use, you'll most likely call up a staggering number of websites. At this point, you want to narrow this list down to the ones most pertinent to your research. For each site listed as a match, most search engines provide a line or two of text that includes the key words you used in your search. You might be able to tell from that context whether the site will prove helpful to your inquiry. In addition, most sites list matches in order from "most matching" to "least but still matches something in the search query." Therefore, you might find that the sites listed on the first page of results prove most helpful to you. In the end, you can always click and open the sites to take a look for yourself and determine their relevance to you. You might instantly realize a site has nothing to do with your topic. Some might be outdated. Others might look like a grad student on a java high churned them out overnight. (We examine more closely how to analyze websites in the next chapter.)

Books, Magazines, and Newspapers

In 2000, A&E's *Biography* series named Johann Gutenberg, inventor of the printing press, the number-one person of the millennium. The power of his invention—and its impact on the written word—remains peerless.

Further, we contend that the written word is your best bet for getting straight facts. True, no one will probably ever be stamping "100% guaranteed truth" on information you receive. Still, safeguards are in place to protect objectivity in the case of books, magazines, and newspapers (in contrast to the relatively unmonitored Internet or breakneck-paced television news).

We're crazy for daily newspapers. Be it *The New York Times, The Toledo Blade,* or *The Wall Street Journal,* they provide an expansive review of the day's events. For spare change a day, it's like your own personal research team goes out all over the world, digging up their own facts, figures, research, and interviews to present you with the top stories. And it can even be delivered to your front door!

Depending on your hometown, the selection of stories can be astoundingly thorough and wide-ranging. Besides world, national, and local news, sections may cover business, sports, health, food, entertainment, real estate, home improvement, and gardening. You just can't beat the breadth and depth a daily newspaper has to offer.

And the best articles are often an information gatherer's dream: you get two well-researched sides to a story that help you form your own opinion. Outside of a newspaper's editorial pages, a daily paper's articles are usually committed to presenting objective viewpoints, relaying the "who, what, where, when, why, and how" of a story with a facts-only-please sensibility.

In addition, newspaper readers are likely to expose themselves to a wider range of information than those who limit themselves to the editorial choices of a news director of a telecast or those who click only on web news stories in which they're interested. Even if you don't read every article in a newspaper, you might pick up more than you would guess just by glancing at headlines and pictures as you page through the newspaper. (You might even be tempted enough by such to stop and read most or all of an article that "catches your eye.")

Joe's first job was writing on the news desk for the *Atlanta Journal Constitution*. Having gone on to write for other media, he was impressed with the commitment to factual reporting and the constant confirmation, fact checking, and corroboration of information for readers.

Cobweb Buster

Versus the net, libraries give patrons access to databases that may be otherwise unavailable or require expensive access. Libraries also can provide a bigger pool of authoritative resources, depending on the topic. And here's another advantage of your local library: Worldcat—which bills itself as "The window to the world's libraries"—has 57 million records and counting. Created and maintained by more than 9,000 institutions, it's the largest and most comprehensive database of its kind, with resources that span thousands of years and nearly every form of human expression from stone tablets to electronic books.

Although often written from a singular viewpoint, nonfiction books can also provide unexpected, excellent insight and information on topics and issues. And, typically, you can quickly determine a book's viewpoint. For example, you know that Al Franken's *Rush Limbaugh Is a Big Fat Idiot* is going to espouse a different view than Ann Coulter's *How to Talk to a Liberal If You Must*.

Magazines often contain timely and well-researched articles infused with well-thought-out perspectives. Depending on the subject you're researching, chances are one or more magazines cover it. For instance, suppose you want to weigh the pros and cons of a honeymoon on Maui or the Big Island. (Clear thinking doesn't always have to be serious.) You could find sugges-tions, trends, tours, and deals in a variety of magazines such as *Hawaii, Sunset, Travel & Leisure, Condé Nast Traveler, Modern Bride, Delta Sky, Arthur Frommer's Budget Travel, Islands,* and *National Geographic Traveler* (to name just a few). Some magazines even have online sites that offer free access to articles from past and current issues.

Words from the Wise

It is a very sad thing that nowadays there is so little useless information.
—Oscar Wilde, Irish author and playwright

Keep in mind that while most magazines are clearly beneficial, some are geared to pander to prurient interests, fabricating or maligning the truth for salacious stories. You'll need to call on your common-sense skills (discussed in Chapter 9) to ferret out the fact-embracing versus the fact-neglecting periodicals.

Interviews

If you're open to the possibility, you can glean valuable information from interview-ing others about their own personal and professional experiences. Someone, somewhere—probably someone you know or who knows someone you know—has firsthand information that you can use. Use discretion (an obvious but important point) in finding someone who may have insights you seek. For example, talking to an accountant accused of embezzlement about setting up a new business is not prudent.

After determining your interviewee subject, consider your answers to these questions before you approach him/her/them:

- ◆ Is this person an expert in this area?

- ◆ What makes him or her an expert?

- ◆ Do I trust this person?

- ◆ What drew me to this person in the first place?

- ◆ Has this person and his/her accounts been helpful to others?

- ◆ What is this person's supposed experience in this area?

♦ What is this person's experience that I'm already aware of?

♦ Was this person successful in overcoming an obstacle or creatively solving a problem relating to the information I'm gathering?

♦ Does this person have an agenda that is selfless, mutually beneficial, or potentially selfish?

♦ Do I have an emotional investment in this person, or can I be objective regarding his or her responses?

Personal Experiences

Nothing quite gives you the lowdown like experiences you've already encountered, mastered, or survived. Personal experience can be a great teacher. Can you consider your experiences objectively? If you can, you can rely on them to provide first-rate information. There's no one you can trust quite like yourself (particularly if you chronicled your experiences via the written word).

> **Mind Fogger**
>
> Directing questions to a newspaper or magazine advice column doesn't really count as an interview. Nothing against an advice column for getting one person's view, but because you're not able to engage the columnist in thoughtful questioning, you're not getting a maximum mind infusion.

Suppose, for instance, that you have a job offer from a firm that reminds you of a former employer (perhaps a company you left on bitter terms). From your personal experience, you might recall unfulfilled promises and unsatisfying achievements at that company. Your experience will cause you to question long and hard whether you are setting yourself up for a similar failed venture with this new company that wants to hire you.

To gain the most from personal experience, you must be honest with yourself regarding your memories and feelings associated with those experiences.

Reviews, Critiques, and Critical Analysis

Information in this area can be scholarly, compelling, or both. Medical journals, movie reviews, doctoral theses, and critical evaluations are just some of the many sources that comprise this category. Authors of such material usually collect a substantial amount of information and spend a considerable amount of time analyzing the data to draw conclusions and release results. In most instances of *critiques* or *reviews*, you'll immediately understand that you're reading someone's opinion.

As for works of critical analysis, opinions have been formed after tests have been conducted and data has been analyzed. For instance, co-author Dr. Ric conducts clinical trials for a new cancer therapy, studying two sets of patients: one group is taking the new drug; the other group is given a placebo. Fellow co-author Dr. Ken has conducted tests on perfectionism with hundreds of middle school students. In each case—whatever the findings—results will provide valuable information.

> **Think Tank**
>
> A **critique** is an analysis or assessment of a topic, subject, or piece of work, devoted to detailing both good and bad qualities. A **review** is a form of a critique; a critical examination of a piece of work.

These doctors have had many reports published in medical journals in their respective fields, so as to inform other doctors and guide them in their treatment of patients. Sometimes medical journal reports even reach beyond professional circles (for instance, when they make the national news because of a major breakthrough).

On the lighter side, it's Saturday night. Do you see the new Brad Pitt blockbuster, a Disney family comedy, or a horror flick? Should your next read be a fashion-world *roman à clef* or a modern-day memoir? If you're undecided, you might go by the reviews, which dispense a critic's view. Well-versed in a particular field, the reviewer can usually draw on a deep reservoir of comparative works for breadth, perspective, and enlightenment.

Many times, all of these formats—critical analysis, reviews, and the like—establish thought-provoking principles worthy of your information armament. Is the information dependable? We give you some tips to determine this in the next chapter.

We also want to point out these formats because, many times, the best and most well-thought-out reviews, critiques, and critical analyses are prime examples of clear thinking. The authors of such materials have set up a premise (or problem), gathered and evaluated the information they have collected, applied necessary thought processes, and then presented their point in a concise and cogent manner.

Other Ways to Reap Information

Whereas the preceding section concentrated on the written word, other experiences—besides previous personal ones—can offer information that can be gifts to clear thinking.

Words from the Wise

No man was ever so completely skilled in the conduct of life, as not to receive new information from age and experience.

—Jonathan Swift, English author and satirist

Information can sometimes come in unpredictable and unexpected ways, so be aware of the possibilities. Many times when you're open to solving a problem or making a decision, you begin to notice all sorts of opportunities that could bring illuminating perspectives.

For instance, have you considered any of these as a means to know more about a topic you're addressing or a choice you're grappling with?

- Museum exhibitions
- Walking tours
- Church groups, meetings, and services
- Classes at universities and community colleges
- Classes at the Y or the gym

- PTA meetings
- Lecture series
- Book fairs
- In-store seminars
- Convention hall expos
- Retreats

And then there's psychotherapy. Arguably a rich research arena, psychotherapy can assist clear thinking by offering a candid and refreshing—and, at times, challenging—resource for probing, sorting, and evaluating accumulated personal information and experiences.

Cobweb Buster

Information really can come from almost anywhere. Have you ever thought about movies for information? Cinematherapy uses movies and their emotional underpinnings to offer insights. In both lighthearted and serious approaches, cinematherapy can delve into such issues as bureaucracy, peer pressure, overcoming challenges, legal issues, co-dependency, and nontraditional partnerships. For instance, *Rocky* might demonstrate rising above challenges, and *When a Man Loves a Woman* shows a family coping with a mother's alcoholism. Cinematherapy draws some correlation to its predecessor, bibliotherapy. Bibliotherapy uses books (rather than movies) to showcase examples of characters coping and handling situations and crises. Both methods are extremely helpful in exploring subject matters from a knowledgeable but non-threatening viewpoint.

Reveling in Research

If you've collected information in some combination of these arenas, you've no doubt amassed an abundance. Approach it enthusiastically; it's your best chance for contributing solid data to your clear thinking.

Research also requires that you use good judgment in bringing your finds together. Many of these information outlets work best in conjunction with another to give you the clearest and most complete picture. For instance, you can probably get a pretty good idea of acupuncture's effects on treating a back problem through acupuncture and Eastern medicine websites and even personal testimonials online. But you should also consult your doctor to make the most informed choice.

Your Very Own Fact-Gathering Mission

To open up your thinking to the vast array of resources available, try this research exercise.

To warm up, run a phrase or question through an Internet search engine, your local library's catalog, and on Amazon.com. See how much you turn up for even "the benefits of drinking organic beer," "off-the-field cheerleading stunts," or "fried chicken addiction."

Now, let's get to work on your mission: you work for a national greeting card company with retail outlets across the country. Sales have been relatively stable across the country for the month of July, except for the 17 stores that dot 3 Midwest markets (St. Louis, Kansas City, and Des Moines), where they have unexpectedly plummeted. You're called in to ascertain what's going on.

What are your possibilities for fact gathering to determine the reason(s) for the decreasing sales?

Here's our approach:

1. Make sure you have all the contact information—including addresses, phone numbers, and store manager names—for each of the stores "affected" by the sales slump, as well as their sales figures for this month of July versus the year before.

2. Determine if each of the stores had a decrease, or if a few stores brought the whole average down.

3. Use the Internet to check out news stories that have happened during July in those cities (use keywords such as the city names, "consumer," "shopping," and "decrease").

4. Check out weather reports for the month in those areas. A heat wave would have kept shoppers in their air-conditioned homes.

5. Check out your industry's publications; find out if other business were affected by a July downturn.

6. Interview store managers to ask about foot traffic, store closures out of the ordinary, and restocking procedures.

Did you think of other research possibilities? Did you notice that research can cause a chain reaction, prompting you to think about other sources to consider?

Sort Through the Information

This step is your chance to give the information you've gathered a first look. Discard what's unnecessary or obviously not serving your needs as you consider and weigh the options of this particular problem. This phase is your first chance for editing. A home-organizing series, *Clean Sweep*, dumps a room's entire contents into the yard, and then has the homeowners complete a 30-minute elimination round, making split-second decisions as to whether an item is immediately disposable or needs further consideration. (Later, homeowners spend the day sorting and sifting through the room's remainders, sometimes eliminating up to 90 percent of the room's original contents.) As in *Clean Sweep*, your initial examination eliminates the fringe elements of your information collection, those pieces that don't really contribute to your cause.

Consider why you need the information in the first place, and then ask yourself these five questions to weed out unnecessary material:

1. Which of this research seems most valuable?

2. Which is more central than tangential?

3. Which is from sources I currently deem reliable?

4. Which is based on my own personal experiences?

5. Which would hold up if I mentioned it during a speech on this topic?

You Wanna Second That Thought?

Now that you've sorted through your information and discarded what you don't need, are there any angles you've missed, any holes in your research? Give your information a second look. Is everything you possibly could have covered, covered? Does any of the information strike you as a launch pad for more investigation? Did any source stir up additional questions that now should be probed?

After you've got all this information in front of you, you might be tempted to think, "Hey, I've got all this great stuff. I can now go forth and ruminate!" But thinking that way would be oh so wrong. Just because it's been written down doesn't mean that it's right. Be patient in determining the truth of your collection's components and in preparing for the critical thinking involved in crafting your clear thoughts.

So, information in hand, you're well on your way. Now it's time for the next phase of fact finding and gathering: hunkering down and asking, "Is that really a fact?"

> **Points to Ponder**
>
> What work of fiction do you wish were actually a factual account?

The Least You Need to Know

- We are a society wealthy in information; it's available on the Internet, in newspapers, in books and magazines, and from other people.

- Facts can be categorized into hard facts (names, figures, and numbers), personal observations (general information accumulated through your senses and reasoning), definitions, and accepted generalizations (time-tested knowledge).

- Don't let the web (or any one source) be your be-all, end-all for gathering facts and information. Use it in conjunction with other sources.

- Consider other research avenues beyond the obvious, such as classes, exhibitions, and other enrichment experiences.

- Edit your info intake to prime it for further analysis and fact checking.

Chapter 7

Sorting Fact from Fiction and Truth from Opinion

In This Chapter

- ◆ Figure out if the information you've collected is valid
- ◆ Ferret out misleading advertising
- ◆ Realize the power of—and formulate—great questions
- ◆ Find out how thinking versus knowing affects your clarity
- ◆ Learn the differences between the subjective and the objective, and the rational and the irrational

This chapter will help you determine fact from fiction in news sources and advertising, and help you ask the best questions—a reliable task to promote clear thinking—to get the job done.

From there, we move on to all the "versus" that truth and opinions face: facts versus statements, thinking versus knowing, the subjective versus the objective, and the rational versus the irrational. All these opposing viewpoints and stances—informed or not—slant and alter or confirm and validate the truth.

Mind Games 7

A man walks into a bar and asks for a glass of water. The bartender pulls out a gun and points it at him. The man says thank you and walks out. Why?

(Turn to Appendix D for the answer.)

Misinformation in the Information Age

With all the amazing information at your disposal in the information age, you have to be even more wary about what to believe (and not to believe).

The information age, according to a Smithsonian exhibition at the National Museum of American History, began in 1837. That year, Samuel Morse's invention of the telegraph put information into an electrical format that could travel a long distance. That paved the way for phones, phonographs, cables, computers, CDs, and even info-driven robots. Not bad for a span of just over 150 years. But in that amount of time, isn't it amazing how much information—and from how many sources—is slung at us everyday?

So what sources can you trust for your information? Is someone's agenda noble or self-serving? Are companies that give you "facts" ever altruistic, or always out to improve their bottom line? How can you determine whether information is credible?

Words from the Wise

Every story has three sides: yours, mine, and the facts.

—Rene Fumoleau, French writer and filmmaker

Before we start breaking down how to sort fact from fiction, consider the various sources of your information: media, other people, ads, your own experiences … a seemingly limitless cavalcade. Obviously, each of your "sources" deserves varying degrees of trust. Even within those trusted groups, some sources are always better than others (depending on the issue at hand). For instance, if you're interested in researching the issue of what most concerns high school students today, your high school student neighbor can most likely provide better information than your grandmother (unless, of course, she's a high school teacher or adolescent psychologist).

For the purposes of this discussion, let's examine the differences in sources we all have in common and are exposed to regularly.

Consider the Source

News sources cover stories in widely divergent ways. Consider, for example, the following headlines for a single story. The American Girl doll company released a Latino doll that came with a book describing her imaginary background. One passage detailed how her family moved from one Chicago neighborhood to another suburb described as safer. Here are some actual headlines collected from local and national newsprint and broadcast outlets, and national magazines. Note how the company's name provided fodder (intentionally or not, your call) for some of the headlines.

"Dollmaker Feels Heat for Depiction of Hispanic Area"

"Latinos Feel Dissed by Doll"

"Doll Flees Urban Violence for Suburbs"

"American Girl Snubs Neighborhood"

"Politicians Beat Up on American Girl"

"Politicians Can Keep Picking on Doll or Fight the Real Problem"

Do some of these headlines hint that the story that follows is more real than sensational? Which ones seem more likely to present facts?

How do you think each of these news outlets would handle information on a topic of interest to you? Ask yourself which might provide the most balanced account of the following:

> **Mind Fogger**
>
> Look out for phrases that conjure up scary images and are just new ways to say old-fashioned words. In the late 1990s, the term *home-invasion robbery* sprung up in local newscasts as the teaser of choice. But as Gavin de Becker, author of *The Gift of Fear* (Dell, 1998), has pointed out, every robbery at home is an invasion of your home. "Home-invasion robbery" just sounds scarier.

- Suicide of a leading man who recently starred in a controversial movie about assisted suicide: *NBC Nightly News*, local eyewitness news, or *Entertainment Tonight?*

- A same-sex couple with kids advising single parents how to raise their children: *Time*, *People*, or the *National Enquirer?*

- An insider-trading scandal involving the company you work for: *The Wall Street Journal*, *The New York Times*, or the *Eagle Eye* (your company's weekly newsletter)?

- A recently revealed conspiracy targeting the president's space program: ABCnewsnow.com, TheDrudgeReport.com, or SciFigotcha.com (a sci-fi fan website)?

Try this clear-thinking exercise: watch an evening newscast. Pick out a story they cover, and then do your own research on it. You'll be surprised at the different aspects, slants, and views of the story you'll find. Print sources you consult will typically have more space to examine the sides of the issue more thoroughly. Driven by visual images, a newscast might cover a story that is given less importance in a newspaper. For instance, a grisly murder-suicide in a distant city might lead a newscast, but your morning paper might carry the story on the last page of the news section (if at all).

Regardless of whether stories emanate from the brainy *New Yorker* or the conservative Fox News Channel, the information provided is funneled through the source organization's perspective. For instance, editors and producers might be trying to make good TV or deliver content that will drive up ratings or readership. To get the story straight, you must put your own clear thinking to the task.

Scrutinizing the Internet

And then there's the Internet. Two words of advice: use caution. To verify facts, a good rule of thumb is to find corroborating evidence on at least three reputable sites. However, you should not rely on the Internet as your sole source of information. The Internet is like the Wild, Wild West; that is, in cyberspace there aren't enough marshals to monitor everything that is going on. Anyone, regardless of credentials, can set up a website and disseminate data. While several credible, reputable sites abound, you should still be both wary and diligent.

Here's a benign example of Internet facts gone awry. An education company needed to gather fun facts about George Washington. They found oodles of sites on the Internet to peruse. One site stated that Washington rode a boat from his home, Mount Vernon, to work as president in Washington, D.C. Well, that fact just won't wash because when Washington was president, New York City and later Philadelphia was the country's capital; Washington, D.C., wasn't until 1800, after he left office. A boat ride for Washington, daily or otherwise, from Mount Vernon to New York City or Philadelphia seems highly unlikely.

> **" "Words from the Wise**
>
> Information on the Internet is subject to the same rules and regulations as conversation at a bar.
>
> —Dr. George Lundberg, physician, professor, and editor

Many informative sites are offshoots of news organizations. (Your metro paper probably has a website, as do CNN and the broadcast networks). You're probably safe getting information about your daily headlines there, but you wouldn't want to rely on such sites for information regarding critical decisions such as in-vitro fertilization or your kid's recent bout with impetigo. Our guideline for the Internet is this: it's a great jumping-off point, but don't make it your only resource.

Although information you glean from the Internet cannot be certified 100 percent accurate, here's an Internet test to determine "trust parameters":

♦ How did you find the source? Were you referred by a credible source?

♦ Look for a date attached. When was the site last updated?

♦ What do you know about the site's origin?

♦ Does it refer you to other credible sources?

♦ How professional does it look? Are there misspellings, notable lapses in logic, shoddy reporting? (And be aware too that a slick-looking website isn't necessarily accurate.)

♦ Is information credited?

The Truth About Advertising

Sure, advertising can be colorful, snazzy, clever, and seductive, but it can really trip up your thinking. When we talk about advertising here, we're not just talking about glossy ads and eye-catching commercials, but also product labels—and basically all the avenues that tout a product's benefits, real or purported, to the consumer.

With consumers slammed with more than 3,000 advertising messages a day, we've entered into an era in which the sheer volume of advertising commands our attention and thoughts. And in the onslaught, the sexy images, talking heads, whiplash editing, and driving music make them all the harder to ignore.

Atlanta's Rich's department store won scads of awards for its classy advertising and became a "poster child" for getting its messages to consumers. One classic from the 1960s featured a child who wished his mother had gotten his measles at Rich's so she could take them back. It was lauded for its effectiveness, without mentioning a single product.

Have you seen an ad like that recently? Probably not.

> **CAUTION**
>
> **Mind Fogger**
>
> Studies show that consumers are on the receiving end of 3,000-plus advertising messages a day in the $278 billion advertising industry; another report found that kids see 40,000 commercials a year. Mind clutter starts very early these days.

Instead, print and broadcast advertising images include himbos and buxom babes luxuriating in cologne and scant clothing, slacker chicks in low-cut jeans, couples embroiled in mean-spirited plotting to get to drive a car … with consumers often confused about the product being advertised, much less its benefits. Regardless of the visual images, the words in ads and commercials often strive to beckon you to a better life, right now, immediately, away from the commitments of job and family.

Intentional or not, advertising—in all its (un)doing—seems to prey on fuzzy thinking.

Lackadaisical Labels

For starters, let's look at a few real-life products. The label on a jar of pickles says a single serving is ¼ of a spear; a single TV dinner is actually two servings; and a frozen "personal pizza" is supposed to be split three ways. Hmm. The image of the serving size and the label's description of the serving size don't quite match, do they? Shouldn't a pickle spear be a whole spear, and a TV dinner and personal pizza each be for one? But making the serving truly single would jack up the fat content, carb count, sodium grams, or calories that we're all so desperate to keep down.

"Buy Me Now" Descriptions

A high-definition flat-screen TV from a major maker was advertised for $3,299, originally $6,999, a whopping $2,700 markdown in an ad that screamed "Hurry! Limited Stock!" The savings seemed unbelievable; they were. The TV was "HD ready," which isn't the same as already being high definition; it would have required an upgrade (and money for the upgrade). The TV was originally almost $7,000 because it had been sitting around in a stockroom for two years, and that was the price point then. Since its introduction, two other models by the same maker had been produced, the latest comparable version selling for even less than the two-year-old model on sale!

If you find yourself drawn in to an ad, dissect the glitzy words and images you see, and determine whether or not they're blurring your thinking. Consider the following:

- If you could tone down the ad's language, how would you describe the product? Is it really "an ultra-plush, sandstone-colored sofa with a suedelike finish that will provide happy, soothing respite to a day's end" or simply a comfortable beige couch?

- Put the product in a different setting. Do those shoes look extra chic because they're propped up on a mod barstool in a hip beachside lounge?

- Strip away the music, the actors, and the voiceover (or copy). What's left of the actual product?

- Is this product really going to make your life better right now?

- Is it a luxury or a necessity?

- When looking at the price, make sure the make, model, style, etc. match. Do your homework; here's a good case for using the Internet to your advantage. Do a search on the product and see the prices and details that are coming up from other stores.

Asking Great Questions

If we didn't question, we'd take a whole lot of stuff for granted, wouldn't we? Throughout this book you'll notice "Points to Ponder," age-old questions and quandaries that can prompt philosophical ruminations. Questions are a crucial asset to clear thinking in everyday ways, too.

> **" "Words from the Wise**
>
> We can have facts without thinking, but we cannot have thinking without facts.
>
> —John Dewey, American philosopher and educator

Throughout this book, we encourage you to ask questions at several junctures, and for several reasons. It's a critical aspect to clear thinking, because it's invaluable in clarifying, expounding upon, and discussing information. It allows you entry into the heart of a matter, where you can get more details and become more fully engaged. Remember Socrates from Chapter 2? Take a cue from him and make questioning an active part of your clear-thinking routine.

Garbage In, Garbage Out: Asking the Right Questions

Too often, we waste our time by not asking the right question to find out what we really want to know. It's the GIGO factor: garbage in, garbage out. That is, the more specific your question, the more information you're likely to extract.

Your question doesn't have to be flowery, just articulate. Get to the root of your question so that you can gain the information you need. To do that, determine if your question has the necessary who, what, when, where, why, and how components.

When you've mastered great questioning, you can direct the flow of a conversation better to gain even more information. Consider these three simple examples of improving a question:

> *Instead of:* How can I get my printer to work?
> *Try:* How can I get my 2003 Computron XL4423 laser printer to print darker?

> *Instead of:* How can I get a business license?
> *Try:* How can I get a business license in Sioux City for my indoor miniature golf course?

> *Instead of:* Why do Catholics do that?
> *Try:* Why do Catholics genuflect when they enter the pew before the service begins?

When crafting your question, consider the following:

◆ What do you hope to accomplish by asking it?

◆ Is it clear and well phrased?

◆ Is it as detailed as possible?

◆ Will an answer to it move you closer to making an informed choice or decision?

◆ Is it *open-ended*—that is, does it require more than just a yes or no answer—for a maximum response, and set up to logically lead to other questions?

Then assess your answers in terms of these questions:

◆ Does it meet the criteria for being objective? Or is it really subjective?

◆ Can it be considered a sensible response?

◆ What makes the respondent an expert?

◆ Does it serve your thinking quest?

◆ Even if it does, can you think of a follow-up question that will be even more exacting?

When Joe wrote for the *Atlanta Journal-Constitution*, part of his "beat" was writing obituaries. Besides being a sometimes-somber task, the post gave him an intense appreciation for deadlines (no pun intended), and a fervent interest in asking the right questions. When you're writing quite possibly the last printed text of a person's life, you want to make sure the facts are right. In many cases, the obit will serve as a lasting reminder of that person for generations. So the commitment had to be in place—and intense—to make sure the facts were accurate. Joe's editor was always a stickler—for good reason—to probe deeper to tell someone's story.

Think Tank

Open-ended questions allow for answers that are more descriptive, reveal more details, and, in the end, are more productive. **Close-ended** questions can be answered with a yes or no.

Be Specific

Joe learned that the more specific your questions, the more compelling the answers usually are. For instance, the vice president of a large conglomerate had died, so Joe interviewed the exec's surviving niece for the obituary. She said his hobbies had included writing. When Joe posed the question, "What kinds of things did he like to write?" a wonderful revelation unfolded. Despite the company's large size, this exec—whose typical demeanor was described as stern—gave each employee an original poem he had written about them for their birthday.

Dr. Ric must ask lots of questions of patients so that he can most accurately assess treatment. That's a given. If a patient says, "My chest hurts," he has to ask a series of questions to define and refine the patient's description of pain. Sometimes an initial diagnosis can even begin, "How would you rate your pain on a 1 to 10 scale?"

Dr. Ken uses Socratic questioning—also known as the Socratic method discussed in Chapter 2—in the interviews he conducts to gather research from doctors in a constant quest to fine-tune and enlighten studies and analysis being conducted.

As you can understand from this section, creative questioning is an integral component of clear thinking that can prompt you to find out what you want or need to know. And sometimes, it can generate further questioning that can bring even deeper understanding and fresh revelations.

Facts vs. Statements

Are you hearing or reading a fact, or is it spin? Remember, a statement isn't always a statement of *fact*. As we've pointed out in this chapter, you can find several occasions every day in which a statement is masquerading as a fact. The statement might be about the $7,000 TV set (that's overpriced), or the headline screaming that an American Girl doll is fleeing a dangerous neighborhood.

Many times statements come in the form of proposed information, policies, intentions, and observations. Perhaps the strongest form of a statement is in an opinion. Opinions often have particularly descriptive adjectives attached—that can be positive or negative—such as disreputable, tired, disorganized, disillusioned, brilliant, etc.

Remember that not all statements (in whatever form) are backed up by evidence, proof, or experience. Unlike a mere statement, a fact must be a statement of truth, an assertion or assumption that can be proven.

Distinguishing fact from fiction is more important than ever. A 2005 Project for Excellence in Journalism study found that information today tends to be "faster, looser, and cheaper" than in the past. Consumers are increasingly forming their opinions based on others' opinions, particularly those showcased on cable news shows and on websites, rather than on actual facts.

To assess whether information you are exposed to is factual, pay careful attention. Ask questions. Don't assume that a declarative expression is the absolute final (and truthful) word. Your clear thinking depends on it.

Cobweb Buster

Statements can be non-language. Consider that "He's really making a statement wearing that leopard-spotted kilt," or "She's making a statement driving that fuchsia Porsche!" Trick question: are those statements or facts?

Thinking and Knowing Are Not the Same

Obviously, you need to think to know the facts and to determine whether or not you've got a fact in hand or just someone's statement. What do you know? What do you think you know? Can you think and not know? Can you know and not think?

We're not messing with you, honest. Thinking and knowing just present one of the most abstract concepts this chapter (and possibly the book) covers. You've read a lot so far about the different ways to think, but you also need to understand the difference between thinking and knowing.

In Chapter 2, we defined "thinking"; it's basically the active version of knowing. We like education gurus Michael Scriven and Paul Fisher's assessment. They conclude that when you think, you process and generate skills and belief. When you know, you "merely" acquire and possess that information, or use those skills. You have to think to know, and because of that, you have to click through information in your mind, analyzing the data—and hopefully divvying it up into fact or fiction—before it becomes part of your knowledge.

Thinking definitely presents a more abstract notion than knowing. Which of the following would you think, which would you know, and which could you either think or know?

1. Ideas

2. The Tampa Bay Buccaneers' quarterback stats

3. Judgments

4. Opinions

5. The name of the author who wrote *Great Expectations*

6. How to use a lawn mower

7. God

8. The value of human life

9. The penalties of perjury

10. The answer to an algebra problem

(You can definitively know 2, 5, 6, 9, and 10; the rest are up for grabs.)

Is It Subjective or Objective?

Now that you've had a primer on questions, and understand how asking the right ones can blow the lid off some advertising ploys and enable you to discern statements from facts, now consider *subjective* versus *objective* statements.

Subjective views definitely take on a personal flair, usually imbuing some sort of judgment call (which isn't necessarily positive or negative). They reflect a person's take on someone or something, and reflect that person's way of thinking and his or her background.

The objective realm should be always impartial, unwavering in fairness, and opinion-free. When collecting information or listening to others, it's incumbent upon you to determine if you're on the receiving end of a subjective or objective view, comment, or statement. Compare the following:

Think Tank

A **subjective** view is derived from one's own consciousness and distinguished from external, impartial observation. An **objective** view represents an outward view "uncontaminated" by opinion or intrinsic thought.

Subjective: A critic's movie review
Objective: A *TV Guide* episodic description

Subjective: A teacher's grade on an essay question
Objective: A teacher's grade on a multiple-choice test

Subjective: An employee's performance evaluation
Objective: An employee's sales for the month of May

Subjective: I hate turnip greens.
Objective: Turnip greens are part of tonight's supper.

Subjective: She looks amazing.
Objective: She has four fashion magazine covers to her credit.

Many people believe that the way to convince others to come around to their way of thinking is by spinning out several subjective statements, vigorously giving their point of view. But often, objective statements—especially those grounded in fact—can be just as persuasive. For instance, although someone can hammer away about their opinion that kids should stay strictly in the home environment rather than be in child care five days a week (the subjective view), pointing out facts from studies and observations that bear out the benefits of staying home (the objective view) will probably be more convincing.

True objectivity is substantially more difficult to achieve than subjectivity. It requires embracing outside sources in an unbiased manner to become completely knowledgeable on a subject, a deep understanding of topics that can't possibly be feigned, and a thoughtful consideration of other people's opinions.

The Rational and the Irrational

Finally, when you're on the receiving end of information or views that you want to consider, you must determine whether they're *rational*—sensible and reasonable—or *irrational*, not conforming to logic. Generally speaking, positive thoughts, feelings, and emotions funnel into rational thinking, whereas negative ones lead to irrational thinking.

To determine whether you're gathering rational information, ask yourself if the thinking behind it is consistent with known facts and reality, is logical, and makes sense.

That's a rational view. For instance, taking an umbrella outside because the Weather Channel has predicted rain for your area represents rational thinking (even though weather can be unpredictable). But guiding your life by the astrology chart is considered irrational because there is no science, no facts that support astrological readings. Irrational thinking is inconsistent or unsupported by known facts.

Think Tank

Rational thinking is sensible and reasonable, and endowed with understanding. **Irrational** thinking is considered bereft of logic, preposterous, or void of reasoning and understanding.

Most of you probably strive to be in the former category. Though none of us is immune from occasional irrational thoughts, the real bane is that they blur reality, distorting it into problematic situations.

Take the following statements, for example. Which pair is rational and can be substantiated by fact? Which pair is irrational and exude a silly notion?

> You shouldn't hug someone who has cancer.
> Bricks make great footballs.

> You shouldn't drive with your eyes closed.
> Black-painted walls will make a room dark.

As you're swamped in messages from all kinds of sources, you must put that information to the clear thinking test to determine whether it is credible enough to deserve your attention and gain your trust. The requirements of that test include deciding if the information you have represents fact—true, impartial, and rational in nature—or espouses a subjective or irrational view.

Now that you're armed with this information, our next stop is "wayward facts," the kinds of data you've got to be aware of … or they'll really fog up your thoughts.

Points to Ponder

Do we have to think scientifically to find the truth?

The Least You Need to Know

◆ When assessing whether information is credible, consider the source and apply appropriate guidelines for print, broadcast, and Internet outlets.

◆ Be wary of the advertising messages and visuals that detract from a product's true description and value.

◆ Craft your questions with a who, what, when, where, why, and how in place so that you get the most detailed answers.

◆ Realize that thinking provides an active channel to knowing.

◆ A statement isn't necessarily a fact. It could be an opinion, and might espouse a subjective or irrational viewpoint. Look for facts that are both objective and rational.

Chapter 8

Watch Out for Wayward Facts

In This Chapter

- Realize the differences between misconceptions, urban legends, hoaxes, and superstitions

- Recognize how to spot a hoax and an urban legend

- Find out why your thinking should steer clear of superstitions and the supernatural

- Prevent wayward facts from infiltrating your thoughts and decision making

These are the ones that'll getcha every time. The urban legend, the superstition, the enthralling psychic phenomena … they're junk food for the brain. And like junk food, they have an irresistible, if detrimental, pull.

What's worse, these "facts" can seem fun and even helpful. So this chapter provides some guidelines for spotting and handling these scrappy and persistent pests—these fact wannabes that will only cloud your thinking.

Mind Games 8

Two friends are chatting on the phone, each in her respective home; one's in a state on the West Coast of the United States, the other's in a state on the East Coast. The West Coaster asks, "What time is it?" When her friend replies, she says, "No way! That's what time it is here!" How is this possible?

(Turn to Appendix D for the answer.)

A Quick Quiz Before We Begin

Answer these five statements with yes or no. We'll return to this quiz at the end of the chapter.

- ◆ I check my astrology chart for sound advice.

- ◆ I've passed along a chain letter before.

- ◆ I've tinkered with and retold a story that sounded true, but had unbelievable elements, so that I could prove a point.

- ◆ Unexplained mysteries—such as UFOs—can't be scientifically proven because a paranormal element is at work.

- ◆ The statement "The sun is between the earth and the moon" is true.

Mulling Over Misconceptions

The first stop in our trip through wayward facts deals with *misconceptions*, those unfortunate pieces of formed—and always mistaken—ideas or judgments. They've been crafted out of a person's misunderstanding. They might be passed off as advice, belief, or fact.

Misconceptions can be so innocuous you may not even realize they pop up in your conversations. You may have even relied on them as fact more than once.

When left untended or unedited, misconceptions can become problematic, leading to falsehoods that are perpetuated—or even bigger misunderstandings.

A Thinking Thorn That's Too Common

Following are some common misconceptions. As you'll see, they're hardly discriminating. They'll happily come to the party of any subject matter, all dressed up and important-sounding:

♦ The only man-made object visible on Earth from space is the Great Wall of China. (This was even a Trivial Pursuit question!)

♦ Loud sound is not dangerous, as long as you don't feel any pain in your ears.

♦ Documents sent from an Apple computer must have a ".doc" extension attached to the filename or they won't go through via e-mail.

♦ If it's in print, you can trust it.

♦ Your insurance company is responsible for selecting the shop to repair your vehicle after a car accident.

♦ Popular vote decides the U.S. president.

♦ A slot machine that's been played for a long time without a win is due to hit.

♦ If a tornado hits, hiding under a highway overpass will provide safe harbor.

♦ Muslims don't believe in Jesus or any other prophets.

♦ Vaccinations cause autism.

♦ Dinosaurs and humans coexisted.

Each of these statements can be fervently disproved. As misconceptions go, these should never be taken for granted just because you might have heard them before or they sound like they could be right. For instance, loud sound can indeed do damage to your ears, even if it doesn't cause pain. That's because a human's threshold for pain is about 120 to 140 decibels, whereas sound can do some damage at 85 decibels, albeit over a sustained period of time. Before the 2000 election, a commonly held misconception was that popular vote decided the U.S. presidency. Wrong again; the Electoral College does that job, although the popular vote certainly plays an influential role (and provides a backup plan, too).

Minding Misconceptions

To prevent misconceptions, ask yourself the following:

♦ Do I really understand the concept, statement, or "fact" being presented here?

> **Think Tank**
>
> A **misconception** is an erroneous conclusion, a false opinion or wrong understanding, whereas a **hoax**—which can sometimes disastrously spin out of misconceptions—is a deliberately deceptive trick or story for mockery or mischief. A hoax that involves bilking others out of money is a **scam**.

◆ Does it make sense?

◆ Does it beg to be verified?

◆ When did I first hear it? At school? At a party? Along a parade route?

◆ Have I heard it more than once?

◆ Has it been couched in a "Would you believe that …?" or "Did you know that …?" type of phrasing?

◆ Is it a piece of "information" that I plan to use for another purpose?

If the answer to that last question is yes, the statement definitely warrants a follow-up investigation. To do that, check out the tips in Chapter 7.

Although many misconceptions are benign, their being left unchecked is cause for concern. After all, misconceptions often leave us open to believe fraudulent "facts." Let's delve into these areas—including hoaxes, urban legends, and superstitions— because their presence in an increasingly volatile world has skyrocketed, particularly as human nature dictates that we constantly seek assurances and protection against fear.

Hoaxes: Frauds Disguised as Facts

When misconceptions go wrong, they can create *hoaxes*, a bane to clear thinking. These are deliberately deceptive, sometimes tantalizing pieces of information that just seem like they can't possibly be true and, in fact, aren't.

Hoaxes, or frauds disguised as facts, have become much more prevalent since the advent of the Internet. The web can be a powerful tool for unleashing loads of these so-called "facts," "know-how," "advice," and "tips," which aren't rooted in any truth or personal experience whatsoever. But hoaxes aren't limited to the Internet; they can be transmitted by mail and conversations. On occasion, even news reports have been the unwitting conduit to disseminating them.

Hoax-y Formats

And boy, can those hoaxes take on many guises! Among the three of us, we've received hoaxy e-mails covering an array of topics:

◆ Free money from computer giants and retail chains (if we just keep forwarding the chain letter being sent to us)

- Requests to help someone set a Guinness world record for number of e-mails received

- Warnings about foreign invasions, unsanitary restaurants, and even poisoned jeans

- Heart-rending messages about aid to sick children

All of these e-mail messages, upon further inspection, were found to be hokey propaganda with not a speck of truth.

Cobweb Buster

Fittingly, the word *hoax* was crafted out of *hocus pocus* during the 1700s. That nonsense phrase was a favorite of conjurers—or magicians—beginning in King James's time. Hocus pocus was probably imitating a Latin phrase—*hoc est corpus*—used by Catholic priests during the communion sacrament (loosely translated "this is my body").

Many hoaxes come in the form of chain letters. These used to come predominantly by snail mail, littering our mailboxes. Now they clutter e-mail inboxes, trapping your time and thoughts by commanding your attention with often-insidious pleas, false warnings, and plain nonsense. We're certain you've received one or two like the ones we've just mentioned, too.

Some hoaxes spin wildly out of a jumped-to conclusion from a news story that did—or didn't—happen. For instance, a few years ago, approaching Halloween, New Jersey residents were warned that trick-or-treaters might receive candy tainted with a virus. This hoax was created when large quantities of Halloween candy were purchased at two warehouse stores. From there, suddenly, the candy had been bought by Arab extremists, the FBI was called in to investigate, and the final finding was that true, a lot of candy had been bought, but it was all for resale … and quite safe.

Particularly troubling, hoaxes are typically disguised as being "helpful," but really just prey on fears of inadequacy, personal safety, insecurity, and health consequences. Have you ever heard of any of these scary health-related hoaxes: sniffing certain perfumes or licking ATM envelopes at a particular branch can cause poisonings; a specific brand of antiperspirant causes cancer; a certain lipstick brand contains lead; or fast-food chains have heroin needles hidden in their bouncy-ball play centers?

Scams—hoaxes that scheme people out of money—can really imperil a good person's name and bank account. One well-documented scam alerts customers of brokerage houses and banks that their account information must be "immediately updated" by clicking a link and turning over vital information (such as Social Security numbers and addresses). Unfortunately, that information then leads to identity fraud, with accounts drained and credit cards issued based on phony information. These scams—particularly in e-mail format—look quite credible, even emblazoned with a reasonable facsimile of the financial institution's logo.

Coax Out the Hoax

In essence, hoaxes (or fraudulent facts) are foolish propaganda, whipped up into a frenzy of mass hysteria that should almost always be ignored, avoided, and kept at bay. Reading or participating in them wastes your time and productivity, and can divert your thoughts into all kinds of errant—and sometimes even harmful—directions.

Not all hoaxes include all of these telltale signs, but follow these guidelines to see if you've got a hoax on your hands:

- There's an absence of reliable references (or any at all) for further investigation.

- It prompts you to take immediate action (do this or else!).

- If an e-mail, it tries to convey credence by using a journalistic tone.

- It requests personal information, such as account numbers.

- There's an overt persuasion to alert you, although the original source doesn't know you.

- It claims to try and help you out, although—again—the original source doesn't know you.

- It defies common sense.

- It contains information that prompts skepticism and suspicion on your part.

In addition, consider the following:

- If it's in an e-mail, does it include a signature from the original "source"?

- If it's a warning in an e-mail, is it the first time you've heard of it? How likely is it that a mass e-mail would be your first alert to a breaking news story?

CAUTION

Mind Fogger

With hoaxes targeting identity theft particularly rampant, check with your financial institution before giving out your account numbers or any other personal information—especially for those too-good-to-be-true "one-time" offers and random pleas for verifying your information.

Rid yourself of hoaxes by, for starters, removing yourself from friends' and relatives' mass e-mail lists. Kindly tell them that your e-mail inbox has been clogged up; keeping you out of the loop on such offerings would be a big help. If you're getting e-mails with hoaxes from those you don't even know, consider signing up for a service such as SpamArrest, which requires that senders verify themselves before e-mail is delivered.

That Hoax Is No Joke

Once in a great while, you may run across a hoax that requires further investigation. When is a hoax not a hoax and actually a warning to be heeded?

If you're on your cell phone often, you may have been troubled by the e-mail that suggested that leaving your cell phone turned on while pumping gas could spontaneously discharge an electrical impulse and cause a fire. Naturally, that's a particularly dangerous incident at a gas station. Signs at some gas station chains do urge patrons to turn off their cell phones, and cell phone manuals have even cited concern over the matter. More recent data suggests that phones from the late 1990s were more prone to these harmful effects, but a chance for a fire—however slight—remains, so caution is merited.

The bottom line: if you're particularly concerned about a warning that may be a hoax but you aren't sure, dig deeper. Go beyond the web to check out the claim. (You can start with the web, but, in these cases, getting corroborating evidence from three other websites might not necessarily pan out if the hoax is rampant and just being repeated harum-scarum.) Do a Google search to determine whether the hoax has already been exposed.

Also check out definitive sources. In the case of the cell phone, that would include your cell phone manual or calling your provider and asking them about what you've heard or read. (Of course, you should call them away from a gas station until you're certain of the facts.)

The Truth Is Out ... Where?

A 2002 CBS poll suggests that 57 percent of Americans believe in psychic phenomena—encompassing the supernatural (events beyond, or exceeding, the laws of nature) and the paranormal (events that can't be explained by scientific knowledge)—with results mirroring previous Gallup polls conducted. This area includes extrasensory perception, psychic healing, extraterrestrial life, ghosts, near-death experiences, and "unexplained mysteries" of all kinds.

Even if most of us believe in such topics, should we? And on what basis? And should the paranormal factor in your thoughts, problem solving, or decision making?

Here, There, and Everywhere

The supernatural has descended on our society with a vengeance through a proliferation of stories and "accounts" in the media. It's at the movies with such all-time blockbusters as *The Sixth Sense* and *The Ring*, on TV with *X-Files* reruns, in best-sellers by John Edward and James Van Praagh, even in a popular late-night radio show hosted by Art Bell.

Many of us were introduced to the "supernatural" as kids with the Ouija board, hoping that some mysterious, unknown force could dole out an answer to life's pressing problems: "Does so-and-so like me?" "Will I get married?" "Will my parents find out if I do such-and-such?"

Even to grown-ups, the supernatural can have a grip on your thoughts. Because supernatural and paranormal events can be so seemingly mesmerizing, they can prompt thinking to head off in many directions, often without any information, knowledge, or personal experience to back them up.

People often want to point to supernatural factors to explain away the unexplainable. But the problem with putting too much thinking or belief into these types of supernatural forces is that you can't really rely on them to sort out issues, problems, or thoughts you're facing today. Sure, seeing a movie about UFOs is entertaining, but will theorizing about extraterrestrial life help us in dealing with the employee who seems bent on demeaning staffers through memos? And who doesn't like a good ghost story? But is blaming a ghost for the draft in your kitchen wise if you've really got a ventilation problem?

Similarly, visiting psychics has become an accepted practice for many. Although palm and Tarot card reading can be interesting, it's not a true substitute for clear thinking.

Take, for instance, those who have lost loved ones and are comforted by clairvoyants who claim they can speak "to the other side." If it soothes your thinking, fine; but usually, this calm is only a temporary fix for grieving thoughts. If deeper issues are involved—which they most certainly are if someone is seeking the help of a clairvoyant—other alternatives should be given more credence. Psychotherapy, counseling, talking with clergy, or working out issues one on one with living family members may be better approaches for longer-lasting effects.

Cobweb Buster _____

We've been looking to explain the unexplainable since ancient times. In 1281, more than 4,000 ships were destroyed—and the lives of 100,000 men were lost—when Kublai Khan tried to invade Japan. The Japanese said a mighty "divine wind," sent from an unknown power, wiped out Khan's force. However, once modern-day science was applied to the 720-year-old tale, a different explanation emerged. The reason for the devastation had more to do with the ships being chained together and a tsunami taking them all down than a supernatural force bent on revenge.

Troll for Trouble

Several people profess to be "psychic healers" who can use their mind to cure diseases. Sometimes patients can be so desperate for a remedy—any remedy—to ease pain and suffering, they put their faith, and money, into such a tactic. Instead, you should direct your thinking toward methods based in fact and that have proven benefits, that can point to evidentiary success, or that can provide a basis for proof, such as experimental drugs or acupuncture.

Coming to Grips with Superstitions

Be it black cats and ladders, staying away from cracked mirrors, or keeping a rabbit's foot around for luck, *superstitions* do have a certain allure. Popular for centuries (and resulting in such mayhem as the Salem witch trials), superstitions enjoyed a resurgence in the 1960s because so many people were disenchanted with the sea changes and radical nature of society. Today superstitions seem to still placate, offering wishes and good luck during troubled times.

Superstitions can sometimes sound like misconceptions, but they usually impart a strange—if not all together irrational—piece of information or advice, usually in the spirit of good or bad luck. Superstitions can also be manifested in some physical object that you can supposedly lord over fate, making you feel like you have control over a situation.

Think Tank _____

A **superstition** is an irrational but typically strong belief in the magical effects of certain objects, rituals, or actions and their ability to bring good or bad luck.

Consider these:

◆ Sleep with a piece of wedding cake under your pillow, and you'll dream the identity of your future mate.

◆ If you enter the back door of someone's home, you have to leave that way, too, or bad luck will follow.

◆ If your palm itches, money's coming your way.

◆ Don't hang up a new calendar until New Year's Day, or you'll have bad luck all year.

◆ Ladybugs bring good luck.

◆ If you plant a weeping willow tree, someone in your family will die.

> **Words from the Wise**
>
> A superstition is a premature explanation that overstays its time.
>
> —George Iles, American writer

If our thinking were always ruled by superstitions, we'd never have to use our minds! We could just consider what's going on currently in our lives, and then look up the corresponding superstitions to follow so that bad things wouldn't happen to us.

Does that last sentence sound like a familiar scenario? That's basically what astrology is all about. The pinnacle of superstitious thinking, astrology—using the stars to chart your life—tempts you with everyday advice to win at life, love, work, money, business, school, and family, urging you to stay away from certain situations and embrace others. Sure, it's fun to say you're a Gemini or a Sagittarius, but you don't really want the stars telling you what to do and when to do it, do you? That's what your mind's for!

Admittedly, particularly when we can't find an explanation for a quandary, and deal with so much uncertainty on a daily basis, relying on a superstition can provide a welcome respite. But resorting to a superstition to make up our minds won't make a problem go away. And it never creates a permanent solution. Instead, to think clearly and face decisions, subjects, arguments—and anything else you need thinking for—head on, you're always better off using your research and reasoning skills, or putting science to the test.

Dispelling Urban Legends

Doesn't everyone love a good story, spun well, with anecdotes thrown in, a little surprise and good humor ... or maybe even a good scare?

That's really the impetus for *urban legends* (or *urban myths*). They thrive on a well-told story that is so mesmerizing (or appalling or unbelievable) that others feel compelled to pass it on.

Heard of the stuffs of these urban legends? Did you hear the one about the poodle that blew up when his owner tried to dry his fur in the microwave, the guy with the hook who massacres a couple parked in a car, or the rampaging alligators in a city sewer?

Think Tank

An **urban legend** or **urban myth** is a modern-day folktale passed around that, although appearing true, contains bizarre and even sometimes macabre elements.

Some urban legends are bent on taking down celebrities and politicians, leading people to stereotype and prejudice: the rumored stories about the leading man and the gerbil, the strumpet who overdosed, the child star who died from downing a combination of Pop Rocks candy and Pepsi.

Urban legends have also been propelled and perpetuated by the Internet. In that manner, they have become folktales for the new millennium. Weirder still, they're prone to a variety of versions that can lead to even crazier offshoots.

Cobweb Buster

The 1998 slasher movie *Urban Legend* followed the exploits of a group of college students as grisly murders shook their campus. All the related mayhem and plot points took a cue from several urban legends. Making light of how urban legends get passed around, the movie's tagline was "It happened to someone who knows someone you know ... you're next."

The Stuff of Urban Legends

So how do you spot an urban legend? Consider the following if a story or "anecdotal evidence" is suspect:

- ◆ You've heard it, or a version of it, with perhaps different names.

- ◆ The players, atmosphere, and objects involved all seem real, and it sounds like it could happen, but still smacks of incredulity.

- ◆ It ends with a twist, a punch line, or a "gotcha" moment.

Set It Straight

If you or your kids are affected by an urban legend and you'd like to find out more, there are ways to set it straight. One story went like this: middle school students were wearing jelly bracelets—those flexible rubber bracelets that have become novelties— and certain colors were described as signifying different sexual activities that the kids were partaking in. Understandably, such a notion horrified parents in areas where the story was gaining steam.

What if you heard this story and noticed that your daughter was wearing one of those jelly bracelets? Do you jump to an assumption about your daughter? Here's where urban legends can muck up thinking. Instead of buying into the urban legend, you've always got other possibilities to check out a story. Just as when debunking a hoax, you need to go beyond the web to investigate the claim, and interview informed sources, such as school personnel. And although you could run the risk of planting an idea where there wasn't one, your best recourse is to communicate with your child. Ask if the bracelet has a "deeper" or "hidden" meaning, and voice your concerns.

Mind Fogger

When it comes to getting facts about urban legends, don't always go by broadcast news reports. Sometimes the news gatherers behind the scenes are looking for the best images and the sexiest stories—which urban legends can sometimes provide. In many major markets, particularly during the months of February, May, and November (when stations set their advertising rates), salacious stories spike. With new, circulating urban legends as a jumping-off point, "news reports"—seemingly ground in hard facts—permeate the airwaves. Notice that many news reports never set out to debunk urban legends you hear; they only seem to perpetuate them by "exposing" darker elements of the story, often with intonations rife with alarm.

Urbananities

Now and again, even clear thinkers can get reeled in by urban legends. Urban legends have become so virulent that fondly remembered stories once thought to be true may also be the stuff of them. We remember a story from our maternal grandmother, who spoke English as a second language, telling us about Chevrolet's troubles introducing the Nova model into Latin American countries in the late 1970s. In Spanish, Nova could be translated to *No va*, meaning "It doesn't go." So she said that Chevy had to rename it with the exotic name Caribe. This marketing disaster has been written up extensively—even appearing in books concerning major corporate marketing foibles such as the 1992 *Classic Failures in Product Marketing: Marketing Principles Violations and How to Avoid Them*. However, in 2004, *Business Week* online and other web reports—such as Snopes.com, which investigates urban legends—actually confirmed that the Nova snafu is indeed an urban legend. In fact, at the time of the *Business Week* article, the Nova was reported as selling briskly in Mexico.

Even having been discredited, the Chevy Nova continues as an urban legend in earnest, repeatedly doled out by the unwitting as a cautionary tale about translating American products for foreign markets. Urban legends can sound amazingly true and realistic, so they can seem all too fitting for evidence and proof. So can hoaxes, the paranormal, and superstitions. But stories, though involving, should always be checked out to see if they're worthy of your thoughts and consideration. When "amazing stories" come your way, keep your gullibility in check. Stay aware and don't leave your believability to chance.

Now let's return to the quiz at the beginning of this chapter. (Hopefully, if you didn't disagree before, you will in the future!)

- ◆ I check my astrology chart for sound advice. (That's falling for a *superstition*.)

- ◆ I've passed along a chain letter before. (That's participating in a *hoax*.)

- ◆ I've tinkered with and retold a story that sounded true, but had unbelievable elements, so that I could prove a point. (That would be those intriguing but untrue *urban legends*.)

- ◆ Unexplained mysteries—such as UFOs—can't be scientifically proven because a paranormal element is at work. (That's the *paranormal* trying to pull you in.)

- ◆ The statement "The sun is between the earth and the moon" is true. (That's a *misconception*.)

Next up, we'll look at logic and common sense, two areas that will also always be on your side to cast wayward facts far away.

Points to Ponder
What's wrong with basing your life on a lie?

The Least You Need to Know

- Wayward "facts" are a bane to clear thinking—appearing as truths but completely false—and come in the form of misconceptions, hoaxes, and urban legends.

- Don't take well-known statements as facts. They could be misconceptions.

- Although they may appear legitimate, hoaxes and scams are just frauds disguised as facts.

- While paranormal topics continue to be believed and are prevalent in today's media, don't rely on them to help clear thinking; they'll only be a hindrance.

- Urban legends are engaging and appear true, but can't ever be relied upon.

Part

The Age of Reason

After you've gotten a bead on the information out there, the essentials of logic and reasoning enter the clear-thinking picture. Here we show you how to apply them to your thought processes. When you do, you'll find out how clarity becomes a key component to developing viable alternatives and making strong decisions, both big and small.

Chapter 9

The Lowdown on Logic

In This Chapter

- ◆ Grasp the terms of logic
- ◆ Apply logic to clear thinking
- ◆ Critique your common sense—and get some more
- ◆ Know about fallacies that can thwart your thoughts

Logic: we know we need it, but we're not always sure how to get it or tap into it. This chapter provides the specifics of logic—most notably the concepts involved—and then shows how you can apply it to your clear thinking.

For this discussion, we also include common sense, a key component of logic, as well as review a list of the ever-present fallacies you should be aware of.

Mind Games 9

Mopping sweat off his brow, a man, thirsty and stranded in the desert, has sliced his arm and is bleeding profusely. If the human body has nine quarts of blood, and he is bleeding such that he's losing a cup every half hour, how long will it be before he "bleeds out" and dies?

(Turn to Appendix D for the answer.)

A Tour Through the Language of Logic

At first blush, logic can seem to be an elusive subject that's hard to define. It's sort of like you know it when you hear it, but capturing it into words might be difficult.

Here's a joke from comedian Steven Wright that hinges on logic: "I used to work in a fire hydrant factory. You couldn't park anywhere near the place." What makes us laugh about this joke? Logical thinking suggests that you couldn't park at the factory because tow-away zones—typically associated with fire hydrants—were everywhere.

That's what logic does: it lets you analyze an argument or a judgment and work out whether it's likely to be correct. Of course, you don't need to know logic to argue, but it certainly will make you a more effective debater. And if use it, you'll find it easier to spot invalid arguments, and make better ones yourself.

Logic does have its place. It's not, for instance, the absolute law that governs the universe. And just because something seems illogical, doesn't always mean it doesn't exist. In addition, logic doesn't govern human behavior. When you see how logic works, you'll begin to understand how it can influence your thinking for the better. For now, let's take a look at the common terms logic employs.

Propositions

Proposition is your setup: a statement or judgment that's either true or false, and that you're trying to prove.

Here's a simple proposition: your pants are muddy.

Arguments and Premises

After you've got your proposition, you try to make arguments to prove it. Arguments are a collection of further propositions that support your case based on the initial one. They refer to the evidence (or reasons) for accepting the proposition posed. They may be indicated by such words as *because*, *since*, and *obviously*. From your arguments, you build a string of premises that make your case.

Premises in an argument for muddy pants would be as follows:

> Your pants are muddy because you've been playing outside.
>
> Your pants are muddy since the backyard outside is filled with dirt.
>
> Obviously, it's been raining because your pants are muddy.

Inferences and Conclusions

At this phase, the premises of the argument are used to obtain even further propositions. Here we start with one or more propositions that have been accepted, and then derive another proposition. Those arrived-at propositions can then be used in further inference. Basically, inference is the process of allowing one truth to lead you to another one. Inference is often denoted by phrases such as *implies that* or *therefore*.

> **CAUTION**
>
> **Mind Fogger**
>
> *Obviously* is a tricky word. Sometimes when someone uses it, you may feel too intimidated to question it. But if it doesn't seem obvious to you, ask. You can always come back to say "That *is* obvious" for yourself after you've heard the explanation.

Here are two inferences regarding the muddy pants situation:

> You were playing in the backyard, therefore you were playing in dirt.
>
> It's been raining outside, therefore the dirt is turning to mud.

Voilà! You've now got information to form a conclusion, which is another proposition. As the final stage of inference, it is affirmed on the basis of the original premises, and the inferences drawn from there. Conclusions are often indicated by phrases such as *therefore*, *it follows that*, and *we conclude*.

The conclusion would be this:

> You were playing in the backyard, where rain was turning the dirt to mud, so it follows that your pants got muddy.

In the preceding example, we just pulled a rather simple proposition that would spin out simple arguments, premises, and inferences for a simple, logical conclusion. These form the building blocks for reasoning, which we examine in its entirety in the next chapter.

Logic, Not Emotion

For logic to be effective, emotion can never be part of the mix. The sci-fi TV and movie series *Star Trek* had a main character, Mr. Spock, who was a Vulcan. Vulcans, almost inconceivably, were a race governed by logic. The Vulcans were supposed to be so much more highly evolved than humans that they'd risen above emotion to embrace logic as their only mode of thinking.

While seeing a Vulcan in contrast to other characters on the series, viewers realize how human behavior is routinely affected by emotion, which makes our point: Logic and emotion are completely separate. Logic has no place for emotion, and emotion can indeed hamper logic.

> **Words from the Wise**
>
> If you go in for argument, take care of your temper. Your logic, if you have any, will take care of itself.
>
> —Joseph Farrell, nineteenth-century priest and essayist

Still, even if emotions can cloud thinking, cause conflict, and prompt bad—and illogical—behavior, we're still better off with them. Otherwise, we'd be robots having mechanisms doing the thinking—and sadly, feeling—for us.

Funneling Logic into Your Thoughts

Let's apply logic to a fictional situation. For the "Yell Like Hell" spirit-cheering competition at Towne Center University, four sorority teams—the Alphas, Betas, Deltas, and Gammas—are vying for first prize. Because they're all wearing the school colors of red and silver, they each have to pick a different-colored ball cap to wear so each of their teams will stand out from the other. The cap choices are green, purple, pink, and orange.

Use these clues to see which team got which color:

> The Alphas refused to wear orange or green caps.
>
> The Betas refused to wear green or purple caps.
>
> The Deltas chose purple.
>
> The Gammas picked the color that both the Alphas and the Betas refused to wear.

Using logic, here's how you know.

The setup: Each sorority has to pick a different color cap—green, purple, pink, or orange—for the competition.

Your arguments include the Alphas' and Betas' preferences, the Deltas' choice, and the Gammas' selection.

From those, you can start to make inferences, which—for this exercise—we actually chart out. Here we've made a chart with an X in each box that can't be right, but an O in each one we knew was definitely right (the premises such as the Deltas chose purple and that the Alphas and Betas refused to wear green).

	Green	Purple	Pink	Orange
Alphas	X			X
Betas	X	X		
Deltas	X	O	X	X
Gammas	O	X	X	X

When you start spotting empty marks on the chart, you can fill in conclusions, leading you to the sororities' final color selection. That is, because "orange" is an open color for the Betas, that becomes theirs. So what color is left for the Alphas?

	Green	Purple	Pink	Orange
Alphas	X	X	O	X
Betas	X	X	X	O
Deltas	X	O	X	X
Gammas	O	X	X	X

The Alphas chose pink (and the Betas chose orange, the Deltas chose purple, and the Gammas chose green).

So by charting out the solutions using logic, you can get an idea how you can apply premises, inferences, and conclusions to everyday situations.

The Virtues of Common Sense

Like logic, *common sense* poses another intangible: you know it when you see (or hear) it. There's great debate over whether common sense can be learned. We believe that it can; you can assess where you are on the commonsense skill scale, and improve your grip from there.

> **Think Tank**
>
> **Common sense** involves beliefs or propositions that seem to most people to be sound and sensible, with no outside need for esoteric knowledge. They are sometimes developed from study, knowledge, research, and experience.

A *Wall Street Journal* article once described how the onetime computer company Compaq was considering changing the Press Any Key command to Press Return Key after so many callers asked "Where's the 'Any' key on the keyboard?" Those callers weren't using common sense, now were they?

To begin, we can tell you that common sense breaks down into two areas: first, the ordinary knowledge that people in our society share, those bits of information that we all take for granted, such as most people sleep at night, and the sky is blue during the day. Second, we use those bits of information—big and small—to solve various problems during the day.

Calling On Your Common Sense

Take a look at these word pairings:

- Marble Cake
- Bed Head
- Pillow Sham
- Fish Tank
- Family Ties
- Great Plains

How do you know that …

A marble cake isn't a cake made out of marbles (or a cake the size of a marble)?

Bed head isn't a head shaped like a bed?

A pillow sham isn't a scheme involving fluffy cushions?

A fish tank isn't an apparatus that a fish straps on its fins?

Family ties aren't neckwear for families?

The Great Plains isn't some of life's magnificent normalcies?

Because you've got common sense—at least a little. Even if, for instance, you didn't know what a pillow sham was, your experience would tell you few if any schemes would involve any type of bedding.

A Logical Approach to Common Sense

Let's take a look at how logic works hand in hand with common sense, and apply those logical terms we talked about previously to one of the word pairings.

Proposition: A pillow sham isn't a scheme involving fluffy cushions.

Arguments (because):

1. Schemes usually refer to secret and cunning plans.

2. Schemes don't usually involve fluffy cushions.

3. A scheme hinging on fluffy cushions seems hardly suited to yield many rewards.

4. The definition of "pillow sham" is that it's a decorative covering for a pillow.

5. A pillow sham is made out of fabric.

6. A pillow fits into a sham.

7. A pillow sham belongs on a bed.

Inferences (therefore):

1. Schemes revolve around plans, and not usually home accessories.

2. Pillow shams are made out of fabric, not plans.

3. A pillow sham must refer to something other than a scheme.

4. Pillow shams most naturally fit on beds, not in plans.

Conclusion: It follows that a pillow sham is a covering for a pillow, not a scheme.

Words for Wisdom

Even if common sense seems difficult to define, let's give it a few adjectives here. Common sense is:

◆ Grounded

◆ Practical

◆ Advantageous

◆ Helpful

◆ Necessary

Because we're all better off *with* common sense than without, let's see how much you've got.

Testing Your Common Sense

In this quiz, you can gauge where you come in on the common sense scale. Let the questions here, and your answers to them, serve as a reference point for common-sense areas. (You may be surprised to learn that you have more than you think!) If some answers seem obvious to you, that's great—that's your common sense working! Answer true or false to each of the following 10 statements:

1. For common sense, clichés are generally a good rule to follow.

2. A high IQ equals a high degree of common sense.

3. Common sense relies on impulsive behavior.

4. It's possible to control your feelings of like or dislike toward others.

5. Common sense has no place in creative occupations.

6. Most people say they have below-average common sense.

7. Common sense is always right.

8. You either have common sense or you don't.

9. In the real world, sheer determination counts for little.

10. In general, ads should be taken literally.

All of the statements are false. Here's why:

1. Nope. Clichés can be convenient to rely upon, but they aren't meant to be practical thought guidelines. Doing that might actually lead to irrational behavior, such as believing you should be separated from your partner after a fight because "absence makes the heart grow fonder," rather than the two of you discussing the conflict face to face.

2. Wrong. This is an apples and oranges thing: You can't attribute one to someone just because of the other. It just doesn't wash. An IQ measures knowledge; common sense involves many other factors.

3. We don't think so. That would be you, looking before you leap. Instincts are great; they're just not always sensible.

4. Controlling your feelings? Common sense would say that's impossible (although you most certainly can control the choices you make based on those feelings).

5. False. Common sense applies to any occupation, whether your job is unstructured or restrictive, in art or science.

6. *Au contraire*. According to a 2004 nationwide study conducted by Yale professor Dr. Robert Sternberg, 43 percent of the respondents said they believe they have "above average" common sense (but only 7 percent of those studied actually had "extraordinary" common sense).

7. No. There are instances when what common sense tells you to do wouldn't be the best thing to do.

8. False. Common sense is a skill that can be developed. (We'll be helping you with that in the sections that follow.)

9. Incorrect: Multiple studies show that a person's passion can greatly influence his or her ability to think better about a project, drink in knowledge, and better apply what he or she knows.

10. Not so—see Chapter 7 for a review.

Cobweb Buster

Thomas Paine's pamphlet *Common Sense*, published in 1776, was a call for the American colonies to declare their independence from Britain. Dispensing practical advantages for independence, it persuaded a majority of colonists to join the fray to fight for freedom. It went on to sell more than half a million copies that year.

Cultivating More Common Sense: A Real-Life Scenario

Common sense has to be used to be developed or improved. Sure, some of you may be more predisposed to it than others, but we're all mighty capable of having it. We believe that common sense relies on these six fairly simple areas for maximum efficiency. Depending on the situation that's calling for the skill, you may need more or less talent in each of these aspects:

♦ **Assessment.** Pay attention and grasp the situation. Ask yourself "How am I coming at this?" Regard details separately without losing sight of their relationship to the whole.

♦ **Concentration.** Think before you act.

♦ **Keen perception.** Call on past facts or experience that may be relevant and ignore extraneous information. This perception also extends to knowing that the commonsense approach isn't always the one that's right in front of you.

♦ **Approximation.** Estimate the capacity or the probable duration of things.

♦ **Logic.** Draw inferences based on what you see and know.

♦ **Calmness.** Keep cool; maintain self-control.

Once mastered, these qualities allow you to have the practical common sense that sees things as they are and does things as they should be done.

Using assessment, concentration, keen perception, approximation, logic, and calmness, check out this scenario and apply common sense.

You've just gotten a new audio receiver that's now elaborately hooked into a DVD player, a satellite dish, a VCR, and a digital recorder. The receiver supplies the audio for all the components, via one remote. On the remote, you must press a corresponding button (marked DVD, DISH, VCR, TV, etc.) before you can control volume. The house is packed with out-of-town guests, and your 3-year-old son has awoken at 6:00 A.M. on a Saturday, and desperately wants to see his brand-new "Thomas the Tank Engine" DVD. Hoping to quell the child and keep the house quiet for the guests, you pop his DVD into the player, which is hooked into the new receiver. As the DVD begins, the audio spews out at an excruciatingly loud level. You press the DVD button on the remote, then try to adjust the volume—but the noise stays at the same level. What do you do?

A. Turn on the DVD player again; it usually follows (particularly with electronics) that "if at first you don't succeed, try, try again."

B. Check whether the DVD, TV, DISH, VCR and DVR wires are crossed. If so, rehook and retry.

C. Pull the plug on the audio, and get the kid interested in another activity.

D. Try to find the 1-800 number and call the DVD maker's customer service line.

The answer is C.; here's how the six common sense steps come into play to solve it. In the following breakdown, concentration and calmness are givens. You've got to keep focused on the task, while not letting emotions run amok.

Assessment: The house is asleep, and noise will wake everyone.

Perception: This whole contraption is new, so your history with it is fresh and you've had little practice messing with the wires. Unless you make your living as an AV expert, cut your losses.

Approximation: The noise could continue until you stop it, which could be the duration of the DVD you've just put in.

Logic: Your kid, though currently obsessed with this DVD, most certainly has other (quieter) interests that can be explored at 6:00 a.m. Because the receiver is the operation's audio "brains," silencing it is your best recourse.

Cobweb Buster

Despite the sophistication of computers, machines still lack the common sense of even a young child. Artificial intelligence researchers at MIT have begun to build that basic knowledge into programs and applications. One device, the Open Mind common sense database, has 527,308 items—and would take more than 20,000 pages to print. You'd probably categorize most of the statements as common sense, such as "Laws are the rule of society," "People generally sleep at night," "If you hold a knife by its blade, the blade may cut you," "A butcher is unlikely to be a vegetarian," and "People go to parties to meet new people." Score one for man over machine.

Fallacies: Logic That Fails You

You're likely to draw on both logic and common sense to determine if a *fallacy* is at work. These are pitfalls that cause arguments to collapse or ways some may try to prove their point of view that just don't hold up. You'll find them everywhere: in politicians' speeches, a CEO's plea, a parental request, and everyday conversations.

Think Tank

A **fallacy** is a logical error. It is incorrect reasoning built on faulty comparisons, information, or language that collapses under closer scrutiny.

Not only should you be on the lookout for them in others' reasoning and arguments, you should also avoid using them to prop up your own propositions! Of the dozens of types of fallacies, here are some of the most frequently used:

- **Ad hominen.** Also known as attacking the person, this fallacy sways attention from the proposition itself to the person backing it. Example: "He's a crook; I don't believe his claim that the magazine will increase ad revenue."

- **Affirming the consequent** and its twin **denying the antecedent.** Because the consequence happened, it must have been because of what preceded it and, conversely, what preceded it is the only way that it could have happened. Consider: "A construction boom in Palm Springs brought the proliferation of modernist architecture." "Modernist architecture blossomed because of the construction boom in Palm Springs." Clearly, in each of these statements, other factors possibly—and, in fact, were—at work to bring about the advent of modernist architecture, and a construction explosion in Palm Springs.

- **Amphiboly.** Conclusions drawn from double meanings. Logically confounding, they are sometimes unintentionally humorous, such as these "church bulletin bloopers": "Don't let worry kill you off—let the church help" and "For those of you who have children and don't know it, we have a nursery downstairs."

- **Appeal to authority.** Tries to invoke the persuasive pull of an authoritative figure or study, by suggesting that you go along with a proposition because it can be trusted. "The mayor thinks the city hospital should be closed, so we should agree with him."

- **Appeal to fear.** Thrives on scare tactics, such as "If we don't pass this bill tonight, crime will skyrocket."

- **Appeal to pity.** You're agreeing with a statement because you feel sorry for the person presenting it. "Let's go along with extending the hours of the after-school program because she's a single working mother with five kids and said it would really help her out."

◆ **Appeal to popularity.** Also known as appealing to emotion, suggests that your proposition holds because so many people feel like it's true. This appeal has often come into play since the start of the war on terror, as in "It's our patriotic duty to hold the detainees at Guantanamo Bay; no one wants terrorists back on the streets."

◆ **Bandwagon effect.** Tries to make its case on the basis of "everybody's doing it." "John, Susie, and the whole gang say that buying into Vitacorp isn't a pyramid scheme, and that it's already paid out thousands to some of its investors."

◆ **Begging the question.** The proposition is never fully satisfied because of circular reasoning. There's always a nagging, unresolved issue left behind because the conclusion is based on the original claim to the conclusion. "Why are vacations in Orlando so popular?" "Because theme parks are there." "Why are theme parks in Orlando?" "Because people love to vacation there."

◆ **False analogy.** Breaks down by striving to compare the outcome of two dissimilar events. "A riot occurred at the Edgetown Arena after the Eagles beat their rivals the Hawks, so we shouldn't stage the 'Battle of the Bands' there."

◆ **False dilemma.** Suggests that you have a choice of only two options (when many more may be available). The operative word is *or*, such as "Take two aspirin or have a headache all day."

◆ **Glittering generality.** Uses virtuous wording to convince rather than actually explain, relying on impressive adjectives over actual facts and statistics. "She's a fabulous designer with exquisite tastes and extensive expertise in upscale, awe-inspiring decorating. You'd be wise to have someone of her stature take a look at turning your drab living room into a luxurious, beckoning vision." However, there's no mention of actual clients, where her work is showcased, or statistics on satisfied customers.

◆ **Non sequitur.** The conclusion just doesn't follow from the argument stated. "If Betty eats that hot-fudge cake, she'll become obese."

◆ **Poisoning the well.** Unfavorable information about the person is presented, causing that person's argument to be tainted. This fallacy has been used in rape trials, wherein the alleged victim's reputation is called into question. "She claims she said 'no' to consensual sex, but how do we really know that's true? She's had dozens of boyfriends."

◆ **Red herring.** You try proving your point by introducing another one under the guise that's it relevant and—in the process—lead the initial point to be abandoned. "That child star can't be blamed for shoplifting, because he's run by his 'people.' Don't you hate how the young and famous are controlled by those around them? Often, they're bilked out of millions and don't even know it."

◆ **Slippery slope.** Tries to get a proposition rejected by showing how its acceptance will snowball into several (sometimes dire) consequences. These fallacies spiral out of if-then statements, and have become increasingly, alarmingly common. Many critics have made the case that going to war in Iraq was based on a "slippery slope." For example, a slippery-slope argument for going to war in Iraq could follow this sequence: "We must go to war because Saddam Hussein is hoarding weapons of mass destruction." "If we don't go to war, then he will accumulate more weapons." "If he amasses more weapons in Iraq, then he can emerge as a bigger player in terrorism and will align himself further with terrorists." "If he aligns himself further with terrorists, then our national security will be imperiled."

◆ **Straw man.** Distorts a person's position so that it's easier to attack. "When you say that we should deposit more money in that hedge fund, you might as well sign away our entire life savings to that broker."

Points to Ponder
Is common sense common?

Now that you've got information on logic and common sense, we take it to the next level by letting it help you understand reasoning.

The Least You Need to Know

◆ Logic in clear thinking involves propositions, arguments, inferences, and conclusions—but not emotion.

◆ Those logic terms and concepts can be applied to real-life problems.

◆ Common sense can be achieved by assessment, concentration, perception, approximation, logic, and calmness.

◆ Watch out for logical fallacies in others' arguments and avoid them in your own.

10

A Recipe for Reasoning

In This Chapter

◆ Reason inductively and deductively, and glean other keys to analyzing

◆ Regard the influences of observations, experiences, and statistics in the reasoning process

◆ Check out how comparisons can elucidate your reasoning process

◆ Apply reasoning to everyday situations

Although reasoning can seem like such a basic skill, doing it well can verge on an art form. Reasoning is the next step from logic: it's actually using that logical thinking we talked about in Chapter 9 and applying it to a wider range of conclusion drawing and result finding. And when you apply sound reasoning to a situation, problem, or decision—or even in discerning whether a statement is a fact or opinion—that's the epitome of clear thinking.

Because reasoning expands your circle of logic, this chapter examines some processes we refer to here as "flows" and "pulls." We'll be calling on two kinds of reasoning "flows," known as deduction and induction. And then we'll call on some "pulls" as we bring in observations, experiences, and statistics to further fortify our reasoning skills.

Mind Games 10

Ace this analogy: Princess is to tiara as cowboy is to …?
    A. Kerchief.   C. Lasso.
    B. Stetson.   D. Chaps.
(Turn to Appendix D for the answer.)

The Keys to Analyze This (or That)

You'll notice that as we head into the great big world of reasoning, we'll be tapping into—in addition to logic—many of the previous thinking areas we've explored. To further delve into this discussion, we break down a few terms in this section that are specifically related to reasoning. As we discuss these concepts in greater detail throughout the chapter, we provide ample examples during our discussion, too.

Deductive Reasoning

In *deductive reasoning*, you take an event, situation, or statement, and then form conclusions about it based on previously known truths. To show how deductive reasoning works—taking a large subject and then breaking it down into smaller relative aspects—let's look at this example.

Think Tank

Deductive reasoning is a thought process that breaks down parts from a whole.

Here's the event: The Federal Reserve hikes interest rates by a quarter point. Deductive reasoning would allow you to draw the following conclusions. (Some of these conclusions would be influenced by experiences and observations, which we detail later in this chapter.)

- The Dow Jones industrial average might drop.

- Banks' prime lending rate will rise, which determines the interest rate on consumer loans and credit card charges.

- This climb could take the bloom off the housing boom.

- This interest rate increase—particularly if it is part of a continuing trend—could spark inflation and slow the economy.

- Consumer spending might slow down.

- High interest rates may lead some to keep their money in a bank account rather than borrow funds.

Now here's how to put deductive reasoning to work for you:

♦ Examine the generalization being presented.

♦ From your immediate knowledge and reasoning abilities, what can be immediately inferred? In other words, what do I already know?

♦ Dig deeper: What other truths are possibilities?

Then, ask yourself the following:

♦ Do all of these inferences hold up under scrutiny?

♦ What proof do I have that suggests those inferences can be made?

♦ Do they all relate to the general information presented?

♦ What are the final conclusions? (List them out if necessary.)

♦ How do those conclusions help me understand the initial generalization?

Keep in mind that deductive reasoning is the force that can drive fervor over certain laws being passed or judgments in high-profile court cases being made. But without applying ample and skillful reasoning, making assumptions and jumping to conclusions can actually be the (faulty) thought processes that are being employed—not deductive reasoning.

Inductive Reasoning

Inductive reasoning works the opposite way from deductive reasoning. In this process, you've analyzed several examples or made several observations to draw a single conclusion.

Let's say you took a tour of Craftsman-style homes, and noticed such trends as:

♦ Stickley and Mission-style furniture

♦ Built-in cabinets

♦ Kitchen booths

♦ Porches with square pillars

♦ Prominent fireplaces

♦ Exterior stone features such as porches or chimneys

♦ Gabled dormers

Think Tank

Inductive reasoning is a thought process that builds up a whole from parts.

Then you went over to your neighbor's home and noticed she had all those elements you saw on the tour. Inductive reasoning would suggest that she has a Craftsman-style home.

So to use inductive reasoning, ask yourself these questions:

◆ What set of specifics or observations do I have?

◆ Are there connections among them? If so, what are they?

◆ From them, what conclusions or predictions make sense?

◆ Do I need to gather additional information to double-check that conclusion?

◆ Then, what would be my "generalization" statement?

◆ Do other examples outside that "observation/examples set" fit or make sense?

Although deductive reasoning seems to be more openly discussed, we often use inductive reasoning. Next time you're drawing a conclusion, decide whether you've tapped into inductive or deductive reasoning.

Syllogisms

Let's look into one more logic-into-reasoning scenario: the *syllogism*. In exploring this concept, we refer to some of the definitions mentioned in Chapter 9.

Syllogisms consist of three propositions: The first two are called the premises, and the last one is the conclusion. The conclusion indeed flows from the premises, suggesting that if they're true, then the outcome is true, too. For instance:

Candles have wicks.

Wicks can be lighted.

Therefore, candles can be lighted.

Think Tank

A **syllogism** is the regular, logical form of every argument that implies a conclusion to be drawn.

However, although conclusions can be correctly derived, they can sometimes be false:

Students in the eleventh grade are 17 years old.

Rita is in the eleventh grade.

Therefore, Rita is 17 years old.

Or:

> Mitch just joined the Wolf Paper Company.
>
> People who work for the Wolf Paper Company are unscrupulous.
>
> Therefore, Mitch is unscrupulous.

Or:

> Sun-Dims are a type of sunglasses.
>
> Sunglasses have lenses with UVA coating.
>
> Therefore, Sun-Dims have lenses with UVA coating.

For each of these, you need to conduct some further reasoning, either by gathering up truths, collecting observations, or relying on experience to ascertain their validity. Rita could be a child prodigy and be only 12, Mitch could be bent on turning around Wolf Paper Company's bad image, and Sun-Dims could be a cheap brand that doesn't coat their lenses with UVA protection.

Analogies

Analogies provide a relationship between two or more things that are similar in one or more respects. Somewhat surprisingly, analogies form the basis for reasoning, either inductive or deductive. Whether you realize it or not, you're using analogies—broadly or finely—to determine comparisons that engage your clear thinking.

Let's start out by sizing up your analogy prowess. What's your take on the following analogy? Egg salad is to chicken rancher as veal picatta is to a ...

    A. Baptist minister.

    B. Cattleman.

    C. Computer technician.

    D. Short-order cook.

Of the choices provided, the answer is B. Chicken ranchers provide eggs, which make egg salad; cattlemen provide veal, which is the main ingredient of veal picatta.

Think Tank

An **analogy** is a found similarity between two things that seem utterly different. With this likeness revealed, a resemblance or relationship between the things becomes apparent.

For clear thinking, analogies are wonderful for better identifying and articulating similarities and differences between topics and things. They can be considerably effective in helping to illuminate and clarify, particularly in the throes of trying to grasp a difficult concept or pattern that's at work.

Analogies are often brought up to explain politicians' moves or bring on support for a particular stance. For instance, to augur popularity, Harry Truman's "Fair Deal" was largely explained by bringing up similarities to his predecessor FDR's successful "New Deal."

> **Words from the Wise**
>
> One good analogy is worth three hours' discussion.
>
> —Dudley Field Malone, defense attorney

However, analogies can also lead to false conclusions. Many factors must be taken into account. For instance, some educators have tried to make the case for using total-immersion language experiences to teach students two or more languages. They may point to a country such as Canada for citizens being proficient in both English and French. However, to draw an analogy and say, "If it works in Canada, let's try it in Peru," would be misguided. For one, Canada has two national languages—English and French—so totally immersing students in the study of both is of prime importance to both continuing education and the nation's unity. For any country considering total language immersion for its students, there may be other economic, social, cultural, and historical implications.

So when considering an analogy, ask yourself the following:

♦ What am I comparing?

♦ What are the characteristics of each that I'm trying to compare?

♦ How is what I'm comparing alike and different?

♦ What dominant pattern/trend/similarity emerges between the two regarding the characteristics I set?

♦ What have I learned in the comparison?

Be an Observation Witness

Valid reasoning requires keen *observation* skills. In combination with or in the absence of *experience*, observation is a commanding backup for reasoning. So how are your observation skills? You don't have to be a scientist or researcher clinically poring over scads of data to perfect your skills of observation.

Good observation skills involve ...

♦ Cogently stating what you see.

♦ Making predictions based on those observations.

♦ Testing those predictions.

Think Tank _____

Observation refers to the act of seeing and taking notice. **Experience** is making practical acquaintance with something, trying it out personally to determine a firsthand account.

Filmmaker Michael Apted observed a group of British-born children of various social strata in a series of documentaries that interviewed the children every seven years—beginning at age 7. Known as the "Up" series, the first program—called *Seven Up!*—was filmed in 1964. The most recent installment was 1998's *42 Up*, with *49 Up* shooting for U.S. theatrical release in 2006. In each program, interviews allow the viewers to observe the children-into-adults and make predictions regarding their growing up. As Apted continues the series, a "prediction tester" is built in for you, because you can determine if your predictions about each "subject" is correct regarding their careers, relationships, woes, and accomplishments.

Observations prove particularly useful when you can't parse out reasoning through experience. Perhaps you attended a college orientation to determine if you wanted to enroll at a particular university. By taking note of classroom sizes, students' interaction on campus, getting a look at dorm rooms, and touring the university town, your observations could provide an aspect for your reasoning—in addition to your research on the school's curriculum, scholarship, etc.—on whether or not that college was a good fit for you. Although you're not actually in the experience of "being" a student, your observations—in this instance—are the next best thing.

What Past Experiences Can Prove

Your own experiences, whether positive or negative, can be a boon to your reasoning. Next time you're facing reasoning in a situation, notice if you're drawing on experience to help you make a case. First, take a look at an incident, situation, or problem you want to resolve. Assess what's already known. Determine what confusion, contradiction, or irregularities exist. Then ask yourself the following:

♦ What has happened historically in this situation?

♦ What does my past experience tell me about the current situation?

- What could happen in the future in this situation; what can my past experience help me presuppose?

- What acceptable resolution could I craft that draws on my past experience?

Try to let your experiences benefit your clear thinking as much as possible. If you're in charge of projects that seem to go careening off-course midway through and always end up over budget, conduct a thorough examination of your previous experiences. You might ask yourself the following:

- At what point have the projects gone off-course in the past?

- What's happening when the project turns south?

- Is my superior involved before then or afterward?

- Have my budget and initial timeline been realistic?

- Have the projects' end results been ultimately deemed successful or disastrous?

The Use and Abuse of Statistics

Statistics can bolster your view and lend credence to a topic at hand. In a sense, presenting a certain statistic can seem to instantly prove your point—sort of like argument shorthand. But quite simply, they can be a bane to the clear thinking that indulges good reasoning.

Think Tank

Statistics is the collection and classification of certain facts from the analysis and interpretation of data.

No doubt, statistics do have their place. They are useful for research, forming thoughts and opinions, making decisions, analyzing ideas and information, and even voting. But that's when they're right.

So often, people rely on numbers to give them the full story on a situation, project, or stance. Crunching numbers has become fodder for legions—and so often, those figures dressed up as facts can be just plain wrong. Many times, statistics are bent, misshapen, or altogether contorted to be wrapped around an existing theory to prop it up and give it substance.

For instance, one insurance company report suggested that women are better drivers than men. If you think that is the case, don't let their statistics be your proof. The company based their findings on a study they conducted. Upon closer inspection of their data, the statistics cited in the study were based on male and women drivers between the ages of 20 and 65 and those of the same age in accidents involving the same kind of car. Although that all sounds kosher, the report didn't take into account fender-benders that had gone unreported. Plus, reporting on drivers of the same age driving the same kind of car seems pretty restrictive for the study's scope and final conclusion. Do all the men and women you know drive the same kind of car? Using those statistics solely to make a sweeping statement that women are better drivers than men would be quite suspect.

> **Words from the Wise**
>
> 47.3 percent of all statistics are made up on the spot.
> —Steven Wright, comedian

The Stature of Your Statistics

You owe it to yourself—others, and the question at hand—to gather statistics with an open mind. And how do you know if a statistic is worth its numbers? To ferret out useful statistics, find out the following:

- Where is the data from?

- Who is responsible for the survey? Might they have an agenda at work for the results going one way or the other?

- How was the data collected?

- What questions were asked, and how were they asked?

- Who was polled?

And follow these guidelines:

- Beware of comparisons. Statistics can often draw a correlation between two instances, episodes, or factors that aren't necessarily related.

- Don't be fooled by bright and colorful visual aids, such as graphs. Sometimes they can be fashioned in such a way that masks the actual results.

- Don't get sucked into *cherry-picking*. This practice cites numbers that are often taken out of context to support a badly wanted conclusion that can ignore other surrounding information.

- Particularly note the sample size and margin of error for a poll that breaks down statistics. Typically, the larger the sample polled or surveyed, the more accurate the results.

> **Think Tank**
>
> Cherry-picking is selecting certain statistics because they suit particular needs, not because of their actual merit.

- Only make statistics part of your story. Good reasoning never accepts just the numbers.

Three M's That Make You Go "Mmm"

Finally, let's look at three statistical terms:

♦ **Mean** is the arithmetical average.

♦ **Median** is the numeric middle.

♦ **Mode** is the most common of the numbers cited.

These three terms are often wrongly deemed interchangeable. Frequently, people regard them as just the same way as saying "average."

Here's how they actually work in action. Suppose you have the following numbers regarding people's salary in a company's marketing department:

$27,000

$27,000

$30,000

$35,000

$65,000

$125,000

$200,000

The mean is $72,714.29 (in which we added up all the numbers and then divided that sum by seven).

The median is $35,000 (in which we looked for the number in the middle of the list; in this case, 35,000 has three numbers above it and three numbers below).

The mode is $27,000 (the number that appeared the most in the list).

If someone cited the department's mean salary to a just-graduated job applicant, the potential hire might think that $72,000-plus wouldn't be such a bad starting salary!

So which of these calculations—mean, median, and mode—do you think most accurately paints a picture of the marketing department's salaries?

Next time you see a mean, median, or mode cited, remember that they've been arrived at differently, and don't consider them just a fancy way of saying "average."

Putting Reasoning to Work for You

In this final section, we put some reasoning to work, using all of the preceding reasoning components (along with some logic and common sense from Chapter 9). To start, take a real-life headline with statistics, then follow up, reasoning through its supporting evidence with analogies, observations, and experience.

Cobweb Buster

An eighteenth-century European intellectual movement, the Age of Reason—also known as the Enlightenment—signaled the advocacy of ethics, aesthetics, and knowledge. The Age of Reason also gave rise to rationalism, wherein thinking moved out of the Dark Ages to provide a foundation for such systems as capitalism and socialism. The "Age of Reason" also has a double meaning; it can refer to the teen years when enlightenment, discovery, and appreciation of knowledge set up a transition to adulthood.

A Study of Silver

Suppose you're in the market for a new car, and you run across the headline "Choosing a Car Color? This One Is Safest." At this point, you're not sure what car you're getting and not set on a color, so you've got an open mind and think the information could be worthy of your consideration.

The information following the headline says that silver cars are involved in far fewer crashes than cars of other colors. "Hmm," you think. "I like silver. And heck, if it's that much safer, why not?" Particularly because, the article points out, 3,000 people die every day in car crashes.

Now, take a closer look at the aspects of the study. Researchers at the University of Auckland in New Zealand conducted the study, which assessed the effect of car colors on serious injury in a survey of 1,000 Auckland drivers between 1998 and 1999.

From the study, researchers learned that silver cars were 50 percent less likely to be involved in a crash causing serious injury when compared with white cars. According to Reuters, white cars are considered a middle-range risk choice (along with yellow, gray, red, and blue); the least safe are brown, black, and green.

Finally, they deduced that silver, a light color that is highly reflective, made cars more visible on the freeway.

Is the Study's Info Sterling or Tarnished?

Now it's time to ask a few questions that you need to answer if you're going to factor this information into your car-buying decision. What can you deduce from the study being conducted in Auckland? In a snapshot, the study was conducted in 1998 and 1999 among 1,000 drivers. You could make such deductions as these:

- The University of Auckland is likely a credible source.

- However, although this article was posted in 2005, the study itself is not current.

- Plus, 1,000 doesn't seem like a huge number to extrapolate such strong-sounding results.

And from that you could also infer the following:

- Each year, car companies introduce new colors for their cars. Other colors that have come out since 1999 could be safer.

- New safety features have been introduced on car models.

- Drivers and driving conditions in Auckland could be markedly different.

What rational comparisons can you definitively make? For this element, some further investigation on your part will probably be necessary.

First, you have to find out more about Auckland and its possible similarities to the town or city where you'll be driving your car. The article didn't say, but further investigation turns up that the greater metro Auckland area has a population of 1.2 million. Is that a comparable number for your area? You might have to do further checking; to put that number in perspective in the United States, the cities of both San Diego and Dallas have populations around 1.2 million.

Then you might want to know, "Was there a greater proportion of silver cars in the study?"

Plus you might be wondering about weather, often a factor to consider in car accidents. Taking in weather conditions, can you effectively apply the study to car buying in North America? What were the weather conditions of the Auckland study? Was it a mix of sunny and rainy days? Silver could be reflective in fog, but it also could be temporarily blinding in sun. Still, the comparisons could be tricky if not downright troubling. For instance, during the months of May, June, and July, Auckland only has an average of four hours of daily sunlight; in the same-population city of Dallas for those months, the average is 10 hours a day.

Bright Input from Your Observations and Experiences

Further, what are some observations that may influence your reasoning?

- In wrecks that you see on the side of the road, do they often involve a silver car?

- From a safety perspective, have you noticed silver cars on the road do have a reflective nature, making them more noticeable?

And what are some experiences that may influence your reasoning:

- Your parents had silver cars when you were growing up, and you were never in a car wreck.

- You were never in an accident when you rode a silver motorcycle you used to have. (This experience would make a useful analogy for consideration. However, having a silver refrigerator that never needed a maintenance call would not provide a good analogy.)

Together, reasoning methods, comparisons, observations and experiences, and statistical analysis provide a potent combination for clear thinking. Now that you've applied them to the silver car study, you can determine how trustworthy the study is.

> **Points to Ponder**
>
> What's the best reason you've ever heard for getting married? Having a pet? Buying a new car?

From this point, we take these reasoning skills to the next level: using them to generate options for the best decisions possible.

The Least You Need to Know

- Deductive reasoning allows you to draw truths from a greater whole, whereas inductive reasoning has you observe truths to make a general conclusion.

- Analogies issue comparisons, helping you to understand a topic or situation by relating its similarities or differences to another seemingly different topic or situation.

- Never discount your own observations and experiences; they provide real-life value to reasoning.

- Don't take statistics at face value; do your homework to determine if they're an asset or a hindrance, valuable or cherry-picked.

Chapter 11

Weighing Your Options

In This Chapter

- ◆ Find out about "free will"
- ◆ Realize the options your thinking faces in a given situation
- ◆ Determine what kind of "choice maker" you are
- ◆ Spin out more choices to consider

Life is not a preplanned multiple-choice test. Every situation you come into doesn't have a pre-determined A, B, C, or D to be the correct answer. Your clear thinking is required to root out the best alternatives and options to—eventually—come to a mentally well-orchestrated decision.

That being the case, we also live in a society that abounds with *choices*. And despite that, we sometimes—given the situation or problem—think that our choices are limited. In this chapter, we want to take the straightjacket off that confining notion so that you'll fully realize the array of choices that are available. And even if it seems there's a dearth of options, we help your elaboration skills to develop more alternatives. Really thinking about choices available—obvious and otherwise—will make our decisions so much better.

Mind Games 11

Which of these words doesn't belong with the others?

A. See   C. Em

B. Cue   D. Gee

(Turn to Appendix D for the answer.)

Get Fired Up for Free Will

Think Tank

Free will is a philosophical doctrine that advocates the power to choose, and our behavior involved in choosing is under our own control.

Think about it: wouldn't we feel like our thoughts were imprisoned without choices? Your ability to choose is fueled by *free will*. That's the philosophical doctrine that proclaims our choices are up to us.

In a broader sense, free will allows that you have a responsibility to gather and investigate all the choices in a given situation. They could be obvious choices or require a little more digging. But without choices and the subsequent decisions or problem solving that result, our minds—and therefore, our thinking—would have very little to do.

Take a minute and think about these questions regarding choices:

- What's the best choice you ever made? What made it a good choice?

- What's the worst choice you ever made? What made it a bad choice?

- What's the hardest choice you ever faced? What made it difficult?

- What's the easiest choice you ever faced? What made it easy?

- How many options were you facing when you made your best choice?

- Did the number of options you had affect your worst choice?

- What's a situation when you had too many choices? Too few choices?

- Do you have a strategic approach to developing choices, or do you just go with whatever comes about?

As we prepare for this part of clear thinking—generating alternatives—we want you to freely come up with ideas. At first, don't limit yourself to only those that seem reasonable, and don't judge the ideas as they come tumbling out. And for the choices you're devising for important decisions, gather ideas on paper so that you can more easily evaluate them.

Oh, Your Possibilities

In the course of each day, you're presented with a litany of choices: oatmeal, fruit, or breakfast bar?; car or train?; talk to the boss about the client's rash of requests or keep quiet?; return that call or not? Then, of course, there are bigger issues with a range of choices that have a greater lifelong impact: what career do I pursue?; what town do I live in?; which preschool should my child attend? And finally, there are those with moral implications: should I return the extra money that flew out of the ATM?; should I lie to cover for my co-worker?; should I support that unfaithful couple's decision to wed?

So is your thinking dogged by the abundance of choices, or do you thrive on the multitude? Let's try an exercise to see where you're coming from—and how creative you are—in terms of making choices. (Note that doing nothing is also a choice, although it may not be your best option.)

Let's suppose you've just been fired from a dream job; what are your immediate options? They could be these:

1. Stay fired and do nothing.

2. Investigate other opportunities at related companies.

3. Go outside your field and pursue another discipline.

4. Go to school to further your own career path, or to start another one.

5. Become an entrepreneur within your own field and launch your own company.

Now here is a completely different option: talk to other people who have been fired and consider launching a cottage industry—such as a book, a play, or a documentary—based on peoples' "getting fired" experiences. (That's actually what actress Anabelle Gurwitch did when Woody Allen fired her from a play he was directing.)

> **Words from the Wise**
>
> I have not failed. I've just found 10,000 ways that won't work.
>
> —Thomas Alva Edison, American inventor

Here's another example: you're in charge of an upcoming annual company retreat that is usually plagued with boredom, executives ditching meetings, and attendees who have Blackberry-itis. (They can't stop e-mailing on their PDAs.) What are your immediate options? They could be these:

1. Stick with the same unsuccessful game plan.

2. Don't call it a corporate retreat; just have a meeting at headquarters.

3. Check out resorts that would be so stunning they'd mesmerize the attendees.

4. Hire a meeting planner.

5. Poll attendees to find out what they'd like to see or do at the retreat meetings.

6. Place a ban on Blackberrys at the meetings.

Here's a different option: schedule the meeting on a cruise or houseboat that commands a more captive audience and obliterates Blackberry signals.

Keep in mind you've always got immediate options; the key is coming up with other viable ones. We address strategies for that in just a bit.

Difficult Choices in Today's Society

Further complicating your thinking and accruing choices may be the difficult issues that seem omnipresent today. Moral implications in situations seem to be increasingly prevalent. And when morals are thrown into the mix, your possible choices can be more confounding than ever.

Let's take a look at two examples.

Example 1: A Midwestern family wanted to prevent being victimized after a rash of burglaries in their neighborhood. The family's patriarch wants to consider his options. What are they?

1. Do nothing and hope for the best.

2. Buy a gun to protect his family.

3. Install an alarm system.

4. Move to another neighborhood.

5. Organize a neighborhood watch.

The second option has moral implications. If the family patriarch is a gun-control advocate who believes citizens shouldn't own firearms, buying a gun for protection—although logical to some—would be unacceptable for him.

Example 2: Gaby feels torn; she knows her best friend at work, Robyn, has been cheating on expense reports. But Robyn recently covered for Gaby when she took some merchandise that was going to be donated, a company no-no. What are Gaby's choices?

1. Don't turn Robyn in and save herself.

2. Turn Robyn in, and suffer the consequences for her own lapse.

3. Turn Robyn in, and hope Robyn doesn't report her.

4. Talk to Robyn and decide together what they should do.

5. Quit the job and hope a situation doesn't ever come up like this again.

In this situation, most of the options will revolve around the central question, "What's the right thing to do?" Although Gaby could generate more choices, she'll still face the central issue of whether she should do the right thing. This example differs from the previous one in that a question of morality totally pervades all the alternatives.

In coming up with alternatives, be sure to consider the moral implications because they may sometimes render choices immediately unacceptable.

Quick Pick or Sluggish Selection?

In mentally crafting your array of choices, is your situation such that you go through those options in a fast trip, or is it so serious you're in it for the long haul?

And within that, where does your thinking fit in? Are you a darter, a sidetracker, a ponderer, or a juggler? We get into those thinker types in this section.

For now, let's look at the possible situation you're drumming up options for. Here are guidelines for choices that shouldn't be fretted about for long. If they require a "quick pick," the situation …

Cobweb Buster

Wow! So many choices! One 2005 estimate reveals that 700 new products are introduced every day. Last year, 26,893 new food and household products showed up in stores worldwide, including 115 deodorants, 187 breakfast cereals, and 303 women's fragrances.

- Is simple.

- Impacts no one else but you.

- Has little bearing on your future.

- Only concerns an immediate need.

- Requires little time, money, energy, or other resources.

- Is reversible.

You'll want to spend more time spinning out alternatives if the situation …

- Concerns others.

- Could impact your long-term future.

- Requires a major infusion of time, money, energy or other resources.

- Has a high risk factor; that is, conveys an all-or-nothing scenario.

- Is complex or has many components.

- Somehow threatens your stability: family, job, housing, income, or otherwise.

Now, in conjuring up choices, where do you fall? We've devised these four categories of thinkers when it comes to drumming up choices. Does one fit your thinking style more than another?

The Sidetracker

If you're a "sidetracker," you get into a mess primarily because you think of too many choices. With too many options—and not all of them relevant to the issue at hand— you get confused, which leads to wasting time trying to decide.

Are you a sidetracker? Do you …

- Obsess over several choices?

- Generate several unrelated options in a given situation?

- Become convinced that there is only one "right" choice that you haven't found?

- Try to corral others into generating choices though they have little interest or input?

- Procrastinate on suggesting choices when a deadline looms?

A sidetracker scenario: Juliette has worked for the same high-profile investment banker boss for 12 years as a highly paid assistant, but the stress has dogged her since she started. She'd like to leave, so she's considered careers in banking, catering, retailing, real estate, and teaching; but nothing seems the right fit. If Juliette continues to check out career options without at least trying out one, she'll probably be sidetracked in her job for another dozen years.

The Darter

The "darter" dives right in, snapping up one of the first choices that comes to mind usually without expanding more from there. That leads the darter to investigate only limited options when it comes to decision-making time.

Are you a darter? Do you ...

- Usually pick the first choice that comes to mind?

- Hate to get bogged down with choices?

- Feel like decision making should be done in a hurry?

- Rarely brainstorm on choices?

- Often have to apply new decisions to fix old ones?

> **Mind Fogger**
>
> If you're a sidetracker, darter, or ponderer, recognize the negative aspects of your particular type of thinking. Then, try correcting one of those aspects. Sometimes, concentrating on and rectifying one weak area will create a domino effect, straightening out the other aspects for improvement you're dealing with as well. That being the case, you may find that you're creating better, quality-choice generation in no time.

A darter's dilemma: In an effort to prop up profits and beef up simplicity, an airline CEO scrapped an in-flight food service program. With great fanfare, he instituted a food-for-sale menu in the skies only to—weeks later—opt to offer snack packs instead. Although his latest move may prove right, the CEO may have needed more time to look at cost-efficiency and consider other options that will be more pleasing to both passengers and the bottom line.

The Ponderer

Though the "ponderer" might not look at it this way, this type of thinker loves to spend lots of time on choices. That doesn't mean you always have a lot of choices to choose from, it just means you take your sweet time in coming up with them. Although you end up with high-quality choices, you typically don't have many.

Are you a ponderer? Do you …

- ◆ Spend a lot of time mulling over choices?

- ◆ Do lots of investigating?

- ◆ Rarely have many choices to choose from?

- ◆ Get stuck on one or two choices in particular?

- ◆ Feel compelled to take action only because of an impending deadline?

A ponderer's predicament: a landlord has been holding on to a vacant apartment building adjacent to a hotel. For years, he has wanted to raze the building and turn it into a retail center that would take advantage of upscale hotel guests' disposable income. He conducted studies of possible income generation and even had an architect draw up plans. Now the hotel has offered him a take-it-or-leave-it proposition to buy his property. Does he stay vested in his valuable property, or give it up? If he hadn't been so fixated on the retail center, might he have come up with other options before the hotel's offer?

The Juggler

The "juggler" takes the best attributes of the sidetracker, darter, and ponderer to devise an attractive list of alternatives for a problem, situation, or impending decision.

Are you a juggler? Do you …

- ◆ Respect the constraints of time?

- ◆ Conscientiously conduct necessary research?

- ◆ Only ask advice of others who may offer valuable insight?

- ◆ Generate many, high-quality choices to choose from?

- ◆ Find worth in the decision-making process?

A juggler's example: A county executive was intent on cutting his city's obesity rates, so he looked at several ways to change the environment. Among his options: create more "walking parks," design more crosswalks and bike paths to link kids and families to neighborhood schools, and organize walking and running teams in neighborhoods that commit to accruing a certain amount of mileage per month. These only represent a few of the executive's choices; he'll test the validity of each of them during the decision-making process, but he's thought up well-formed choices to initiate that process. (We'll go through the entire decision-making process in the next chapter.)

Needless to say, work toward being a juggler type. If you find yourself in one of the other categories, eliminate the traits that are dogging you by adapting them to the juggler's attributes.

Obvious Options

We mentioned earlier in this chapter that, when you're looking at your options, there's always one obvious one: doing nothing. But as you gather up your options, we want to encourage you to look beyond the obvious. Sometimes that may be the one you go with and it might prove to be your best option. But to really delve into your situation, do yourself a favor: create alternatives! Your decision making will have so much more fodder if you go beyond existing alternatives, or a "hunch" that just feels right.

> **Words from the Wise**
>
> There are always two choices. Two paths to take. One is easy. And its only reward is that it's easy.
>
> —Anonymous

It's important to briefly go back to the logical fallacies we discussed in Chapter 9, because many of them hinge on "false" choices and suggest that you only have two options. The most forthright example of this is the false dilemma: you only have the choice of A or B. (Choices C, D, E, F, and G aren't even mentioned, although they may be considerably more viable.) An appeal to fear proposes that your decision or opinion has to go one way or else the sky will fall, tragedy will strike, etc.

Before we look at ways to generate commanding choices, try this exercise to break out of the regimen of the obvious. The Coca-Cola Company is interested in launching a coffee-flavored soda. Although "Coffee Coke" is probably the most obvious, that name doesn't sound exciting to marketers or consumers (though it probably does a pretty good job conveying the product).

Here's a bit of information to get you started: previous coffee colas have included Pepsi's Kona and Starbucks' Mazagran. What choices can you come up with? Here are a few possibilities: Jitters, FizzBuzz, Smooth Blend, Cola Café, C3, and Sweetbrew.

One of the Coca-Cola Company's names for the proposed drink: Blak. Obvious, but with a twist. Sometimes, as you learn in the next section, that's the best advice for identifying choices.

Elaborate to Devise Alternatives

As you move from the obvious, let's now consider ways to come up with other options for a problem, decision, or situation. This "elaboration" is a form of brainstorming, in which you follow a string of instructions to come up with a range of choices.

Cobweb Buster

In many cases, the more choices you brainstorm, the better the decision will be.

Say two foreign dignitaries—one from Fandangostan and one from Valanya—whom you'd really like to impress are coming over for a dinner party. Fandangostanians don't eat meat, berries, or dairy products, but the menu you devise has to be for both dignitaries. Let's investigate ways that you can dream up more alternatives:

◆ Do research into the related elements, and similar situations. What are Fandangostanians' favorite foods; what are popular Valanyan dishes? If you cross-reference them, will any meals pop up as possible options?

◆ Check out case studies of similar experiences. For instance, what did the White House serve last year during that state dinner when the Fandangostan prime minister visited? Are there blogs that discuss preparing meals for "mixed marriages" of Fandangostanians and Valanyans? What was served at the reception of a Fandangostanian who married a Valanyan?

◆ What's the ideal scenario? (We consider time and money constraints in the evaluation stage, which we discuss next.) You decide the ideal alternative would be to have it catered. Are there companies who specialize in serving Fandangostanians at meals with other guests?

◆ What's the fantasy scenario? How much of that can be reserved with real-world constraints? Wouldn't it be great to have Wolfgang Puck cater it? If that option is too expensive, what if you designed the menu yourself using some of his recipes?

- What's a generic option? State that, and then fine-tune it to be a custom-made option. If you can't have meat in the main course, what about tofu or seafood? Would Asian crab cakes with wasabi sauce be plausible?

- Conduct a literary review of books, television, and film to determine fictional characters' options in similar situations. If you searched books and movies on Amazon.com, does any media feature a Fandangostanian and/or Valanyan meal?

- Look at alternatives you may have faced in other situations and see whether they're applicable to this one. You've had other dinner parties with both vegetarian guests and meat-eaters. What did you serve them that was impressive to both?

- Take the location where the situation "lives" out of the equation. In other words, take the focus off the focal point for a spell. What if you didn't concentrate on the food to impress? What if you had other rousing elements that contributed to the experience: favors, games, music? Or consider a buffet where guests can pick and choose from several foods.

- Look at solutions you've reached in previous situations. Obviously, these are all unique to your own solution set, but oftentimes "gettin' creative" with your past can be a boon to generating alternatives in your present.

- Tweak the preceding ideas either by magnifying, minimizing, rearranging, substituting, or combining components.

A Choice Checklist

Armed with a healthy list of options, let's review the criteria you need to test alternatives for a decision you may face. Here's where we start the fine-tuning process that will enhance your decision making:

- **Cost-effectiveness.** Will the choice break the bank, or does it fit within the necessary budget?

- **Communicability.** Does it "translate" for you; in other words, if implemented, would it convey the message it should?

- **Compatibility.** Does it fit into a bigger scheme if necessary?

- **Flexibility.** Could it be easily adaptable if it had to be?

- **Hardiness.** How invulnerable is it? Could it fall apart easily?

- **Merit.** Can it stand up to the problem/situation as a viable alternative?

- **Relatability.** Does your option relate back to the problem/situation at hand?

- **Simplicity.** Is it too complicated for its own good?

Also take the following points into account when collecting your choices to ensure that you haven't slipped into any wayward thinking:

- Break your thinking free of past experiences with certain choices. Don't be confined by notions that a particular choice didn't work for one scenario so it shouldn't be considered for this one.

- Capture ideas and insights through listening, writing them down, or tape-recording them.

- Don't rule out alternatives too early.

- Make sure to reconsider discarded alternatives if conditions change.

- Don't feel compelled to go with an option just because it seems like it could be the right one.

- Get all your alternatives down before making a decision.

When Is Too Many Too Much?

Not to rain on your choice parade, but there can be such a thing as too many choices.

In a 2004 issue of *Negotiation*, a Harvard Business School newsletter, the article "Too Much of a Good Thing? The Role of Choice in Negotiation" by Michael Wheeler pointed out that people have enough trouble making a decision. Then that's made more difficult by too-many-options overload. That's especially apparent in Wheeler's concept of "anticipatory regret": We're bummed to say no to all but one of the choices.

Cobweb Buster

Sometimes wading through the choices is the hardest part: A 2000 *Journal of Personality and Social Psychology* report showed that when shoppers were given a wide array of jam flavors to choose from, they showed more interest than they did with a smaller array. But when it came time to buy a flavor, they were 10 times more likely to actually make a purchase if they chose from among just 6 jams rather than 24.

Having lots of choices doesn't necessarily make anything easier. The benefit stems from coming up with good choices to select from and not feel overwhelmed. A 2004 Stanford Business School study bore that out: Colgate offered up two types of toothpaste in the 1970s; they now offer 17. The credit card industry only had a few types to offer in the 1960s and 1970s; now you can say "Charge it!" with hundreds of plastic plates. But interestingly, the more choices a company offers doesn't necessarily translate into higher profits. Quite the contrary. This study learned that a significant percentage of product lines don't financially benefit by offering more alternatives.

The disadvantages to clear thinking when you have too many choices to consider include the following:

- Confusion.

- More time must be allotted.

- Possibly energy-draining.

- Procrastination in decision making can result.

- Overall, it makes arriving at a decision more difficult.

In the end, your clear thinking must judge if you've given adequate time and consideration to the number and quality of the choices you've generated. And the number and quality will almost always relate to the seriousness or lightness, magnitude, or unimportance of the situation.

In the next chapter, we look at how to whittle down your choices for decisive and insightful decisions, judgments, and opinions.

Points to Ponder
Sure we have free will, but are we ever really free?

The Least You Need to Know

◆ Free will gives us the power to have control over our choices, which extends to generating as many choices as possible to solve a problem or make a decision.

◆ When it comes to generating alternatives, determine if you're a sidetracker, darter, ponderer, or juggler; strive to be a juggler.

◆ Moral implications can eliminate or add to your choices.

◆ The most obvious option may not be the best option.

◆ Build upon ideal and fantastical options, and check into case studies and previous solutions to give you the fullest complement of choices available.

Chapter 12

Decisions, Conclusions, Judgments, and Opinions

In This Chapter

- Use your mind wisely in the decision-making process
- Try out popular ways to test alternatives
- Realize decision making's role in devising conclusions, judgments, and opinions
- Be mindful of decision-making pitfalls

Most decisions we make barely command our attention, but important ones—to be the best they can be—demand clear thinking. In this chapter, we continue to outline how logic and reasoning provide pronounced measures in decision making.

With that approach, we go over some ways to direct your mind to reap the best outcomes. And we discuss how decisions also play into conclusions you draw, judgments you make, and opinions you form.

Do I Hafta Decide?

Did you know you make thousands of decisions daily? Most you just don't spend that much time on, because they're part of a routine: what time to get up, what to wear, what to buy at the store. Estimates suggest that 80 percent of the decisions we make are "unimportant," meaning they bear little or no *consequence*.

Think Tank

Consequences are the results of a decision that are directly determined by your actions (or lack thereof).

But what about the major ones—those with potentially major consequences—that need a more disciplined approach? Because, let's face it: making any ol' decision is easy, but making the right one requires skill and knowledge. Making a decision implies that several courses of action have been presented to the mind, and that a choice—usually requiring a deadline and energy—is made.

One pundit opined that the average person spends more time deciding where to go on summer vacation than on choosing a career. Sometimes faced with so many decisions—both big and small—that we have to make every day, we just don't want to decide. (But even deciding not to decide is a decision, and hopefully if that's the route you take, you'll have used clear thinking to arrive there.)

So if the answer to the question is, "Yes, I hafta decide," then let's look at the steps involved in coming to a decision.

Articulate Your Decision

First, identify the decision you're trying to make. Size up the situation and, if necessary, break down a complex decision to be made into clearer, simpler steps.

You can size up your situation by suggesting the goals or mission you're trying to accomplish with your decision. These factors will also form *criteria* you'll establish in ascertaining which of your alternatives is the best one in making the decision.

If the decision's not easily put into words, then try saying (or writing) it several different ways. And be sure the phrased decision is clear about what you're trying to achieve in making this particular decision.

Get Your Facts Together

Second, depending on the scope, intensity, or depth of your situation, spend some time getting facts and doing your research. Use all available resources. Perhaps you're trying to decide whether to hire someone. You'd want to check out that person's references and work samples, and investigate his or her resumé further. If your decision requires several venues of information, check out resources discussed in Chapter 6.

> **Think Tank**
>
> **Criteria** refer to the standard or measure of judging; the established rules of the game that you're using to test out an alternative for a decision related to your action plan (or lack thereof).

After Careful Consideration

After you've got the decision outlined, your goal understood, and your facts straight, you've got an initial decision to make. Are you deciding between two—or more—possible options?

> **Cobweb Buster**
>
> Recent technological experiments have made stunning findings in the way our brains make decisions. Companies around the globe want to know how and why we respond to certain products. To the delight of brand managers, a team at Caltech has been conducting a remarkable study to peer into how and why people decide. They're scanning participants' minds—recorded by an fMRI (functional magnetic resonance imager) that maps brain patterns. The participants "decide" on images of designer products and celebrity faces by labeling them as cool (iPods were an example in this category) and uncool (Patrick Swayze was cited as such), while the researchers note where the brain "lights up" as they make their decision.

The Multiple-Choice Decision

Is yours a "which" decision that will require your conjuring up several options?

Multiple-choice decisions include the following:

- What should my college major be?

- What brand of piano is the best to purchase?

- Which agency do we hire for that ad campaign?

- What insurance company should I go with?

- Who should we select as "Employee of the Month"?

If the answer is a multiple-choice decision, start now by creating choices and listing them. Be creative; consider combining the best features of several different ideas for a completely new option.

In Chapter 11, we suggested some ways to generate alternatives for decisions or situations you're facing. Now's the time to start drumming those up.

The Two-Choice Decision

Or are you facing a two-choice decision: are you deciding yes or no, or either/or? (These may be the paring down of a previous multiple-choice decision, or could have always been a two-choice decision.)

Two-choice decisions include the following:

- Should we paint the bedroom aqua or rust?

- Do I pick door 1 or door 2 for that prize?

- Will Best Buy or Target have the better CD selection?

- Should I marry Alex or Eli?

- Do I take the job with Bank of America or Washington Mutual?

CAUTION

Mind Fogger _____

The greater the potential consequences of a decision, the greater the need for careful decision making. That said, when making a decision, you're choosing from the options you've created; you're not making a choice between right and wrong.

As you can see, though there are only essentially two choices involved, your decision can still have monumental ramifications. However, by the very nature of only having two choices in these instances, many two-choice decisions can be swiftly disposed of with cold, hard facts. For instance, a phone call to the stores will give you an idea of their CD selection.

A Further Delineation

We can also divide decision-making strategies into four major approaches:

♦ In **optimizing,** you're discovering as many options as possible and choosing the very best one. (This—appropriately—is the optimal goal of decision making.)

♦ In the **satisficing** strategy, you're plucking the first satisfactory choice over the best one. (This term was coined by psychologist Herbert Simon as a combination of satisfactory and sufficient.)

♦ The **maximax** approach usually throws caution to the wind to look for the biggest payoff and most dramatic upside. It's widely considered the optimist's strategy because with it, you're set on finding the no-holds-barred, best end result. But beware: in actuality, this could turn out to be the most foolish approach, akin to a gambler letting all his winnings ride on one roulette spin.

♦ With the **maximin** approach, also considered the "least of all evils," you're looking to offset risks. You're predicting the worst possible outcome of each option, and choosing the one with the least downside.

In the next phase, we show you how to put your alternatives through some testing to find out which one will work best. But first, let's make sure you won't let your mind slip into a wishy-washy mode before we get there.

Mired in Indecision

Whether you're looking at a two-choice or multiple-choice decision, sometimes you just get stuck. You just don't want to make that decision. Don't let your mind wallow in that mire.

Here are some tips for keeping your mind focused:

> **Words from the Wise**
>
> Nothing is more difficult, and therefore more precious, than to be able to decide.
>
> —Napoleon Bonaparte, French military leader and emperor of France

♦ Choosing the right alternative at the wrong time is not better than the wrong alternative at the right time. You've got to make the decision while you still have time!

♦ That's not to say you should rush into a decision. In fact, you shouldn't make the decision until close to your deadline. You'll find that, in the realm of decision making, your information and alternatives will continue to grow as time passes. So to give yourself access to the most information and the best alternatives, don't make the decision too soon. (However, realize that if too much time passes some options may no longer be available.)

♦ Be cognizant that time, manpower, money, and priorities may all be factors in your decision making. Remember from the outset that they'll naturally pose a challenge, but don't let them be the specter of uncertainty that ominously looms over your decision making.

♦ You'll help your case for straight-on decision making with the best possible decision "environment," having employed clear thinking to include all possible information, all of it accurate, with as many alternatives as possible.

♦ Although valid alternatives are excellent and exciting, be wary of too much information. A surplus could bring a delay in decision making as you spend time getting and processing the extras. Plus you risk the chance of overload, which could lead to mental—and decision making—fatigue.

Decide and Abide

Now we're into the nitty-gritty. At this stage, you're trying to see how your alternatives match up against your criteria. In looking at that, you're trying to determine which of your options will render your best decision by applying all the criteria that you've determined your best decision needs to espouse.

Cobweb Buster _____

> While we're focusing here on individual decision making, you could give group decision making a try if you're stuck, or your particular situation depends on it. Its advantages include bringing a wider range of knowledge and experience to the table, the possibility of more energy and resources, and the fact that people may work harder when others are depending on them. But drawbacks may also be present: feeling pressure to fit in and that your ideas aren't "good enough" to share; socializing substituting for real action; and the real work falling on just one or two people's shoulders.

Next we delve into two decision-making exercises for selecting the best alternative by putting your options under review. They'll work for decisions where you face two options ... or more.

C × A = Criteria Times Alternative

With this popular approach, you rate alternatives on how well they possess a set of assigned criteria and make your choice from there. Begin by listing your options, and then list the important criteria in making the decision.

Let's take a look at some of the decisions the Atlanta-based airline Song faced when it launched in 2003. A division of Delta, Song wanted to go head to head with such upstarts as the profitable Jet Blue, who appeal to their clientele with friendly service and stylish amenities for a "cheap chic" milieu.

Cobweb Buster

No one makes the right decision all the time. But by developing your clear thinking, you can increase your success rate.

Obviously, in starting out, the airline—to be competitive in this new "cheap chic" arena—had several decisions to make regarding the "look," including flight attendant uniforms, meals and cocktails, seats and legroom, and high-tech and low-tech frills.

Let's look at the decision that might have influenced the uniforms the airline wanted their flight attendants to wear. Here's one way they may have articulated the decision they had to make:

Who/what label should design our flight attendants' uniforms? The goal of the decision would be to have attendants—both male and female—in uniforms that convey Song's hipness, friendliness, and how flying is both fun and fashionable once again.

After some research, Song management's design choices may have been these:

- Juicy Couture
- Kate Spade/Jack Spade
- Lacoste
- Lands' End
- Ralph Lauren

Next, using a scale of 1 to 10, Song management could have assigned a number to each of these criteria, with 10 being the most important. Here, the "cool factor" may rate an 8, whereas "throwback to air travel's glamour days" may only warrant a 5. In using this method, remember to spin the criteria out of the decision you're trying to make by looking back at your initial goal for the decision. In that vein, Song management could have selected the following for their criteria:

- Cool factor
- Appeal to women (Song's core audience)
- Cost
- Competitive edge
- Stand-apart/distinct
- Fashionable but sensible
- Professional but fun
- Throwback to air travel's glamour days
- Versions for both male and female attendants

Now to determine how each option rates with the criteria, the management would have assigned each option a score for each of the criteria.

The airline ultimately chose Kate Spade to design their uniforms; let's see how some of the scoring may have been conducted.

A Score for the Equation

Say the cool factor was an 8 to Song, and Kate Spade was a 10 in that department. That's 80 points. Say cost was also important to Song; it rated a 7. Kate Spade's kind of pricey, so for that criteria the designer may have only gotten a 4, for 28 points. But having versions for both males and females is a must; it's a 10, and Kate and her husband Andy—with the Kate Spade and Jack Spade labels—can provide both genders. That scores a 100. For a total score, first add up all the individual criteria times option categories, then combine all the category scores together for a grand total.

If you prefer, you can lay your options and factors out in a table. You can list your options vertically down a page, and then your factors horizontally. This is also known in some circles as "grid analysis." It might look like this:

	Factor 1	Factor 2	Factor 3	Factor 4
Option 1				
Option 2				
Option 3				
Option 4				
Option 5				

Although the scores are subjective, this approach is compelling because it offers the opportunity to assign a numeric value to alternatives. It works for an array of decisions to be made. For instance, suppose you are considering a career change: to manage a bed and breakfast versus a local hotel, or to become an independent contractor working from home versus a long-term employee with a company. Criteria to consider would be your rise in income, time-to-productivity ratio, the risks involved, free time, and skills utilization.

Remember, though, you're in control of your decisions. If your selected alternative throws you for a loop, consider changing the scores, and/or adding or dropping criteria.

Decision Avenue

A decision avenue is a variation on the "decision tree" approach to decision making—a kind of flow chart in which you list all the possible outcomes of a decision you make. You can visualize this with your decision being the "tree" and your outcomes being its "branches." A decision avenue allows you to freely associate the different paths your options may take. By charting out the pros and cons, you can predict possible repercussions of your decision. This strategy clarifies your thinking, and allows for a better decision to be made.

Start with a decision you need to make and, moving outward from it, draw lines that reflect possible options. Write the solution on the line, keeping lines as distant as possible from one another to allow for your notes.

For each alternative you've written, ruminate as to the positives and negatives that could occur if you took that road. As you chart each possibility, ask yourself, "What might go wrong if I go this way?" "What might go right if I go this way?"

Cobweb Buster

With an etymology that dates back to a 1380 Latin origin, the word *decide* literally means "to cut off."

Now, You Try

Here's a decision you're considering: In what entrepreneurial endeavor should I become a partner and invest $10,000? Putting the question in the middle of the paper, your alternatives might be:

♦ Dateme.com, a dotcom start-up

♦ Cutters, a new hair salon that caters to men

◆ Fry-days, a restaurant that just broke off from a national chain

◆ Hallelujah!, a company that distributes inspirational DVDs

◆ Ace2Luv Inc., a scoring system for collegiate tennis tournaments

You write each of those options on lines that radiate from your central question. Often, the avenues generate other thoughts regarding consequences and even other alternatives. For instance, taking the alternative of the new hair salon, you start thinking about your "avenues," perhaps the following:

◆ In the "what might go wrong?" arena, the salon could go bankrupt and you'd lose your investment, or the business might come under attack for discriminating against women and you'd be a target. (However, in the consequence department, what is the likelihood of this actually happening and your being implicated?)

◆ In the "what might go right?" realm, the business is founded by a former haircut chain executive, so he knows the market's niche potential; your investment represents only a fraction of the overall picture, so it's a well-financed operation that could have longevity. (And, because of that, there could be the chance to build a chain, franchising opportunities, and an even greater return on your initial investment.)

Decision avenues present the possibility for a powerful brainstorming session that—with a little concentration—identifies scenarios that will immediately nullify some alternatives and give greater credence to others.

The Art to Drawing Conclusions

Your decisions should feed into well-thought-out conclusions. In so doing, a conclusion basically terminates the question or issue at hand. The conclusion makes a case for the decision that's been reached—or case presented—having successfully addressed all the criteria that had been outlined.

For instance, Song would have concluded that they should hire Kate and Andy Spade to design the airline's new uniforms because they'd be striking and hip, fit the company's stylish image, and have comfortable, professional versions for male and female attendants. Or a conclusion was reached to invest money in the hair-cutting salon, because it represented the least risk-averse venture and was the best capitalized.

But the best conclusions will not just offer a summary of the decision, they'll also plot out the next steps. In the case of Song, that perhaps might be setting up a meeting with the designers, drafting a wish list for the uniforms, and conducting a poll among the flight attendants to determine their feedback on uniform wear and care.

Good decisions should breed definite conclusions that easily spawn the next steps of action. When they do, the art of conclusion drawing is simple to express.

That's Your Opinion

We discuss opinions at length in Chapter 7, but they're important to bring up here because they're a form of decisions. Opinions are really decisions you've made—factoring in your background and experience—about a person, place, or thing. It's your decision to think a certain way about that something.

With the most fully formed opinions, we've gathered up facts or experience, or a combination of both, to decide our thoughts concerning the topic.

> **Words from the Wise**
>
> A wise man makes his own decisions, an ignorant man follows public opinion.
>
> —Chinese proverb

If you deem Austin, Texas, a "lovely cultural hub," your visit there coupled with research you conducted when you took on a client from that area props up your stance. Similarly, if you've followed the career of and regard cyclist Lance Armstrong as a great and philanthropic athlete, you're prepared to reel off statistics about his Tour de France wins and his Livestrong Foundation.

That's not to say you'll be necessarily discounted if you spout off a slew of opinions about any topic you wish to. It's just that opinions need your decisive thoughts to be their most credible and persuasive.

Judgment Day

A *judgment* is your decision based on interpretation of evidence presented. Again, like opinions, people slight the importance of judgments when they profess them willy-nilly with nary a fact or thoughtful consideration to back them up.

> **Think Tank**
>
> Passing **judgment** is making a decision that involves comparison and discrimination in the process of using or acquiring knowledge of values, the relationships of things or people, moral qualities, intellectual concepts, logical propositions, or material facts.

Judgment can present an even tougher case for clear thinking than opinions because it sometimes involves some moral aspect. Judgment comes up a lot these days in discussion circles; it's really become this millennium's version of "opinion," but opinion taken to the nth degree.

Many hot-button topics have brought up "judgment calls"—thoughts that convey an opinion—in the past few years, particularly in light of the spate of white-collar crimes, Patriot Act imbroglios, and court rulings relevant to gay marriages, abortion, separation of church and state, and capital punishment. Every day, news stories present a figure who might prompt judgment: be it a murder suspect, a fallen CEO, or a disgraced politician.

Plus there seems to be plenty of opportunity for judgment to go around in how our friends, relatives and business associates handle their money, raise kids, take time off, and indulge hobbies.

What judgment calls pop up as you read over the following list?

 ◆ Gun control

 ◆ A family bed

 ◆ Celibacy

 ◆ Illegal immigration

 ◆ Assisted suicide

 ◆ Transgender operations

As you perused that list, did you just go for a gut feeling, or were there actual facts that influenced your thinking to decide the way you did?

The next time a topic comes up that you seem ready to pass judgment on, take a step back and review your thoughts. Have you decided to pass judgment as you have because you've done your homework, or have you erroneously or sloppily arrived at your decision? Make a conscious decision to mentally review the following before passing judgment:

 ◆ Consider collected data carefully.

 ◆ Regard what that data suggests you didn't know equally to what it confirms you do know.

 ◆ Be open to others' points of view and the data surrounding that.

 ◆ Don't readily dismiss criticism, particularly if it's well founded and researched.

 ◆ Be willing to discuss your interpretation of data with others.

Common Errors in Decision Making

Pertinent to decisions, conclusions, opinions, and judgments, let's look at some no-nos to stay away from as we make choices and form our thoughts. First, ask yourself these questions:

♦ Did you gather all the information you could in the time allowed?

♦ Is your goal realistic?

♦ Are you operating in a "thought bubble"? In other words, have you relied on the same information, people, etc. you always do in trying to decide issues?

♦ Did you automatically go to only one right answer?

♦ Is your decision attempting too much too soon?

♦ Did you seek advice that could be deemed too risky?

Now do the following:

♦ Be honest in identifying the decision to be made and setting goals.

♦ Accept responsibility for the decision.

♦ Learn from your mistakes.

♦ Use time wisely, and take as much time as possible without creating more problems.

♦ Move quickly on reversible decisions, and slowly on irreversible ones.

♦ Think through the alternatives.

♦ Give thought to the risk involved.

Don't:

♦ Make snap decisions without generating multiple options and analyzing them.

♦ Fool yourself by taking the path of least resistance with choices that are easy and comfortable but bear little impact.

♦ Make decisions that aren't yours to make.

♦ Take a shortcut (think that "I always do it this way when this situation comes up").

♦ Rely too much on expert information, or overestimate or underestimate the value of information received from others.

♦ Hear or see only what you want to hear or see.

The Final Arbiter: Truth and Consequences

The fact is, after you've made a decision, you'll probably come down with a—brief and temporary—case of buyer's remorse. In California, there's a "lemon law" in effect, where after you make a big purchase such as a car or piece of furniture you have three days to take it back if you decide you don't want it. And that's even if you've signed a contract. Don't you wish the whole world had a lemon law in effect for decisions? But because that's not the case, it's time to make lemonade: put that decision to work.

Keep in mind that every decision follows from previous ones, enables future ones, and also prevents other future ones. So the important ones will have far-reaching consequences.

Which brings us to "evaluation station." This is where you look back and determine how your decision performed. To make an effective decision, you must adequately consider your choices in terms of longer-term consequences. You may accomplish short-term objectives, but at the cost of long-term goals. So in revealing that decision, be ready to ask yourself: does the decision advance my purposes? And in the evaluation of it: am I satisfied with the results?

Let's go back to the Kate Spade–designed Song uniforms. From our perspective, that's a decision that advanced the airline's purposes on many, perhaps even unexpected, fronts. For starters, the news brought an avalanche of press coverage, much of it in magazines geared toward women, which raised Song's profile with a target audience: women business travelers. Plus other magazines picked up on the stylish element of Spade designing the uniforms, which lent credibility to Song's positioning as a "cheap chic" airline. Song must be satisfied with the results; they recently added more routes and bought more planes. And the Spade uniforms were mentioned as a key component to their popularity and success. That decision was a good one!

Points to Ponder

What decision have you made that impacted the most people? And did it have a positive or negative impact?

Having taken on the reasoning necessary for choices and decisions, we're now ready to move into the next phase. We'll put clear thinking to good use to define and solve problems, and to articulate thoughts verbally, in writing, and for creative endeavors.

The Least You Need to Know

- Clearly articulate your decision with a defined goal for maximum decision-making effectiveness.

- Decisions can be made from two or more choices. For the latter, your goal is to take an optimizing approach, in which you spin out several viable alternatives to consider.

- Choose among alternatives by weighting them against predetermined criteria, or subjecting them to a scenario of speculative pros and cons.

- Decisions also form the basis for opinions and judgments; in either case, make sure your decision is well grounded in clear thinking and stable facts.

Part 4

Resolve, Express, Engage!

Ready to articulate those clear thoughts? Now's the time! Having gathered up information and learned how to transform it with reason, you're ready to tackle this phase. Here you channel clear thinking into concise, cogent communication. We show you how to transform clear thoughts into clear verbal words to define and solve problems, to communicate effectively in speech and in writing, and even to express yourself creatively.

Chapter 13

Knock, Knock: What's the Problem in There?

In This Chapter

- ◆ Identify types of problems
- ◆ Learn ways to define problems
- ◆ Prepare a statement of your problem
- ◆ Evaluate your definition

Clear thinking comes in handy for so many reasons, and certainly one of its prime uses involves solving life's problems. So let's take this opportunity to figure out how to tackle a problem. More specifically, we look at what goes into articulating a clearly defined problem that can yield the best and most positive results for you once it's solved.

Now you might not have the language, the understanding or the know-how to accurately and adequately identify the problem. But fear not: you can redirect yourself with the methods described in this chapter. And when you do, solutions are guaranteed to follow more easily.

Mind Games 13

Everett is having a party to celebrate his twelfth birthday. However, his mom won't let him—or his seven party guests—have any cake until he can figure out how to create eight pieces with only three straight knife cuts. And his mom won't allow any funny business with Everett touching the cake with his hands to get the job done. How should Everett cut the cake?

(Turn to Appendix D for the answer.)

Gray Is the New Black

Clearly defining the problem is the first step in conquering it. And today, more than ever, that's a tough one because problems are not always what they appear to be. Life as we know it has become increasingly complicated.

We're no longer a society of cave people who worried only about food and shelter, activating their fight-or-flee mode when survival was threatened. A post-9/11 world fraught with escalating fears and worries along with a blur of pulse-pounding images can't help but make an impact on your internal psyche. The pervasiveness of the Internet and a proliferation of television talking heads don't help much either. The whole shebang makes the go-go 1990s seem pretty quaint.

Complicating that chaos, a multitude of advice columns, talk shows, and magazines espouse simpler living. Sure, their goal may be to ferret out disorder. But the mere onslaught—and the conflicting input you're getting from those sources—really only makes clarity harder to achieve. There's just too much information to live the "simple life" anymore.

Cobweb Buster

The word *problem* was derived from two Greek words that, together, form *proballein* and literally mean "throwing a thing forward." We also like that within problem, you can find a call to delve into it—the word *probe*.

All those forces working in tandem hardly jibe with human nature's quest to look at problems and their solutions in black and white. Still, isn't that always the most tantalizing option? To pigeonhole a quandary into a neat and tidy, quick solution?

However, as you know from personal experience and see on television, problems and their solutions aren't always so cut-and-dry. Ethical dilemmas unrelentingly pop up in such series as *Law &*

Order and *ER*. You see a character in the midst of an almost-impossible situation: a lawyer bound to honorably defend his guilty client or a medic barred from divulging to a woman that her boyfriend has AIDS, and wonder, "What would *I* do?"

In the end, media representations truly can reflect the real world. The specter of Supreme Court cases, dealing with terrorists, and understanding new cultures provide a backdrop to the day-to-day challenges you already experience—whether managing a household, an office staff, or schoolwork.

And wouldn't you know it? You don't even get to sum up and solve your problem in the span of a 60-minute episode.

So What's Your Problem?

Ah, *problems*. They come cloaked in controversies and posed in predicaments. They take on forms from bureaucracy in the workplace to arguments at home, from finding ways to improve your disposition to seeking cures for what ails you, from choosing a politician to defending your religion.

Symptom Alert!

Many times, we overlook the most important step in problem solving: defining the actual problem. And the truth is, you might not know how to clearly state exactly what the problem is. You may tend to focus instead on the upheaval the problem has caused—the *symptoms* that come with the problem, but aren't the actual source of it. However, when your focus strays that way, fuzzy thinking reigns and chaos ensues. Because if you just wipe out the symptoms, the problem will come back. It always does.

Think Tank

Psychologists refer to **problems** as situations in which some of the components require further investigation. From the Greek word for occurrence, a problem's **symptoms** describe instances or changes that cause disorder or distress.

While a patient suffering from an unknown disease "presents" a physician with a laundry list of ailments, the doctor has to analyze those to determine their underlying cause. When that's treated, the symptoms disappear. If the doctor just went about doling out prescriptions for the various bumps and pains, those might go away for a time. But the disease would stay. And because it would, the ailments would return.

Problems Classified

We've devised five areas to classify problems. Some areas may overlap with others, but laying out this groundwork will allow a more productive discussion, and will help you in defining problems you face:

- ◆ **"It's all about me"** or **intrapersonal.** These types of problems strike at your core, and entail areas you'd like to target for personal improvement or empowerment: thinking outside of the box more, making better choices, beefing up your reasoning abilities, or thinking more with your head than your heart.

- ◆ **"Between you and me"** or **interpersonal.** In this realm, you're looking at your relationships with others and attempting to communicate more clearly, listen, and understand better. These kinds of problems may include mending fences, building stronger friendships, being less combative or more intimate, and maintaining a healthy and happy marriage.

- ◆ **"Angel vs. devil"** or **moral/ethical.** Ooh, the hot-button area. Moral dilemmas frequently encompass those topics that prompt and provoke the most passionate discussions. These may be religious or political in nature, and can even spread to such tangential topics as astrology. These types tend to concentrate on what's right or wrong, and are invariably shaded by your personal experience, beliefs, and values. Problems you face here may include how you can figure out your position on an issue, and state your case persuasively for the side you take.

- ◆ **"It's the workplace, baby"** or **occupational.** These on-the-job quandaries may involve increasing sales, improving marketing, launching a new product, initiating a new program, communicating better, or getting a raise.

- ◆ **"Citizen [insert your name here]"** or **social.** Your responsibilities geared toward citizenship and your role in society including, but not limited to, voting for public office and taking stands on community issues.

Set It Up: Your Problem's Parameters

The winner of the Nobel Peace Prize in 1978, Herbert A. Simon, along with fellow psychologist and artificial intelligence pioneer Allen Newell, devised a two-tier concept categorizing problems as—appropriately—well defined and ill defined. In their view, well-defined problems have a fixed, completely specified outcome in a determined space of time and refer to games, puzzles, and simple math and science.

Ill-defined problems must grapple with factors of uncertainty that could produce a variety of outcomes. Ill-defined problems could be as simple as what to have for dinner, or as complex as how to cure cancer.

When a problem comes along, you should decide will its solution have definitive outcomes, or endless possibilities?

You may further help your approach in defining a problem by drawing bounds for it. The two key questions here are these:

◆ What's the worst that can happen?

◆ What's the best that can happen?

Often a problem pulls you into negative thinking: "If I don't fix this, I'll (fill in disaster here)." Irrationality takes over, and you think the problem unsolved will lead to death, divorce, or the country going to pot. Your perspective can be measurably brightened when you realize that most problems won't automatically translate into your worst fears coming to pass.

> **Mind Fogger**
>
> Make sure that what looks like a problem really is a problem. Although all problems signal a disparity, difference, or inconsistency, not every disparity, difference, or inconsistency represents an actual problem.

On the Road to a Definition

Don't worry if definitively naming a problem isn't obvious at first. It could be that you lack information to define it, or that you're confusing symptoms with underlying causes. If either is the case, state your problem in broad terms first.

Perhaps the best way to define your problem—and what you'd like to make a case for in your own best interest—is to pare down the possibilities surrounding it. That means shearing away all the mistaken identities that might be covering up the true problem. It's also important to be completely honest with yourself about the problem that you're trying to define. To get to the heart of the problem might require some hard—and maybe even painful—work on your part.

Here's a tack worth trying to get to a problem's root. Starting with a general statement, note how you can arrive at the eventual true problem:

The problem is I don't get along with my mother.

The problem is I don't get along with my mother when she comes over.

The problem is I don't get along with my mother when she comes over with her new boyfriend.

The problem is I don't get along with my mother when she comes over with her new boyfriend and they argue a lot.

The problem is that reminds me of my relationship with my husband.

The problem is that reminds me of my husband and I arguing.

The problem is my husband and I argue over his playing golf.

The problem is my husband and I argue over his playing golf on Sundays when I want him to go with me to church.

Now obviously, that final statement taps into an entirely new realm than how the supposed problem initially started out. But the problem-ator (that's our term for the person who has the problem) is much closer now to the root cause and therefore, the real problem. In this example, each statement draws nearer to being a clear statement of the problem. Yet only the last statement could prompt clear action. That one verges on being well defined and ready for problem solving. You now have a scenario that can lead to a solution.

Cobweb Buster

Newspapers rely on the who, what, where, when, why, and how of a story for their leads. That approach is also a boon for defining a problem. Identify the who, what, where, when, why, and how of your problem. Compile a comprehensive statement of all the facts as you know them surrounding your problem, even those that seem obvious. Detailing these can help you make sure the apparent problem is in fact a problem, gives a reliable record that can be used to gauge success, and provides a reference in case the same problem comes up again.

The Toddler Take

You could also try stating your problem with another method called root cause analysis. This process involves repeatedly stating a fact, followed by the question "Why?" We like to call this way the "Toddler Take," for its steady stream of inserting the "Why?" question. For instance, "My friends always seem smarter than me." "Why?" "Because they're always referencing works and books I've never heard of." "Why?"

"Because they had a better education than I did." "Why?" "Because I never finished school like I planned."

These and similar techniques help overcome the natural human tendency to rush into a solution for a problem. Too often, you find out too late that you're solving the wrong problem, or that you're actually addressing only a symptom of the real problem.

Give That Problem a Face and a Name

Now that we've looked at the types of problems and possible parameters, let's go to the next step: preparing a statement of the problem.

Here's a list you can use to get started. Not every problem will need every one of these questions answered. Being stuck in a high-rise elevator or saving someone trapped in a burning car requires a different perspective—and begs a different and more immediate outcome—than considering a troubled relationship or facing a career change.

Words from the Wise

If I had one hour to save the world, I would spend the first 55 minutes defining the problem.

—Albert Einstein, American physicist

- ◆ What is the problem? Can you describe it in one sentence?
- ◆ What are you being asked to find out or solve?
- ◆ Is it your problem or someone else's problem?
- ◆ Is it possible for you to solve the problem?
- ◆ Is the problem worth solving?
- ◆ If this is an old problem, what was wrong with a previous solution?
- ◆ Does the problem require an immediate solution?
- ◆ Is the problem likely to go away by itself?
- ◆ Can you risk ignoring the problem?
- ◆ Does the problem have ethical implications?
- ◆ Does the problem potentially have more than one solution? (Most problems do.)
- ◆ What conditions must the solution satisfy?

♦ Will the solution affect something that can't be changed?

♦ Is this the real problem, or merely the symptom of a larger one? In other words, is it masking a deeper problem?

If it will help to craft your statement, commit your problem to paper. Write it down. Use the next list as a guide for all the particulars. This list is similar to the previous one, but is a little easier to work from for writing out a statement. You should have a clear description of the following:

♦ The problem

♦ The negatives involved

♦ The positives involved

♦ The owner

♦ The parameters, including length and scope of problem

♦ The consequences, or how it would impact your family, job, marriage, or school performance (Here's where "What's the worst that could happen?" comes in.)

♦ The affected parties

♦ You as the problem's primary caregiver or solver

If the problem concerns you and someone else, you both need to be on the same wavelength in tackling the problem. That is, you both must have defined the problem as exactly the same, with no variance, no extras, and nothing left out.

CAUTION **Mind Fogger**

A poorly defined problem is just begging for a solution that yields poor or no results. Too often we approach a problem by being too general in defining it. To guarantee success in finding the eventual solution, specificity is key.

In going through the lists, review what you absolutely know in terms of evidence and what can actually be measured. From here, you'll be making assertions and staking out the unknown elements. That will most likely mean fact-gathering missions to accumulate relevant information (some of which could very well turn out to be irrelevant).

Practice Defining Others' Problems

Sound impossible to state your problem? Sometimes we have better luck examining our own dilemmas by seeing how others identify and learn from theirs. Some television series and films give us an opportunity to state someone else's problem. In the movie *Finding Nemo*, Marlin (voiced by Albert Brooks) has a specific problem: he must find his son. In the pilot episode of the TV show *Frasier*, the title character was faced with the prospects of looking after his injured and alone father, and had to decide whether to return to Boston or stay in Seattle. *Seinfeld* made television history with a litany of absurd problems, such as Kramer being banned from a fruit shop or Jerry having to wear a puffy shirt on a television show. Many episodes of TV's *The X-Files* were set up for Agent Mulder making a case to prove that a UFO, crop circles, or a poltergeist existed and Agent Scully making a case against the unexplained mystery.

Name a problem you're facing right now. Is there a character on TV, in a book, or in a movie who has had a similar problem? Try defining it in that character's words.

A Little Help Here

If putting a problem into words is still giving you grief, you might give these problem-defining busters a go:

- Leave it be and let it steep for a while.

- If necessary, move to a new setting; this will prompt new insights.

- Talk it over with someone you trust.

- Involve people from relevant areas of expertise and experience.

Some Perspective on the Problem

Let's say you've defined your problem, but you're terrified of it. Sometimes a little perspective is all you need to help out. This exercise, called "It's All Relative: 12 Just Bad or Really Bad Problems," is devoted to that. How would you prioritize this list in terms of worst to best problem to have? Can you see how further defining each of these might make it easier to handle? Each one needs a cogent plan of attack, but you'd probably be more willing to take on some of these than others:

1. Trying to buy a house

2. Living in poverty

3. Discovering that your spouse is cheating

4. Coping with a life-threatening disease

5. Suffering from colorblindness

6. Dealing with the death of a loved one

7. Contending with an in-law moving in

8. Being the victim of a hate crime

9. Considering becoming a vegan

10. Surviving the fallout of a natural disaster

11. Wanting to make more money

12. Creating world peace

An Evaluation: Make Sure Your Definition Ranks

After you've got a statement you're happy with, and feel like your problem is well defined, you still should evaluate it to make sure it strikes at the heart of the matter you're trying to solve. You may need to dig a little deeper, and ask yourself more questions.

With your definition in hand, put it to this test:

♦ Is the definition striking at symptoms or the core of the problem as you know it right now?

♦ Do you have a vested interest in the definition—as it stands right now—being solved?

♦ What goal would be accomplished if the defined problem was solved?

If you have a specific, well-put problem that affects you and, when solved, will produce a desired outcome, you've done it. You've got a problem ready for solving! Congratulations!

Again, the most common reason for a poor solution is an incorrectly or inadequately defined problem. Let's look at this true-life example, in which the principals involved shunned analyzing and specifying the problem and just jumped to action.

A hot new website selling trend-setting accessories was trying to get more traffic (and sales), so the company launched an extensive publicity campaign, getting mentions in several fashion magazines. Customers materialized in droves, but the site—which was still only accepting payment by check—hadn't taken the time to set up a payment system with credit card companies, so the business evaporated.

The website owners believed that to be successful they just needed some solid publicity—and fast. After they solved what they thought was their clear problem, loads of people were visiting the site. Unfortunately, the owners realized too late that those people weren't becoming paying customers because they were turned off by having to send in a check or money order. If the owners had put their business under the harsh light of reality, they might have realized that the real problem was that the website wasn't offering enough payment options to their customers, particularly for trend-setting merchandise sold via the net. It didn't matter how much publicity they garnered because they hadn't adequately defined their problem.

Here the problem-ator didn't take the time or the opportunity to probe further into the problem's underlying cause.

For their too-hot-to-handle-credit-cards website, the owners were all too aware, and probably a little frustrated, by their problem's symptoms: low sales, zilch visibility, limited exposure, and slow site traffic. But their eventual approach—more publicity— really wasn't getting at part of the larger problem (or problems). With that approach, people were coming, but no one was buying. Breaking their problems down and asking more questions about them might have helped them define the problem better, and redirected them to concentrate on organizing their payment infrastructure. That way, they could have ensured that they could handle more traffic and, in the end, more actual sales.

> **Words from the Wise**
>
> A problem well stated is a problem half solved.
>
> —Charles F. Kettering, inventor, teacher, and longtime research head for General Motors

In the end, the definitions for problems can be posed as questions or statements. Either way, a problem's best chance for resolution relies on its framing. Spell it out as specifically as possible. One way to do this is to channel the problem into its imminent domain, and ask yourself, "What's really at work here?"

You'll have a chance to do that by doing the following two exercises that look at the problems of others. Test out your problem-identifying skills by examining these situations. In each of them, see if you can identify the areas of problems in which the problems fall—such as interpersonal or occupational— discussed earlier. Ask yourself if they fall into more than one category. Dig deeper by posing some questions to help define the problem. And, in each case, assess for yourself if answers given would serve in getting to the very heart of the matter.

Date Night Dilemma

Ella and Mark really want to spend more time alone, yet they can never organize a date night. With three kids, evening work commitments, and a dearth of babysitters, a night out seems to be a luxury impossible to nail down.

This couple's problem would be interpersonal, but could extend into intrapersonal issues, too. Their problem is "We want to spend more time alone," although some root cause analysis may be helpful for them to define it further. Is sealing the deal for a date night the true problem, or is that masking bigger issues? Could they be avoiding each other, or do they have mismatched priorities? To define their true problem, they might start with such questions as "Why would we be avoiding each other?" or "What are our priorities concerning spending time alone with each other?"

The Low-Paying Gig

Riley is a marketing consultant who is locked into a low-paying contract for a very demanding client. Although he is only committed to 10 hours per week for the company, he finds himself often working weekends, taking late-night calls, and offering his counsel on tangential projects. Worse, the more he gives, the more the company comes to expect of him. When he tries to increase his fees, he is summarily shot down. Riley really needs the account—his financial situation borders on dire—but feels taken advantage of and wonders if his time wouldn't be better spent, and compensated, working for someone else.

Riley's problem is both occupational and intrapersonal. Does Riley have several problems at work here, or just one? Is he grappling with a financial problem, a respect problem, a time management problem, or a combination of all three? One way to state his problem might be, "I want to spend my work time more profitably." Some ways he could begin articulating his multilayered quandary might be by asking, "Am I allowing this job to prevent my finding a better opportunity?" "Should I subcontract out some of this work to pursue a more lucrative assignment for myself?"

Your Burden of Proof

After you've defined the problem, and taken it on, own it! You have the *burden of proof* to solve it, which we delve into in the next chapter. Devising the solution—and making the best of it—will now be up to you. And you'll be in great stead with that crystal-clear problem defined in hand. So take the risk and pursue that solution to its fullest potential.

Defining problems can be messy and time-consuming. Solving messy problems requires commitment, assigned tasks, and resources. But great rewards may also be in the offing. You're better off casting problems in the positive light of opportunities or challenges than wallowing in the negative dim of uncertainty and doubts.

Take heart: Almost all problems can be solved! But remember, when you can't solve a problem, it's often because it hasn't been identified clearly.

> **Think Tank**
>
> The person taking on a problem has the **burden of proof** in solving it, or substantiating his or her position. In some cases, that may include making a case for experts or skeptics that his or her belief has the greater probability of being "right." So he or she has the responsibility to justify, to show and to confirm.

> **Points to Ponder**
>
> When is a problem not an opportunity?

The Least You Need to Know

◆ Different kinds of problems abound, and encompass personal choices, interpersonal relationships, moral dilemmas, workplace woes, and civic responsibilities.

◆ Take the time to break down your problem into less-complex parts.

◆ In a productive problem-solving process, defining the problem is the first step and will guarantee stronger resolutions.

◆ The more clearly you can define the problem, the more success you'll have in solving it.

Chapter 14

Have a Flair for Solutions

In This Chapter

- ◆ Understand the problem-solving process
- ◆ Determine if you're primed for problem solving or prolonging the problem
- ◆ Find out about time-tested ways to check out your possible solutions
- ◆ Get the lowdown on brainstorming
- ◆ Analyze possible solutions
- ◆ Evaluate the solution to see if it works

Now that you've got that expertly defined problem that's itching to be solved, it's time for the tips, tools, and processes—proven and newfangled—that'll help you devise definitive solutions.

And as we proceed, keep this notion tucked into your clear-thinking mind: our goal in problem solving—aside from the relief associated with bringing closure to an issue—is finding solutions that bring sound results.

Mind Games 14

Mindy has been trying to figure out which city would make the best place for her to relocate. Rather than spend time researching and delving into why she wants to move, she's decided to pick a city by playing a word game with three friends' names. She's going to live with one of these friends, the letters of whose name can be rearranged to spell out a hot and sunny U.S. city where the friend lives. The letters in the other two friends' names can be rearranged to spell out cities with colder climates where they live. Who's the friend with the sunniest letters? (Hint: No punctuation is given, and the city names may be more than one word.)

    A. Annie Polsimi

    B. Bette Sprrugs

    C. Katy Laticles

(Turn to Appendix D for the answer.)

Where Are You Headed with That Problem on Your Back?

Whatever the problem, you gotta have a plan. To see where you're going with that problem, here is a step-by-step look at the process to solve it. As we head into problem-solving land, grab your "problem backpack." That should contain your well-defined problem, but also the following "tools":

◆ An open mind

◆ Creativity (if you don't think you're a "creative type," don't worry; we show you how to activate this trait for problem solving)

> **CAUTION**
>
> **Mind Fogger** _____
>
> Make sure that your problem has been properly and articulately defined so that the facts you collect—once analyzed—will really work for you.

◆ A desire to generate options, alternatives, and possible solutions

◆ A willingness to examine and analyze those options with logic, reasoning, and common sense

◆ A mental commitment for follow-through: determining the solution and evaluating it

Then as we proceed through the land of problem solving, let's keep in mind the process that we'll be implementing:

♦ First, gather up your pack. Throw into it all the information pertaining to your problem—facts, knowledge, beliefs, and opinions—to help you in your quest.

♦ Be ready to lay out and use those contents at the next stop, Creativity-ville. Here we generate ideas for solutions—using a variety of methods.

♦ Then at the weigh station, you determine which of those ideas are worthy solutions and which should be tossed out.

♦ Before you leave town, select your solution.

♦ Now you're off and running with that selection to new and different worlds. At your stops, you'll be ready and eager to evaluate its effectiveness—and make adjustments if necessary—at the appropriate, predetermined intervals.

♦ Finally, it may be necessary for you—in, say, a workplace setting—to share your solution with others, in thoughts, words, or in writing. (See Chapters 15 and 16 for tips on effective communication.)

Assess Where You Stand

As we start this process, we move through a few problem-solving methods out there that are well established. Then we give you insights into brainstorming—your very own transportation mode on the Problem-Solving Express. But first, let's take a few considerations into account, determining where you stand before we begin.

> **Words from the Wise**
>
> No problem can stand the assault of sustained thinking.
>
> —Voltaire, French writer and philosopher

Rain Maker or Drought Baker?

Let's take this consideration before we begin the problem-solving process in earnest. Answer for yourself: "Am I a Rain Maker or a Drought Baker?" A Rain Maker takes on problems with enthusiasm to find workable and often inventive solutions. Conversely, a Drought Baker resents problem solving, often creating other obstacles in the process.

We all know them. They're the people in your workplace, or maybe even in your family, who naysay ideas or project pessimism into the problem-solving process.

Instead of seizing a problem and delving into the opportunities they present (Rain Maker), they squelch the process, drying up possibilities and the ideas that come with them (Drought Baker).

Are you secretly a Drought Baker? Let's hope not; take this test to find out if you're into egging problems on … or sizing up effective solutions. For each statement, decide whether you agree or disagree:

1. When a problem arises for me, I like to take responsibility for determining a resolution.

2. While solving a problem—if I'm honest with myself—I actually use questions as more of a delay tactic than for fact or idea collecting.

3. I believe finding a solution brings a rush—a sense of exhilaration—with it.

4. It's my responsibility to show others the impediments to their solutions.

5. I think solutions often mask bigger problems.

6. I know the obvious may be an option, but it usually needs a makeover.

7. I think details matter more than the overall picture.

8. Even if I'm working on a project that's just a piece of a much bigger one, I think vision is a must.

9. I don't like to offer suggestions that aren't part of my job, even if they will bring positive impact.

10. I'm not deterred if my suggestions aren't readily accepted.

11. If I criticize an idea, I offer at least a couple of alternatives.

12. Problems are onerous and defy a sense of humor.

How'd you do?

If you're a Rain Maker, you agree with statements 1, 3, 6, 8, 10, and 11. Drought Bakers agree with 2, 4, 5, 7, 9, and 12.

So let's concentrate on being a Rain Maker. A Rain Maker …

◆ Views problems as opportunities.

◆ Takes ownership of a problem.

◆ Regards situations with vision.

- Only asks questions to get to a solution, not stagnate on the problem.

- Is willing, ready, and eager to move past the obvious for solutions that utilize creativity and—in the process—will likely be productive and successful.

Be Ready to Hit the Bull's-Eye

Now, finally, make sure you're set up to squarely deal with the problem at hand. With a Rain Maker approach in mind, answer the following questions:

- Do you have all of your information gathered?

- What's your ideal solution?

- What are the obvious options?

- What barriers/restraints/restrictions do you see in your way that need to be overcome?

Do the Dig

In the problem-solving process, always be prepared to dig deeper. Check, double-check, and triple-check your defined problem. Make sure you're not only addressing a symptom of the problem, and that your solution is set up to get to the heart of the matter.

For instance, Vera thought her immediate problem was she wanted to get married. But when she delved deeper, she realized that want was masking another issue. She agreed that she was lonely and wanted companionship, a life with a partner. But she also didn't feel good about herself. Vera realized a correlation existed between her feelings about herself, and projecting a positive image that was attractive to others. Further, she didn't feel good about herself because she was unhealthily overweight. Instead of concentrating on finding a husband, she decided that her initial problem was shedding the pounds that had been steadily adding up. And in dropping that weight, she could also get at root issues that had caused her to gain that weight in the first place.

So if Vera had only concentrated on getting married, her true problem would have lived on—and, more than likely, festered.

Check Out These Tried-and-True Methods

In the problem solving we'll be delving into, these methods rely on investigating multiple choices for your solution.

> **Mind Fogger** _____
>
> Here's a good question to keep on hand as you move through the problem-solving process. If we solve this problem, will we just create one in another area? A physical demonstration of this answer's importance is in an example from the U.S. Forestry Service: if we build levees and dams here for flood control, will the floods simply move downstream? Make sure your final solution isn't creating another flood somewhere else.

First, we examine the most logical, straightforward approach to solving a problem: you just gather up what you've got, and extrapolate from there.

This problem-solving method is akin to writing a business proposal. Right off, you've got the following:

- The objective, or your goal in solving the problem
- The tactics, or your obvious options

Here's an example: your company is manufacturing Suzy-Q dolls targeted toward preteens, and you're getting battered by the competition. The doll's profile isn't very high and has very little distribution in stores.

The objective: beef up awareness of Suzy-Q with consumers and toy stores.

The tactics:

- Produce commercials to air on prime preteen programs.
- Feature Suzy-Q prominently on the company's website.
- Get Suzy-Q reviewed in *Doll Reader* and other consumer publications.
- Arrange for Suzy-Q booths at upcoming industry toy fairs.

In looking at your tactics, you have to consider economic and even political constraints before moving on, asking such questions as these:

- What's the budget?
- What timetable will be assigned for implementing the proposed solution and evaluating results?
- Are there other factors, such as, "Is this a pet project of the boss?" or "Is Suzy-Q just a stepping-stone to the rollout of the Vivi-V doll, which will command more resources and attention?"

Now, of course, you could just take a look at what we've just outlined and be on your merry way to solving a problem. But stick around, because this is when the fun begins … and when even more productive, effective, and substantial solutions can take hold.

It's Brainstorm-y Weather

We're crazy for brainstorming—working with others to devise ideas or processes, either separately or in tandem—that prompts new directions or methods. It is hands-down the best way to quickly generate a slew of ideas for possible solutions to a well-defined problem or predicament. We've found that it works in both personal and professional arenas. And in the throes of allowing yourself or the situation to be focused on quantity and not quality, you'll find that a bounty of ideas can often naturally lead to and produce a winning solution.

Cobweb Buster

Ad guru Alex Osborn is credited with inventing brainstorming in 1953 while at the advertising agency BBDO, where groups attempted to find solutions. He said it was so named because "brainstorming" meant using your brain to storm a problem. However, he didn't take complete credit for the method because he believed that this "conference procedure" approach had been used in India for more than 400 years as a Hindu teaching practice known as *Prai-Barshana*. In Indian, *Prai* means "outside yourself" and *Barshana* means "question."

Here's how to set up a brainstorming session. In this step-by-step approach, we concentrate on how an "office" brainstorming would work. But you'll see it's easily adaptable to other venues; hype them up or tone them down to be appropriate to the problem you face.

1. Gather participants whom you respect. Selectivity from the outset breeds better results in the end. That doesn't (and shouldn't) mean you're only calling on colleagues or higher-ups to brainstorm with you. You no doubt know some within your company who may work in a junior or assistant position whose competence or brightness inspires your confidence. Call on their creativity, too. Regardless of those joining in, don't feel inclined to give anyone an intense briefing before the session's appointed time.

2. Before they gather, outfit your room with thinking stimuli: that could include snack foods or healthful munchies, sodas or water, colorful wall decorations, playthings or toys that are relevant to the discussion at hand.

3. When the session begins, give it a time limit. Although these can vary, we've found that 50 minutes to an hour is prime. At the 30-minute mark, creative juices are still flowing, and some are just getting started. But by 50 minutes, attention may begin to wane. Don't exceed an hour, unless you're in an emergency situation wherein lifesaving or crisis communication is involved.

4. Make sure the brainstorm leader designates someone to man a flipchart and magic marker to record *every* idea that's uttered.

5. At the session's start, the brainstorm leader should download all the particulars of the problem, including possible constraints. However, participants are not to be restricted in any way—by cost, time, manpower, etc.—in the ideas they offer up. Literally, anything goes!

6. In tandem with the preceding guideline, no negative comments are allowed to live at a brainstorming session. Without belaboring this point, we've got to stress it again: no negatives! The brainstorm session isn't the time for that. Even if someone doles out an idea that seems absolutely far-fetched and/or beyond budget, don't let yourself belittle it out loud. Here's why: it's often the off-kilter, crazy ideas that someone can build upon and recraft to be the perfect solution.

7. Participants are encouraged to dive in, freely contributing whatever ideas they can, no matter how wild and crazy. Further, participants should try to build on others' ideas whenever possible to generate even more possible solutions.

8. At the session's conclusion, each participant should number the solutions that have been recorded from favorite to least favorite.

Words from the Wise

When the only tool you own is a hammer, every problem begins to resemble a nail.

—Abraham Maslow, one of the founders of humanistic psychology

9. After the session has ended, the brainstorm leader should—as soon as possible while the session remains fresh in mind—draft a "brainstorm report" that includes the ideas, the build-upons, and the assessments. The report will then come in handy for evaluating the possibilities and determining the best, final solution.

10. After preparing the report, you might want to apply some criteria you've determined that will

help you whittle away your possibilities to the ones that will be most appropriate to your final solution. Criteria may include budget, time involved, etc.

Analyzing Possible Solutions

After you've collected your obvious options and the top choices that brainstorming has produced, let's put those solutions through some stringent tests. These will be instrumental in helping you pick your final solution.

May the Forces Be with You

In 1951, social scientist Kurt Lewin devised force-field analysis, which allows you to look at the forces involved in implementing a change. According to Lewin, you would have "driving forces" and "restraining forces."

Here we've adapted that for a more focused pros-and-cons approach to problem solving. You divide a page into two with your two "forces" at the top. If a solution that you're considering is implemented, what will be a positive outcome (driving force), and then what will be a negative one (restraint)?

Let's take a look again at the Suzy-Q doll, and apply the force-field analysis. Perhaps a brainstorming session has given you an idea: have models dress up like Suzy-Qs and have them featured in "live" store windows or displays.

Driving Forces	Restraining Forces
High-visibility locations would heighten awareness.	Would take research to determine feasibility.
Tactic itself could generate publicity.	May be limited on locations that specifically target preteens.
Few costs involved.	Few major toy retailers have display windows.

And for each column, consider tweaking. Is there a chance that if one of the forces was slightly altered, another solution may come into play? For instance, you might not have a ready-and-waiting contact for FAO Schwarz to put a real-live Suzy-Q in one of their store display windows. But one of your colleagues has a contact at the nationwide Toys-a-Rama chain, whose management has been wanting to do more exciting, visual, and interactive in-store displays.

As you move down your list of driving and restraining forces for each possible solution, you need to draw in your subjective views. In true force-field analysis, you would assign a subjective score to each driving and restraining force. Then, when you add up each of the columns, you determine if you have a valid solution on your hands that can be evaluated further.

Hats Off to Putting These Hats On

Edward de Bono is known as the architect of several *lateral thinking* concepts, which apply creativity to logical thinking. One of his myriad exercises is six thinking hats, which has been adapted for a variety of uses and meetings in mulling over possibilities for problem solving. The six "hats" allow you to look at possible options from each one of six perspectives. Here's our take on the approach.

Think Tank

A concept invented and pioneered by Maltese physician Edward de Bono, **lateral thinking** prizes a creative approach to solving problems. Rather than tackling a problem head on with preconceived right-and-wrong answers, you approach it from different angles, employing many methods.

With the white hat, you focus on available data and analyze trends to see how your possible solution measures up. In our adaptation, you'd ask, "Has it been done before?" If so, was it successful? If it wasn't successful, can we implement changes that would make it flourish?

The red hat allows you to look at the solution with intuition, and respond with your guts and emotions. What do your instincts tell you about this possibility?

You look at the negative aspects and weak points with the black hat. What's wrong with this picture? Can obstacles be overcome?

Meanwhile, the yellow hat lets you in on the sunny, optimistic components of your solution. What is unique and compelling about this possible solution? Why do we think it will work?

As for the green hat, you bring creativity to the mix to make the solution stronger, or build on it yet again. Will it do what we need it to?

Finally, the blue hat is the hat monitor, if you will, making sure that the hats stay focused on their particular area. Did every hat do its job in analyzing this possible solution?

And staying in the color vein, we like to take the solutions from the six thinking hats to a traffic light. You have to go into subjective mode again and ask yourself if the possible solution is a go (green light), a go but with reservations (yellow light), or an absolute no-go (red light).

In most cases, you're best off with those options that have gotten the full-on green light.

Now, It's Up to You

In the end, determining your own best solution is up to you. Although we can give you some guidance, problems are always under the guise of such different factors as the people involved or budget assigned. Take these considerations into account as you select your solution:

- Which one is most acceptable in terms of solving the problem?

- Are the consequences of putting the solution in place acceptable?

- Which solution will be hardiest and have more permanence? In other words, select one that will have staying power so that you're not re-addressing the problem again shortly after you've put yourself through problem-solving school.

- Which is most cost-effective? For instance, am I heading toward one that will drain finances and manpower?

- Which is most time-conscious? Am I picking one that will fit into a prescribed timetable, or will this one take me off track?

- What are the risks involved? Are they too numerous for this solution to be practical?

Answer those questions, and grab the solution that earns the highest marks. With that, you're ready for the next step!

Apply Your Results, Evaluate Your Solution

You've got a solution, but to be most effective, a solution must be monitored and evaluated. Set up an action plan to think about the following:

- What deadlines need to be put in place to manage the timetable you had assigned to the problem and its solution?

- Who's implementing the solution? You and, if appropriate, who else?

- Have financial resources already been diverted to the solution, or do they need to be set up?

- What needs to be changed within yourself, the current structure, the staffing and/or the organization, the household, etc. to put the solution in place?

- What plans will be made to notify all those involved of the solution being proposed? People are more apt to contribute to what they know and understand. Give a solution its best chance for effectiveness; get everyone involved or affected to climb aboard to make it work.

- What criteria do you need to meet for this solution to be deemed a success?

Then have key dates locked in to monitor the progress, and determine if you're seeing what you expected. During this aspect, ask the following:

- Is the solution working?

- Is it on track time-wise and budget-wise?

- If the "solution" seems off track, take a hard look at it. Was it realistic? Were appropriate resources allocated? Was a solution as important as you thought? In other words, has another matter taken priority?

- Does this problem seem likely to occur again?

- After the solution has run the course you determined time-wise, answer the key question: Was it successful?

- How will you know if it's successful? What does success look like? Can you see it? Can it be measured? Did it meet the standards of the prescribed criteria?

- Looking back at your stated problem, did an accomplished goal—or a series of improvements—result?

In a best-case scenario for problem solving, the solution will have been successful, and you'll have learned from the problem-solving process. So at the conclusion of each process, make sure to give the process another once-over to answer for yourself "What did I learn?" Because you're probably closer than you think to your next problem coming along, you'll also be more equipped to tackle it head on and winningly.

> **Points to Ponder**
>
> Is there really ever a problem that can never be solved?

The Least You Need to Know

◆ The ins and outs of the problem-solving process require a well-defined problem; all appropriate information; and creativity in brewing up options, selecting your solution, and evaluating it.

◆ Determine for yourself whether your thinking is geared toward being a Rain Maker (with an enthusiasm for solving problems) or a Drought Baker (with a penchant for perpetuating them).

◆ Take the time to assess where you stand before you begin problem solving with your obvious options (that can be primed for bigger-and-better solutions).

◆ Brainstorming can bring an avalanche of possible ideas, but efficient sessions require guidelines.

◆ Analyze possible solutions to choose one that sounds best.

◆ After selecting your solution, put in place an action plan to evaluate and monitor the solution to make sure it's effective.

Chapter 15

Clear Thinking Out Loud

In This Chapter

◆ Make your point the best way you can

◆ Engage in conversations that are productive for all participants

◆ Get the ground rules for presenting your case effectively

◆ Learn about speaking foibles that muddle clarity

So you're well equipped with clear thoughts, and you want to voice them out loud? In this chapter, we help you do just that, giving you tips to verbally present your case, and deploying versatile tactics in the process.

Putting your thoughts into words can be tricky. Obstacles loom in ambiguous words and double-edged phrases, but we help gird your thoughts for effective speech.

Mind Games 15

Each of these sentences contains three different homographs—words that sound the same but have different meanings and spellings. Can you figure them out? (The dashes indicate the number of letters per word.)

They love to – – – – – her: She brews up a variety of green – – – – before she sets up her – – – – on the course.

Honestly, that topic is such a – – – –, it'd be more interesting if a wild – – – – taught it than hearing that loutish – – – – drone on.

Despite his looks and talent, that rising star will never be an – – – – if he's – – – – for too long, squandering all his time reflecting on an – – – – – idea of life.

(Turn to Appendix D for the answer.)

Cogently Stating Your Point

How many times have you clearly known what you wanted to say, but then completely floundered the delivery, leaving you flustered and frustrated? Let's look at some ways that you can recover, and thrive under similar circumstances the next time.

Are You Speaking in Circles?

Where are you on the clear-thoughts-into-words scale? Are you a salient speaker or do you speak in circles, inarticulately or indirectly addressing a topic or subject? Honestly answer true or false to the following:

Think Tank

To **imply** is to explain something without directly expressing it; to **infer** is to extract meaning out of that explanation. To differentiate between the two, realize that the sender of the message implies it, whereas the receiver of it infers it.

1. I have a good grasp on grammar. For instance, I know the difference between *imply* and *infer.*

2. When I set out to make a stand, I've done my homework.

3. I'm a good listener. (You may refer to the LQ quiz in Chapter 4 before you answer this one!)

4. In discussions outside of formal debates, there's never a winner and a loser.

5. I'm guided more by organization than emotion in putting my thoughts into words.

To clearly state your point, you needed to answer true to all of the above. This chapter explains how each of the preceding enables you to clearly communicate your thoughts.

Gathering, Interpreting, Organizing

As you know from earlier chapters, to present your position clearly you first need to have done your homework on the topic. Only after you have mastered your facts can you verbally express them articulately. So prepare for your conversation or speech event. Collect your arguments, and to test your coherence, try the following:

♦ State your stance in a single sentence. If you have trouble with that statement, consider breaking down your stance into smaller components.

♦ Review your arguments. Which seem strongest? Weakest? Order them from strongest to weakest.

♦ Follow your initial stance with several arguments or propositions that support the stance. Begin with your strongest argument, to capture the audience's attention.

♦ Consider whether some arguments might make listeners glaze over, ignore the initial proposition, or refuse to consider your main proposition? If so, consider discarding those.

♦ End your presentation with a snappy conclusion that summarizes the points and memorably drives your case home.

Beef Up Your Vocabulary

Using the right words is all-important and can make your message more powerful. Clear thoughts deserve to be expressed clearly. So really think about what words best describe your thoughts.

> **Words from the Wise**
>
> The difference between the right word and the almost-right word is the difference between lightning and the lightning bug.
>
> —Mark Twain, American author and humorist

Know that the right words don't have to be overblown or "intellectual." They just have to be appropriate and well suited to your cause. Here are some tips to improve your vocabulary:

♦ Read magazines and books that you find mentally challenging. In other words, treat your mind to pithy articles in respected periodicals rather than superficial and short pieces in tabloids. Be mindful of which words have gravity and substance, and which are just sass and sizzle.

◆ Pay attention to the words experts use to make their points. When watching an interviewee or program guest who strikes you as particularly articulate, turn on the "closed-caption" option on your television and read the scrolling text. Newspaper columnists William Safire and Maureen Dowd are prime examples of people who turn clear thoughts into artful conversation.

◆ When you encounter an unfamiliar word from whatever source, look it up! Then try to use it yourself.

◆ Go a step further and look up the etymology (origin) of the word. Many words are interconnected within our own language and have "relatives" living in other words. Further, many are variations on words from other languages. That deeper understanding of a word might further your understanding of other words or phrases.

CAUTION **Mind Fogger** _____

Words such as _um, like, uh, y'know,_ and _okay_ hamper clear communication. Pay attention when you speak to determine whether you needlessly dot your sentences with those distractions. Do you use them to fill up silence, as a "pause" when your mind is racing, or because you're uncomfortable or unknowledgeable about the subject at hand? If so, try to eliminate them. Spend some time listening to your speech patterns, learn from them, and then consciously take out the needless clutter that you hear.

A Verbal Case for Casual Fridays

Consider this example of gathering facts, organizing thoughts, and using the right words to convey a message. Suppose you're trying to convince your company's standards and practices committee that "casual Fridays" should be instituted for all employees at your company, Flower Power. In a meeting with the decision makers, here is one tactic you could use to present your case.

The Proposal:

Casual Fridays should become a common practice for the Flower Power corporate offices.

The Arguments:

Productivity at chief competitors Heidi Hydrangea and Roses 'n Riches soared by 87 percent and 98 percent respectively after they instituted casual Fridays.

An employee poll indicates overwhelming support for the idea, so casual Fridays would undoubtedly boost morale. In addition, implementation of casual Fridays would entail no actual monetary cost.

Ideas Unlimited has found that companies that allow casual Fridays benefit from a surge in profitable ideas.

Evidence culled from *Mid-Size Company Reports* shows that in companies Flower Power's size, the practice of casual Fridays fosters teamwork among all employees that extends to the rest of the workweek.

The Conclusion:

The implementation of casual Fridays is a no-cost, potentially high-return endeavor with a high probability of boosting employee morale and teamwork, increasing productivity, and generating profitable ideas.

Use Supporting Arguments

Whatever verbal case you're making, you want your arguments to logically support your proposal. In this example, the arguments do just that.

Remember to use reasonable points that aren't fraught with emotion. Notice that no argument in this example relies on "We have really cool clothes that we can never wear to work unless there's a casual Friday" or "Our company will be more hip if we have casual Fridays." Although those may be true statements, they don't necessarily help prove your points. (However, you might be able to link hipness to a better performance for the company—in which case, the arguments would be valid.)

If You're Still Not Making Sense

If you think you have relatively sound arguments but still have trouble expressing them, review the basics of what you are thinking. Consider the following:

- What fundamental information do you want to convey?
- If you think your thoughts may come out inarticulately, write them down in short, simple sentences. Then rewrite them using enhanced vocabulary.

◆ Review the arguments. Do they state an opinion? Remember, relevant facts will strengthen your arguments.

◆ Can you present the information another way that sounds better?

◆ Can you draw a helpful comparison to explain the point better?

◆ Do you have additional information that might prove helpful to include?

◆ Do you need to omit any of your arguments because they don't contribute well to your cause?

Head-y Conversations

The best way to see if your clear thoughts are effectively verbalized is to engage in robust, productive *conversations*.

Spark up your best conversations by following these guidelines:

◆ Be ready to listen.

◆ Don't answer questions with a simple yes or no. Nothing stagnates a conversation more. If you find yourself answering yes or no, follow that by asking "why?"

◆ Pay attention to those with whom you're engaged in conversation; listen carefully to what they're saying so that you can ask intelligent questions.

◆ Don't rush your thoughts into words. If you need to, pause—and even take a breath—before responding and between sentences to collect your thoughts. In fact, pausing can be an effective communication technique to let points sink in.

Think Tank

Conversations are informal dialogue between two or more people. This dialogue— which is usually familiar rather than formal—allows for the oral interchange of sentiments and observations.

◆ Don't use terms such as *kind of*, *sort of*, *woulda*, *coulda*, or *shoulda*, which can distract from a message and even mitigate the power of your other well-selected words.

◆ Use examples to support your points and back up your arguments.

Understanding Another's POV

Now it's time to consider how well you actually listen and understand during conversations. One of our favorite examples of a conversation gone awry involved someone misunderstanding the K.C. and the Sunshine Band's song "Keep It Comin' Love." Two people were discussing the meaning of the song's title, and their disagreement was becoming heated. Unfortunately, their argument escalated because they weren't listening to each other. If they had been, they would have realized that one of them thought the title was "Keep It Common Law."

To understand and engage in meaningful conversations, you must listen carefully. You can test your listening and understanding by questioning and encouraging feedback. To confirm whether listeners understand what you have said, don't be afraid to check in. If you don't understand something, repeat what you think you heard, as in "Did I hear you say …?"

Words from the Wise

Use soft words and hard arguments.
—English proverb

If you think you're not making your point effectively, consider what you are saying from a listener perspective. For example, perhaps you think you're giving easy directions to somewhere, but you can tell that the listener does not understand you. Take a crack at "hearing" yourself. How might you rephrase the directions to make them clearer?

There are other ways to gauge your presentation. Watch for signs of confusion in others. Are brows furrowed? Is someone grimacing? Does someone ask a question that is totally unrelated to what you think you're talking about?

Further, be aware when assuming knowledge or skills of another person. For instance, if you suggest that the Oporto Museum of Contemporary Art in Portugal is a stellar example that all U.S. museums should follow, you are assuming listener knowledge of the museum. Your statements might not be meaningful if those you're talking with aren't familiar with your references.

And finally, take diversity into account. Different ethnicities have different styles of communication, so, if necessary, and depending on the situation, be prepared to adapt. To make sure that your clear thoughts translate appropriately, you might have to do further research about your intended audience.

Debate Tactics

Debate encourages a formal approach to clear thinking because you must prove your claims. To validate your claims, you need the right words—which have been formed from clear thoughts—to back them up.

Here are a few terms that are important to understand as you endeavor to transform your clear thoughts into words:

Arguments. Reasoning and evidence that supports your position or claim.

Case. Your arguments as a whole.

Claim. The point you're trying to make.

Debate. To argue for or against; to contend for in words and arguments; to maintain a stance by reasoning.

A debate is a discussion between sides with different views; people speak for or against an issue in hopes of swaying a decision to their side. In the best case, debates initiate and foster critical thinking, personal expression, and tolerance of others' opinions.

Cobweb Buster

September 26, 1960, marked the first of four "great debates" between presidential candidates John F. Kennedy and Richard Nixon. Although Kennedy received higher marks in these first-ever televised debates from those who watched, polls showed that those who only heard the debates on the radio thought that the men were evenly matched. That finding suggested that the candidates' verbal abilities may have been equal, but Kennedy's charismatic on-screen persona tipped the scales in his favor, or his presence may have helped him drive his points home.

Today heated debates seem to be increasingly common in professional, social, and family environments regarding topics ranging from abortion and assisted suicide to "buying American" and drilling for oil in Alaska. The more information available to everyone means there's more fodder for issues to be discussed and debated.

You probably have an image of two people—one pro, one con—standing up at a podium, taking turns to present their case. But a debate doesn't have to take place in an official forum. Typically, you'll just find yourself engaged in a conversation when a debatable issue arises. In these cases, you want to coherently and concisely present your view.

For starters, try to ascertain the following:

♦ What bothers you about the information presented? Does the information seem misleading?

◆ Is someone trying to influence your thinking/actions?

◆ Can you identify specific errors in what's being presented?

◆ Is the speaker's thinking clear? Are fallacies, incorrect information, or shaky statistics at work?

Then you must decide: "Can I challenge their thinking properly and effectively with counter-information?"

If so, do the following:

◆ Weigh your words carefully. Think before you speak, and make your point simply and concisely. Be specific. If you do so, people will respond better and you'll be in for a more productive discussion.

◆ Think of the debate as a friendly tennis match, with messages being the ball that goes back and forth. You serve (speak) and then wait for the return (listen).

◆ Be a fair player: don't resort to fallacies yourself or use cherry-picked facts and figures.

Sparring with Grace

When you spar with grace, you work to incorporate all of the preceding into your thoughts-into-words machinations. No matter how forceful the debate or conversation, respecting others during the discussion should always be paramount. You undermine your own arguments when you make judgments about the intelligence, integrity, and background of those listening to you.

Follow These Rules

Debatable issues inherently are not wrong or right. Therefore, you don't have to prove that you are "right." Instead, clear thinkers want to use reason in their arguments to reinforce them; they're not out to put a checkmark in the win column.

Good manners require that you not be rash in your discussions, debates, and conversations. In addition, don't make claims you can't prove. Listen carefully. Make honest attempts to understand what others "mean" to say. And pause before you respond so that you can truly take in what the other has said.

Don't attack the other person with words in any way. Address thoughts, not the other person's personality.

In the end, be willing to agree to disagree. A conversation that's deteriorated into prolonged debate has stopped being productive. Because not everyone will share the same opinion, be ready to appreciate and respect someone else's. In that spirit, look for any common points of agreement, however, so that the next conversation, debate, or discussion can start fresh.

Finally, don't judge another's views. Even though the views may differ from yours, judging them isn't in the domain of a clear thinker.

Negotiation in the Clear-Thinking Mix

In both professional arenas and everyday living, negotiation skills come into play. Although negotiation tactics aren't described in detail here, the subject is considered briefly because clear thinking can make negotiating more effective. Routinely, negotiation is fueled by the zero-sum perspective, which means that what I gain, you lose; and what you gain, I lose. However, once again, when you focus on putting clear thoughts into words, you move away from the concept of winning. You move toward a thinking person's dream: the best outcome prevailing from a productive discussion. And that's a point that needs no negotiating.

Verbal Snags

Let's review some major verbal entanglements that can hamper effective oral communication. First up, the three H's—*homonyms, homographs,* and *homophones*—which can lead to misunderstanding.

Think Tank

A **homonym** is one of two or more words that are spelled or pronounced alike but have different meanings, such as arms (body parts) and arms (weapons). A **homograph** is one of two or more words that are spelled alike but have different meanings or pronunciation, such as present (gift) and present (make a presentation). A **homophone** is one of two or more words that aren't spelled alike but sound alike, such as hoarse and horse. Homonyms has also become the umbrella term to include homographs and homophones.

Whether words sound alike or are spelled alike, the worst offense is that they might have a different meaning than what you intend to say or what you hear. "Err" can come across as "heir," so the meaning can be misconstrued as someone receiving an inheritance rather than a mistake that's about to be committed. A "bazaar" can be taken as "bizarre," and your facts can be in a "sink" rather than in "sync." But you can also mistake a ship's "bow" for one that accompanies an arrow, or the railroad "tie" for neckwear.

The best way to avoid confusion with the three H's is by being an active listener. Also pay attention to the speaker's *syntax* (the arrangement of words and their relationship to each other and additional structural elements in sentences), which gives clues to meaning. And when presenting your own point of view, take special care to determine whether you've included words that could be unclear.

Malapropisms—a grotesque misuse of a word, usually to (unintentionally) humorous effect—have a habit of causing unrelenting glee in a message's recipient. Although no one minds a hearty chuckle, malapropisms can bring inopportune moments that can make a good point crumble and prevent clear thoughts and messages from getting across. A malapropism can even have a lasting effect, preventing further valid arguments from being taken seriously.

Malapropisms often result when a word switches off with another one, either one that sounds similar to the intended word, or an exact opposite of it. Here are some examples, with the word the speaker meant to say in parentheses:

> Passing that law was beyond my apprehension (comprehension).

> He's not thinking for the long term; he has channel (tunnel) vision.

> After she became a manager, she plummeted (skyrocketed) to the top.

Cobweb Buster

The word malapropism derives from the character Mrs. Malaprop in Richard Sheridan's 1775 Restoration comedy *The Rivals*. Her name borrowed from the French term *mal à propos*, which means "inappropriate," and describes her terrible (and funny) grasp of the English language. Some of Mrs. Malaprop's lines in the play are as follows, with the correct word in parentheses:

- ◆ "He is the very pineapple (pinnacle) of success."
- ◆ "I have since laid Sir Anthony's preposition (proposition) before her."
- ◆ "Sure, if I reprehend (apprehend) anything in this world it is the use of my oracular (vernacular) tongue, and a nice derangement (arrangement) of epitaphs (epithets)!"

You can avoid unintentional malapropisms by being certain that you're familiar with all the words and terminology you use. Here is just a sampling of some common words prone to malapropisms that can dog and detour your clear thinking-into-words efforts. Do you know the differences between each word in the following pairs? If so, can you think of how using one instead of the other might provoke inadvertent laughter or offense?

adverse, averse	elicit, illicit	moral, morale
affluence, influence	eligible, legible	precede, proceed
allude, elude	emanate, eminent	predecessor, successor
antidote, anecdote	empathy, sympathy	pundit, pungent
conservation, consumption	jibe, jive	secede, succeed
deprecate, depreciate	livid, vivid	thong, throng
	malady, melody	travel, travail

Points to Ponder

Why are politicians so prone to malapropisms?

Now that you're familiar with some tips—and traps—to put your clear thoughts into articulate verbal messages, let's take that a step further and turn those clear thoughts of yours into powerfully written words.

The Least You Need to Know

- Before speaking, make sure you can clearly state your thoughts in concise sentences that can be backed up with valid arguments.

- Expand your vocabulary to select the most appropriate and precise words for the message you're trying to convey.

- To truly understand others' points of view, engage in respectful conversations and debates, ask open-ended questions, and be an active listener.

- When you find your thinking being challenged on an issue, pinpoint the suspect information and then provide counter-information to it.

- Homonyms and malapropisms can make speech unclear; homonyms breed confusion, and malapropisms cause unintentional gaffes that disrupt trains of thought.

16

Transforming Clear Thoughts into Written Words

In This Chapter

◆ Decide when written communication is more effective than verbal communication

◆ Articulate clear thoughts into well-worded letters and e-mails

◆ Find out about written-word etiquette and netiquette

◆ Ascertain the clearest ways to frame your writing

◆ Look out for language barriers

You've got clear thoughts that you've just got to get down on paper—or up on that computer screen—and you're looking for the best way to do it. If you can turn your clear thoughts into verbal expressions, you'll be primed and ready to transfer them to a written forum.

Writing truly can provide you with the most potent form of expression available. In this chapter, we demystify that process, help you decide which written form is your best course, and show you how to avoid patches of murkiness.

Mind Games 16
Name a word that when capitalized is pronounced differently than when lowercased. (Turn to Appendix D for some examples.)

The Power of the Pen (or Keyboard)

Let's face it, speaking—no matter how clearly it can communicate your thoughts—isn't always the right mode for presenting or persuading. Take a look at the following list. Can you make a case for why a written communication would be better than an oral one?

◆ A public-relations campaign

◆ Post-surgery care instructions, including prescriptions

◆ A customer service complaint

◆ A recipe for chicken lo mein

◆ A work order for installing different-sized shelves at multiple heights in several departments

◆ A new business proposal to handle public affairs for the state lottery

◆ A focus-group summary of results from test-marketing a new video game

◆ Directions from a Chicago residence to an Oklahoma City home

◆ A bid to be the electrical engineer for a downtown high-rise

In each case, you can probably immediately understand the problems that might result if any of the preceding were only communicated verbally. Details would have been lost or misconstrued. And without the clear organization that writing can provide for several connected thoughts, rambling tangents might have overtaken the intended message(s).

Words from the Wise

If any man wish to write in a clear style, let him be first clear in his thoughts.

—Johann Wolfgang von Goethe, German poet

Besides ensuring that you've included all your facts and opinions in a coherent manner, the written word can often leave a more lasting impact. And in many cases, that lasting impact means that your words persuade or prompt action much faster.

The next time you're debating whether to speak or write, answer these questions to help you decide:

- **What will be more time-effective in the long run?** Too often, making a telephone call to get business out of the way seems like the expeditious route. But will that only prolong what needs to be written down at some point anyway? Or will you waste more time explaining in words what might be picked up faster if it were written down?

- **Am I opting for speaking because I don't have the time to put it into words on paper?** Does that also mean I don't have time to effectively put it into verbal words either?

- **Am I asking for a call to action?** If that's the case, you're more likely to get a response if your case/proposal/suggestion is made in writing.

- **Is my targeted message too complicated or does it contain too much information for the spoken word?** We're usually not geared toward memorizing large chunks of information at once. Sometimes our information flow is just too much to grasp and we need it to be written for reference.

- **Would the message require more study than a general conversation would allow?** Sometimes we need to hold on to information for a while, to review it and then act on it.

- **Is it just too important to trust the spoken word to someone's memory?** In the case of patient-care instructions, you don't want to risk someone's safety. And you don't want to waste company money (or your own) by leaving instructions for hanging shelves to chance. When in doubt, go with the written word. It's your permanent record of clear thoughts.

Determining Your Best Form of Communication

After you decide to put those clear thoughts into writing, you must make another decision: paper or computer, letter or e-mail? When making your decision, consider the following:

- What's my role as the writer? Am I the consumer, boss, or employee?

- Who's my target audience? A prospective client, a relative, my manager?

- Does what I'm communicating need to be kept confidential?

- What's the topic?

- Taking the preceding into account, should the communication take on a formal or informal tone?

- And most importantly, what do I want to accomplish here?

As you're making your decision, also consider the following attributes to determine what mode of written communication best suits your needs (and the recipient's):

Timing

E-mail: Immediate; and in business, so often, speed rules.

Letter: Nicknamed "snail mail," delivery could take a few days (unless overnighted).

Message Effectiveness

E-mail: It's all in the wording.

Letter: Letterhead, colored paper, and attachments/embellishments can look professional and forceful (and they're not always possible with e-mail). In addition, the personal nature of a letter can add more impact.

Personal Nature

E-mail: Depending on the approach, it can seem formulaic, nondistinct, and—unfortunately—indistinguishable. Your font choice can only go so far in making your e-mails look different from other ones.

Letter: Handwriting can tip off personality traits of the sender; typically, letters take on more permanence with a recipient. (You rarely hear someone say they "love to keep an e-mail written to them.") As such, a letter usually has more resonance with its intended audience.

Delivery Confirmation

E-mail: You'll have to ask for it.

Letter: You can send via registered mail.

Cobweb Buster

When you send a clearly worded message via e-mail, you may find it difficult for yours to stand out. Consider these statistics. Jupiter Communications estimates that nearly 12 billion e-mail messages are sent every day, and spending on commercial e-mail has soared to more than $7 billion in 2005 (up from $164 million in 1999). And in 2005, the average consumer will receive 2,000 pieces of spam.

The Rules for Making Your Case in Written Form

As you take up that pen (or keyboard) to communicate your clear thoughts, follow these rules to avoid coming across as a fuzzy thinker:

♦ Remember that you're not speaking face to face. Therefore, you cannot rely on body language or inflections in your tone to soften a message, which means you need to take care that your writing doesn't come across as too blunt.

♦ In e-mails and memos, make sure your subject line accurately conveys what will follow. And make sure your subject line is pithy and precise.

♦ Avoid mixing personal with professional written communication.

♦ Keep private matters separate from public ones. In other words, would you be embarrassed if someone outside your intended audience saw this message or memo?

♦ In the e-mail world, observe netiquette. For starters, don't engage in flaming or posting derogatory messages, which can turn a heated online discussion vicious. In addition, don't write in all capital letters (which can be construed as shouting), and avoid offensive humor. These are all hindrances that detract from a clear message and risk offending your reader.

♦ Take the high road. Follow standards that foster and promote productive discussions so that clear thinking can naturally flow from your written communications.

Articulating Your Decisive Thoughts

When you have committed to following the rules of written communication and determined your role, the audience, the topic, and your goal, survey your armament. You want the following at your command:

♦ Facts

♦ Statistics

♦ Examples

♦ Anecdotes

♦ Evidence

" "Words from the Wise

The skill of writing is to create a context in which other people can think.

—Edwin Schlossberg, artist and designer

A Checklist for Crafting Clear Thoughts

Here's a checklist to help you craft your message. The examples that follow illustrate these points.

- Organization is paramount in laying out clear thoughts. You want to lead the reader through your train of thought and connect your points for optimal flow. If you're dealing with a sprawling topic, draft an outline that will help you plot out your points better. The outline will show you how the pieces fit together and how your writing will flow.

- What's your most important point? Grab your audience by stating it up front. If it's a multilayered approach or a communication with several sections of information, make sure you begin with a cogent, attention-attracting summary that encapsulates what you want to say.

- Stay on the topic. No matter how enticing it might be to dally in tangential areas that might be interesting, steer away from them. Relate all sentences to the topic delineated.

- If you're making claims, defend them and offer reasons for your assertions. To that end, rely on facts, statistics, and other research.

- If appropriate, acknowledge opposing opinions. Doing so will enhance your own point by demonstrating that you have considered those contrasting views.

- Go for specifics and details. The mind craves these, and you'll find more rapid and involved responses when you include them. In addition, specifics reinforce clarity. Think about the impact of just this simple statement: "The book gave us good information on welfare." That simple statement will receive a markedly different reaction than "The scholarly biography about LBJ provided deep analysis on the rise of welfare in the 1960s."

- Proofread. Sloppy grammar and misspellings simply aren't in the domain of clear thinkers.

- Make sure you're saying something! Avoid flowery phrases used just to decorate your writing. Beware of the latest buzzwords, too, that infect most modern workplaces. While buzzwords almost call out to be used, they often are just that: words that substitute the drone of a buzz for actual substance. Terms such as *synergy, value added, paradigm, redeployed,* and *core competency* might needlessly muddy your communication. If you're going for these words, use substitute and precise language, which will sound more original and, in effect, enrich your writing.

- Edit your words. The written word rarely succeeds in its first draft. Even if you think it seems clear, it can probably still be improved upon somehow.

- Have a plan of action that includes follow-through as part of the equation.

It's helpful to look at prime examples of clear thoughts into written words. The following e-mail, proposal, letter, and memo exemplify staying on topic, using precise wording, and—if necessary—calling up facts to back up messages. All of these also present an easy-to-follow style. Take notice of what's striking to you about clear communication in each of these examples.

The Eloquent E-Mail

Following is an e-mail from a lawyer regarding an application for a trademark. In this e-mail, she succinctly lays out existing and potential uses for a trademark and outlines next steps for action.

TO: Marge@PeppyPreppy.com

FROM: Daphne@JKLLaw.com

SUBJ: Peppy Preppy Trademark Uses

Hi, Marge:

As discussed, we will now move forward with obtaining a trademark for your brand, Peppy Preppy. Following please find a list of potential places to which you want to apply the Peppy Preppy trademark. Because you are branching the Peppy Preppy brand into several areas (publishing, merchandise, etc.), we will be investigating whether you will be able to secure a trademark in each one. In the following list, I've indicated our understanding of each line item to ensure our grasp on your intent for each area. When you sign off on this list, we will proceed with the application.

A Peppy Preppy trademark will be used to identify the following:

1. Your website, which provides editorial content and online shopping for your products.

2. Your Peppy Preppy columns, which have been appearing in *Alumni* magazine for at least a year. With this usage, you own the Peppy Preppy mark featured with the column, and that's clear with the magazine.

3. Peppy Preppy Books, a series that will espouse the virtues of incorporating college life into the real world. Subjects under discussion include dressing youthfully, continuing your education, and tailgating recipes. You currently have no trademark use on books yet.

4. Peppy Preppy products, such as sweatshirts, stadium blankets, and coolers.

I'm going to send you a separate letter that details the fees/costs involved. After you've had a chance to review it, please let me know how you want to proceed. Let me know if my understanding is wrong on any facts presented here. And if you have any questions whatsoever, don't hesitate to contact me.

Please acknowledge receipt of this e-mail. I look forward to talking with you soon.

Thanks,

Daphne

The Particular Proposal

In this example, clear thoughts have preceded putting together a new publicity campaign for a television show. The weekly half-hour program, *Marquee Mavens*, features a team of four critics who review current movies. Each of the proposal's categories has required fact gathering, an understanding of the current situation, research, and analysis. Those thoughts were then translated into coherent sentences. Particularly notable in this proposal is the organizational methods employed as the thinking moves from general assessments to specific actions to be taken. "Goals & Objectives" sets up the proposal, and the "Strategies" and "Tactics" sections flow logically from it, with each point appropriately relating back to established information.

Situational Analysis

As *Marquee Mavens* heads into its fifth season, the series has posted year-to-year ratings and demographics gains, particularly during the key advertising sweeps periods. Further, the critics have all become highly regarded, hip authorities on movies. They're often quoted in studios' movie ads, and are often called upon to provide expert perspective on films and film stars.

Goals & Objectives

- To heighten awareness even further of *Marquee Mavens* with viewers and the studios

- To make the *Marquee Mavens* critics team a studio's best resource for intelligent, consumer-friendly quotes that embolden their ads with unsurpassed credibility and vivid descriptions/endorsements

- To gain even more respect from the studios for *Marquee Mavens* quote offerings and placements

- To further position *Marquee Mavens* as the hipper, happier, friendlier, faster-paced, more-accessible movie review show

- To exploit ratings successes and point them out to the industry

- To broaden the reach of *Marquee Mavens* in the consumer press

Strategies

- Get exposure week-in and week-out for the critics' quotes in the studio's newspaper advertisements for movies

- ◆ Continue to be proactive, timely, and responsive regarding studios' needs: servicing advance quotes when possible and keeping track of release dates and critics' screenings

- ◆ Feature all the critics as valuable resources for release-heavy times of the year for both print and broadcast opportunities

- ◆ Point out ratings successes—whenever possible—against other movie review shows, particularly for industry publications

- ◆ Secure items with columnists for the *Marquee Mavens* feature segments and, when appropriate, star quotes

Tactics

Quotes/Studio Relations

Target: Studio publicists

Timing: Year-Round

- ◆ The distribution of quotes will continue on a per-show basis, while taking full advantage of opportunities to service advance quotes during time crunches or upon studio request (on a case-by-case basis).

- ◆ Provide the studios with shining ratings articles (such as the May *Variety* piece), which serve to give them an idea of the show's national standing, and the influence the show could/does wield in a multitude of markets.

- ◆ On a weekly basis, continue staying in touch with studio publicists to keep them apprised of featured segments and run dates for their films.

- ◆ During Oscar season, provide additional quotes to studios for their Oscar contenders.

Critics Positioning/Ratings

Target: Film and television writers, top 25 market newspapers

             Columnists, top 10 market and national newspapers

             Radio, top 15 markets

Timing: Year-round, with special emphasis in November-December (for holiday releases), February-March (for Oscar stories), and May-June (for summer releases)

◆ Using the TV season advertising sweeps months of November, February, and May, send e-mails to targeted press/major newspapers in top 25 markets offering the *Marquee Mavens* critics as experts for:

November—Holiday movie releases

February—Upcoming Oscar news

May—Summer movie releases

◆ During those above target dates, also contact radio satellite tour companies to arrange radio tours for the four critics in top 25 markets.

◆ During those above target dates, also pitch the critics to LA-based talk shows.

◆ Throughout the year, provide items—when appropriate—to columnists at newspapers in top 10 markets about feature segments on the show.

◆ Approach newspaper TV critics to "turn the tables" on *Marquee Mavens* and review an episode of the show.

A Broader Reach

Having had a relationship with *Awesome Movie Magazine* for the past two seasons, explore other possibilities with magazines, offering the following:

◆ A weekly venue to have their logo seen

◆ Possible tie-ins for their covers to be seen

◆ Website tie-in

◆ The show's critics as "expert" columnists/interviews for their publication

◆ Possible publications to approach include *Box Office Weekly*, *Dear Cineaste*, and *Celebrity*

The Lively Letter

In this letter, notice how facts, observations, and experiences have all been used to present the consumer's case. Again, the details are concisely laid out regarding a bad customer service experience. The letter is well thought out in its organization and presents a call to action at its conclusion.

January 3, 2005

Mr. Peter President
Big Box Family Department Store
100 Big Box Boulevard
Uncle Sam City, CA 90000

Dear Mr. President:

My family had an unpleasant experience at your store located at 2307 Uncle Sam Street in Uncle Sam City, today, 1/3/05. Unfortunately, talking to a manager at the store only exacerbated the situation, so we thought we should bring the matter to your attention.

On several occasions, my husband, our toddler son, and I have found shopping carts scarce while shopping at this store. Further, last time we shopped at this Big Box Family Department Store (on 12/7/04), a store employee scolded us for borrowing a cart from another nearby store in the same shopping center. Worse, she demanded that we give her the cart—while we were standing in line with our toddler in his seat and our cart full of merchandise. Again today we could procure no cart in the Big Box Family Department Store.

When I brought the matter of hardly any carts to the store's manager, Rudy, he regretfully admitted he has not had luck in remedying a situation he agrees has become problematic. To quote him, he's "been asking for more carts from regional headquarters since he started two years ago and only has 12 carts for 3,000 customers. Customers are complaining constantly, and there's not a thing I can do. My bosses at regional just don't care." I find it troublesome that a manager would complain so openly to a customer about an internal lack of respect for store consumers that Big Box executives apparently have.

You advertise quite liberally about being a "family" department store. Yet, as I told Rudy, if Big Box management is unwilling to help a consumer shop, then your store doesn't make me or my family feel very valuable as customers.

We have been longtime Big Box customers, but this store is remiss in providing a pleasant shopping experience for the families your company stresses it caters to. How can I further patronize a store that seems to disregard our patronage? I expect a response to this letter in the next 10 days to explain why Big Box chooses to conduct business in such a manner. My address and phone number are included below.

Sincerely,

Sally Shopper
4278 Pleasant Way
Uncle Sam City, CA 90000
858-555-6423

The Detailed Memo

In this example, clear thinking has led to an organized request for a quote. All the necessary details are included to allow the vendor to follow through. The memo writer leaves little to chance, offering illustrations of his needs and a deadline for getting back to him.

MEMORANDUM

TO: Evelyn Branson/LABELICIOUS, INC.

FROM: Charlie Quilson

SUBJ: Quote Request

DATE: 2/11/05

Following please find the details you requested to give us a quote for surfing wetsuit labels. I've included a summary of the information below, as well as three attachments that provide reference points and further details.

The Attachments

—Artwork sketch with PMS color callouts

—Diagram of sewing edges

—Sample label that we'd like to emulate

Summary of Specifications

Quantity: 1,000

Fabric: Satin

Label Size: 1 1/2 inches x 1 1/2 inches

Background color: White

Lettering colors: Pampas green and aqua (per attached artwork; please notice PMS callout colors on the artwork)

Sewing edges: Please see attached diagram and refer to attached sample label for sew folds and size

Font: Berkeley Bold Italic

As we are in the process of collecting quotes from several vendors, please supply yours back to us in writing by close of business on Wednesday (2/14/05). Fax the quote to 708-555-0001.

If you have any questions in the meantime, please call me at 708-555-0004 or e-mail me at Charlie.Quilson@surfsup.com.

Whichever format you're writing for, make sure you've thought through what you're putting down on paper. You always want to have your communication relate succinct, appropriate details that meet your end goals. Don't be afraid to ask yourself questions and put it through the checklist we offered earlier. By following those guidelines, your communication method will benefit immeasurably, conveying pertinent information that keeps the reader's interest and becoming most effective in getting your message across.

Cobweb Buster

Do you know someone who you think writes well? What do you find admirable in his or her writing? Part of your appreciation may stem from this person getting a point across in a way that you immediately understand (an advantage that all clear-thinking writers share). And that suggests another advantage a clear-thinking writer has: an audience that will readily read the writer's next document/proposal/memo, etc., because they know it will be articulate and easily understandable.

A Hazy Shade of Semantics

Semantics is the study of language and meaning. In a sense, semantics is a science that detects if writing or the meaning implied therein has gone off-course. When you apply semantics to your own writing, you can often determine if your clear thinking is sticking to the words or coming unglued somewhere in your message.

Punctuation usage, word definitions, and sentence structure all assist in helping you glean meanings in a written message. But those are just the mechanics. Semantics also can extend further to help you get underneath written words to churn up deeper meanings.

Let's dissect a real-life example where clear thinking unraveled in writing. It involves a controversy that erupted in November 2003 concerning the Macy's Thanksgiving Day parade and that prompted one blog to comment: "Same-Sex Mrs. Santa: The Semantics Are Confusing."

On November 26, 2003, *The New York Times* ran an editorial by actor Harvey Fierstein, who played cross-dressing mom Edna Turnblad in the Broadway musical "Hairspray." His piece

Think Tank

Semantics refers to the interconnectedness of words, phrases, and sentences that can relay clear—or fuzzy—meanings.

described how he would be dressed as Mrs. Santa, accompanying Santa Claus on a float in the revered Macy's Thanksgiving Day parade. As such, he basically would be making a political statement as one half of a same-sex couple. The next day, *The New York Times* reported how Macy's, anxious to keep the parade from turning into a political fiasco, had issued two statements relaying how Fierstein would be on his own float as his character Edna Turnblad. On a totally separate float, a "Mrs. Claus"—who wasn't Fierstein—would be riding with Santa Claus. Next, a costume designer weighed in on how Fierstein's Turnblad character would actually be dressed as another Mrs. Claus on his own float. The designer further urged parade watchers to suspend disbelief to see Turnblad dressed as Mrs. Claus, not Fierstein dressed as Turnblad dressed as Mrs. Claus. In an apropos statement, he added, "The semantics are confusing."

Admittedly, many situations today get mired in confusing semantics, as different viewpoints are espoused. And many times, semantics get confusing because people don't focus on the core of the subject matter or try to sidestep an issue—rather than write clearly and precisely what they mean. Be warned: when you don't focus on clarity, you risk having more conveyed in your message than you intended—and most likely, to your disadvantage.

In a similar vein, when you're reading other writing, apply semantics to determine what's really meant. Put semantics' friends, logic and reasoning, to work, and see how phraseology and tone can give you clues to underlying and overt meanings.

Is the Writing All Right?

Ensure that your writing is on course and making sense. In finally sizing up a piece you've written, put it through this 10-point evaluation:

1. Have you clearly stated your position on the issue?

2. Does it come off as clear, with sentences that make sense and display a good use of vocabulary? Could anything be misinterpreted?

3. Does it convey an appropriate tone for your intended audience?

4. Was it expressed in an interesting manner to satisfy attention spans you might not have for long?

5. Did you reinforce any arguments with facts, research, observations, etc.?

6. If appropriate, did you use impactful examples?

7. Did your conclusion prompt action?

8. Did you just go with a first draft or did you revise and fine-tune?

9. Did you proofread?

10. Is this so important that another set of eyes should review it, particularly someone who's an expert?

Double-Edged Expressions and Other Potential Language Barriers

Finally, when communicating your clear thoughts on paper, be mindful of double-edged expressions, those clunker phrases or sentences that can be taken two ways … one of them the very wrong way.

Some examples are these troublesome headlines:

> Include Your Children When Baking Cookies
>
> Drunks Get Nine Months in Violin Case
>
> Two Sisters Reunited After 18 Years in Grocery Aisle
>
> New Obesity Study Looks for Larger Group to Study
>
> Panda Mating Fails, Veterinarian Takes Over

Can you find how each of these can be taken two ways?

These headlines can also be referred to as *double-entendres*. Double-entendres are actually usually laced with sexual *innuendo* or some impropriety that's even more inappropriate for the intended audience.

Although none of us would intentionally insert these problematic language barriers into our writing, they present another reason for proofreading—or getting someone else's opinion. Sometimes a sentence you've written seems perfectly benign. However, to someone else's mind, it could raise red flags. By being aware of the possibility of double-edged expressions and double-entendres, you decrease the likelihood that they'll pop up in your writing.

Think Tank

A **double-entendre** is an expression with two meanings, one of which is humorous or inappropriate. **Innuendo** refers to a remark or implication that carries a negative or improper connotation.

Points to Ponder

Do you respond more to the written or spoken word? Why?

The Least You Need to Know

- Sometimes your clear thoughts need a more extensive, expansive forum that only writing can provide.

- Consider both manual and electronic writing methods to determine which format is best.

- When presenting your message, make sure you can express it verbally, and state your information clearly in an organized fashion, with research if appropriate. If necessary, draft an outline first.

- Use semantics to deconstruct sentences and investigate underlying meanings.

- Avoid double-edged expressions in your writing.

Chapter 17

Chasing Thoughts into Creative Pursuits

In This Chapter

- ◆ Draw in creativity for ideas that will thrive in work, home, and life scenarios
- ◆ Develop fertile thinking ground for ideas
- ◆ Cast your thoughts out of the box and into new territories
- ◆ Discover ways to elaborate and strengthen creative thought processes

Is that million-dollar idea kicking around in your head? Have you been able to commit it to paper? Do you have a desire to take up creative pursuits but think you're completely uncreative? Where do ideas come from? And how can creativity assist in clear thinking? Conversely, how can clear thinking enhance the mind's creativity?

In this chapter, we survey imagination, innovation, and design and show you how to explore and develop those dimensions in your thinking. When you do, you'll gear your thinking to ideas bound to be more inventive and productive.

Mind Games 17
Give yourself 30 seconds to come up with five uses for a trivet. (Turn to Appendix D for some possibilities.)

Your Thoughts = Great Works

This is when thinking turns creative. As we begin, let's look at the creative side of thinking with these terms you need for your very own idea vault:

Create. To bring into being; to form out of nothing; to cause to exist; to form or fashion.

Design. An outline or pattern of the main features of something to be executed as a picture, a building, a decoration, a delineation or a plan; a plan or scheme formed in the mind of something to be done; the realization of an inventive or decorative plan.

Imagine. To form images or conceptions; to conceive; to devise.

Innovate. to bring in as new, to introduce as a novelty; to remodel; to revolutionize.

Invent. to discover, as by study or inquiry; to find out; to contrive or produce for the first time, applied commonly to the discovery of some serviceable mode, instrument, or machine.

Putting your clear thinking to the ultimate test would be transforming thoughts into a creation or invention. Now we're not getting all Dr. Frankenstein-y here, it's just that your creativity can bring a mental idea to physical magnitude.

As you inject creativity into your thinking, you'll find that you won't just produce good and bountiful ideas. You'll also develop innovative approaches to business strategies, inventions for the home front, scheduling scenarios—all kinds of implementations.

Quizzing for Creativity

How conducive is your thinking to engineering creative pursuits? Take this quiz to find out by answering each multiple-choice question. Afterward, we give you a question-by-question breakdown of the traits each question fosters in clear-thinking creative pursuits.

1. Thinking out of the box is …

    A. Approaching situations with new perspectives in hopes of innovation.

    B. A good approach sometimes.

    C. Intimidating; I prefer proven methods for problem solving.

    D. A cliché that needs to be put out of its misery.

2. In the workplace, you …

    A. Encourage ideas of yourself and others.

    B. Believe ideas have their place and time in the office.

    C. Offer ideas only when prompted, and then it's kind of a strain.

    D. Feel creativity has no place at all.

3. Which of the following are true? (Circle all that apply.)

    A. Wal-Mart began when Sam Walton couldn't convince the Ben Franklin store chain to open outlets in rural areas.

    B. Martha Stewart's empire began with a catering business called "The Uncatered Affair."

    C. George Washington Carver developed 325 products from peanuts, 75 products from pecans, and invented a process for producing paints and stains from soybeans.

    D. Steve Jobs's Apple product failure, a model called the Lisa, actually paved the way for the Macintosh model, which first introduced the "mouse."

    E. Thomas Edison failed thousands of times before creating the incandescent light bulb.

4. When you're trying to generate ideas, it's important to …

    A. Give yourself a break now and then so that ideas can incubate.

    B. Stay focused and on schedule; allow for a break only if time is on your side.

    C. Keep moving until your mission is accomplished.

    D. Set a timer and, at the end of the day, what's done is done.

5. Drawing in attributes of both the left and right brain—or, simply put, linear and lateral thinking—is …

   A. Absolutely crucial to creativity.

   B. Sometimes helpful to the creativity process.

   C. Worthy of consideration; I'd have to know more about left- and right-brain modes of thinking to implement them.

   D. Just a bunch of hooey.

6. The more I know, the more I …

   A. Can put great information to work in my thinking and the more curious I become.

   B. Can use information in different pursuits.

   C. Become scattered.

   D. Cringe.

7. Creativity …

   A. Is available to any occupation: building on existing ideas to give them a fresh twist.

   B. Has some advantages in most workplaces, but most advantages in only a select few occupations.

   C. Isn't always appropriate and would be subject to further investigation.

   D. Is strictly in the domain of artists.

8. Creativity also …

   A. Requires skills that can be acquired.

   B. Presents a tough challenge, but is worth the effort.

   C. Is difficult for me to access.

   D. Would get in the way of my real job and life.

9. If someone comes up with an idea I think is mediocre, I ...

    A. Immediately try to analyze it and build upon it to take it from mediocre to sizzling.

    B. Assess whether it's worthy to build upon, and then go from there in helping them.

    C. Encourage them to discount it and move on.

    D. Tell them to try harder.

10. Which of the following are true? (Circle all that apply.)

    A. Sales of packaged cake mixes that only required adding water before baking were stagnating in the 1950s. A General Mills researcher discovered that homemakers would have more emotional attachment to use them if they could add in eggs as well ... and sales soared.

    B. Leo Baekeland was trying to develop a shellac substitute for varnishes, but instead produced a substance too tough to be a coating. He made it stronger, moldable, and dyeable, and one of the first plastics—Bakelite—was born.

    C. Other uses for Krazy Glue include closing stitches after surgery and lifting fingerprints from a crime scene.

    D. A 3M chemist was trying to create a stronger adhesive for tape, but ended up with a weaker one that another employee appropriated for use in Post-it Notes.

    E. Trying to invent a rubber substitute, James Wright could only come up with a gooey substance that bounced ... but Peter Hodson encased it in plastic eggs and turned it into Silly Putty.

11. Inspiration can be found in ... (Circle all that apply.)

    A. Poetry.

    B. Company newsletters.

    C. Children's artwork.

    D. eBay listings.

    E. NASDAQ stock quotes.

Tally Up!

To add up your score:

For numbers 1, 2, and 4 through 9, give yourself 5 points for each A answer, 3 points for each B answer, 1 point for each C answer, and 0 points for each D answer.

For numbers 3 and 10, all the responses are true. Give yourself 2 points for each one you gave a true response.

For number 11, all of the answers are correct. Give yourself 1 point for each one you checked.

How did you score?

56–65: You're a clear creative type. Your thinking basks in the challenge of using creativity for a host of opportunities, and you know the value of building upon others' ideas and looking at all options in new, fresh ways.

> **Words from the Wise**
>
> The best way to have a good idea is to have lots of ideas.
>
> —Linus Pauling, Nobel Prize–winning chemist

38–55: You're a fair-weather creative. Sometimes your thinking revels in the thrills and advantages of being creative and sometimes your mind spurns it.

0–37: You're a cloudy creative. It's time to consider challenging your thinking to find the benefits in employing creativity.

The Quiz, Question by Question

In the following list, we provide insights into the background and meaning for each question posed in the quiz. Refer to your answers to determine your position on each one.

1. We give a description of thinking out of the box later in this chapter. However, all this quiz's components weigh in on the methodology and practice of that kind of thinking.

2. Ideas naturally build on ideas. So whether you're in the workplace, at home, or at the carwash, your thinking flows better—and more creatively—with each idea that comes along. Don't squelch yours and don't squelch others'!

3. All of these accomplishments are true, and excellent examples of using clear thinking in innovation and invention, not being deterred by the fact that ideas sometimes need to be repeatedly tried.

4. In the area of crafting ideas, your thinking requires breathers. Not long, extended ones, but pauses for mental refreshment. When you do that, you're

allowing yourself to tackle it again with renewed (and quite possibly better) perspective and insights.

5. We delve a bit more into coming at ideas with thinking from both the right and left sides of the brain later in this chapter (and also see Chapter 3), but it's a necessary and appropriate approach. It's what we like to call "Renaissance thinking," accessing both your artistic and administrative modes for the best outcome possible.

6. Creative thinking needs information, and lots of it. It's the fuel for thoughts to flourish, build, and consider new slants. Curiosity is inherent in that; when you're curious, you automatically gain more information that a creative mind will undoubtedly—at some point—put to use. You never know when random information will be called in for duty, but a creative mind is waiting and willing for it to come.

7. Creativity can and should be employed no matter what the business or situation. Some view creativity as improving on others' thoughts. What business or home doesn't want to be improved for the better?

8. You're not born with creativity. You acquire it. True, you may be more naturally predisposed to it or grew up in an environment where it was encouraged more, but your thinking can always begin the journey toward being more creative. You only need to follow a few guidelines (such as those described in this chapter) to start finding and figuring out ways to employ it.

9. Creative thinking loves a challenge, so a mediocre idea just presents a prime opportunity to make it better.

10. All of these examples are true. In each instance, a fresh twist from a clear-thinking creative mind brought a raging success.

11. Inspiration is everywhere! No outlet is exempt from providing you with a winning idea.

Cobweb Buster

Clear thinkers can always find their creativity! Before you say you're not creative, think outside the box about your creativity. Consider strengths that aren't always labeled "creative." For instance, you could probably find someone who's an example of creativity in home improvement, athletics, organization, and computer programming, even if those aren't immediately regarded as creative domains. If you suddenly realize you are creative in a particular realm (and you most certainly are), analyze the traits that make you think so, and try transferring them into another area you feel less proficient in.

U2RCRE8IV

Too often, creativity is characterized as a heady distraction zone, where thoughts can only develop if a wild and crazy mind-set takes hold. But infusing creativity into your thinking mix doesn't mean that willy-nilly thought processes take over. In fact, an organized approach is necessary for it to be optimally effective.

And before you make an assumption that "I can't be creative, I don't have it in me," know that creativity is in everyone. We'll repeat that: creativity is in everyone. And after you realize how to tap into it, devising better, bigger, and more ideas is a snap. What's more, creativity grows—seemingly exponentially—as it's used. The more you use it, the more you'll find it in your thinking.

Imagine That!

Nurturing your imagination can develop a fertile mind for clear thinking and creativity. Here are some methods to be a Renaissance thinker; that is, tapping into both your left and right brain to parlay them into creative strengths.

> **Words from the Wise**
>
> You can't wait for inspiration. You have to go after it with a club.
>
> —Jack London, American author

- Brainstorm! As we indicated in Chapter 14, brainstorming presents a steady stream of ideas. And although a good idea is great, good ideas can often lead to even better ones in a brainstorming situation.

- Embrace diverse activities, approaches, and people. When you do, your mind opens up to new possibilities and perspectives.

- Flexibility is key: Let your thinking be agile enough to jump around, free associate, and not be bound to conventional wisdom and approaches. Don't be confined to the shackles of the routine and regimen.

- Look for inspiration for your ideas in all kinds of places: cereal boxes, comic strips, catalogs, in people watching, a first-grade schoolbook.

- Try to solve other people's problems (that you're not connected to personally). For instance, how should Yellowstone National Park handle the influx of tourists who have crammed the area to see a rare wildflower bloom? What would you recommend for someone's course of action if that person finds out he is the victim of identity theft? How would you end a recent movie differently?

- ◆ Where do your thoughts naturally give over to free and flexible thinking that is more prone to creativity: mowing the lawn, in the shower, exercising?

- ◆ Don't give in to creative thought-buster phrases, proclamations about "not enough time, money, or resources," "it's been done before and it didn't work," or "that's pie in the sky."

- ◆ Consider maintaining idea files or a journal in which you keep a record of your brainstorms. Although some may seem worthless for your present predicament, some could be a possibility for another situation down the line.

Also be mindful that creativity thrives on these attributes:

- ◆ Wide-ranging knowledge.

- ◆ Curiosity about several topics; the ability to ask why and find out reasons behind a choice or decision; or to figure out why something does or doesn't work.

- ◆ A challenge of the status quo.

- ◆ Letting go of judgment and criticism. As we know from brainstorming, these are danger zones for imagination, too, and prevent other ideas from flourishing.

Creating and Gauging Ideas

With a mind that's now more suited to idea generating, now's the chance to put it to creative use. To apply clear thinking and the ensuing strategies to your own creation—of ideas, inventions, concepts, etc.—answer these questions:

- ◆ What's the challenge you're facing that requires creativity? What do you want to make or make better?

- ◆ What information can you gather that will help?

- ◆ What's been tried before in this situation?

- ◆ How many ideas do you have for it?

- ◆ Can you think of more, or build on the ones you have?

Before you continue, leave the process for a while and let your ideas "incubate." Then ask yourself, what format could you use to "illustrate" the challenge? A sketch, a diagram, an outline, a model, a prototype?

Cobweb Buster _____

Clear thinking brings inventions that are must-haves, but not always must-likes. In 2005, the annual Massachusetts Institute of Technology survey, known as the Lemelson-MIT Invention Index, found that 30 percent of those surveyed regarded cell phones as the most-hated must-have invention, followed by alarm clocks (25 percent) and television (23 percent). Other must-have but hated inventions included shaving razors, microwaves, coffee pots, computers, and vacuum cleaners. What do you think is the world's best invention? What about the worst?

By answering the following questions, you can determine whether an idea for a concept, innovation, etc. will connect or face barriers. Criteria you should consider include the following:

- Will the idea bring desired results?

- Can it be easily explained/expressed/understood?

- Is it a valid improvement over the norm?

- Does it seem too familiar? Could it be mistaken for the status quo? If so, can you tweak it to improve upon it?

- Is it within budget and practical for the resources involved?

- Does it "pop" and excite others?

- Will existing technology work with it? Or will other innovations/inventions need to precede it?

- Is it a cover-up or a true solution?

- Could it produce continued success or is it more of a temporary fix?

Thinking Outside the Box

When faced with a situation or problem, do you let your thoughts stick to the tried-and-true? Or do you relish the opportunity to try a new way to accomplish a task or solve a predicament?

If you're an out-of-the-box thinker—which you want to strive to be—you're willing to do things differently and face situations with new perspectives. This type of thinking brings an openness to explore, nurture ideas, act on them, and secure results. But thinking outside the box doesn't always have to be directed toward some grand plan. Sometimes it's just bringing a fresh twist to common sense. Consider these examples of out-of-the-box thinking:

◆ Sarah Susanka, author of the successful *The Not So Big House* books and magazine, banishes preconceived notions of what a nice house is supposed be. She has pioneered a design take on how to fashion elegant, comfortable living areas in smaller, more manageable, and intimate spaces.

◆ The Global Idea Bank has an international suggestion box for "socially innovative, nontechnological ideas and projects." Some of their submissions have included a rage center—complete with a laughing room and batting cages—to relieve pent-up frustration over traffic, bad customer service, etc.; and a cooperative neighborhood equipment library to check out such infrequently used—but necessary—communal property as a circular saw or scuba gear.

◆ Dr. Patch Adams takes an unconventional approach to medicine that led him to found the Gesundheit! Institute in 1972. "Friendship and fun" are instrumental to patient healing as patients' and caregivers' lives are integrated in treatment that eschews the traditional norms. You can check out the "Patch Adams" version of thinking outside of the box in the popular movie of the same name starring Robin Williams.

To practice thinking out of the box for innovation and inventions, refer back to the section in this chapter on stimulating your imagination. Also follow the tips offered after the quiz at the beginning of the chapter. Putting those tips and tools into constant practice will reinforce how your clear thinking can snap creativity to attention quickly and efficiently.

With Design in Mind

In this section, we take an idea and suggest some creation and design possibilities. Cast off the restraints of thinking inside the box, and get ready to employ the attributes of imagination and creativity.

A small Florida town located miles from a big city wants to build a music club to serve as an entertainment mecca for the town's many teenagers. However, past efforts have failed because of the community's diverse mix of teens. They've cliqued off into the heavy metal heads, Broadway balladeers, disco divas, and country cowboys. How can one club serve all the groups and maybe even unify them more?

Cobweb Buster

In Hawaii, a design trend spotted in 2004 was known as "clear thinking," wherein glass and acrylic were used in interior décor to make living areas seem bigger. Philippe Starck polycarbonate swivel chairs, a Louis Ghost armchair (so named because it's practically transparent), and acrylic lamps and waterfall-style tables lent to a look that physically fostered openness and clarity.

Some design possibilities:

The First Idea

Divide the building into four quadrants or four floors.

Limitations: Keeping the cliques separated by designated spaces won't foster much unity. Plus, what if the groups divide further and the building has only four spaces? Can it easily be divided further?

Build on It

Make the club one big space and issue a pair of headphones to each guest. They can turn their headphone to one of four channels, each of which is streaming a different music genre.

Limitations: Will headphones be costly? What logistics are involved with channeling the music? Also, will a bunch of headset-outfitted teenagers further dilute their social interaction with each other?

Getting Closer

Keep the club one big space, but have a DJ rotate sets of the four different types of music.

Limitations: What will teens do while their music isn't being played?

Now Workable

Make the club an "entertainment" mecca in different ways: Divide the space, but develop different uses for the spaces. Keep one as a music/dance floor that changes out music for predetermined, timed sets. Teens not interested in that music can head off to the other rooms for pool playing, snacking, board games, darts, DVD playing, etc. An outside area could even be set up for a separate dance floor or an outdoors activity. This approach might find teens learning to like music they previously didn't enjoy. Plus, they might find common ground in the other activities so that crossover social interaction among them also increases.

Limitations: Check out costs for other rooms' activities.

For this design, which relied on ideas and innovation, each idea built on another, keeping the helpful and weeding out the hindrances. The final one presents a design that not only could be quite workable, but also could have other positive side benefits.

As you come to a design or invention endeavor, keep in mind that clear thinking is a must to assist you in fine-tuning for impressive results.

Creativity That Enhances Clear Thought

Finally, let's survey a trio of activities that can be deemed creative and have a lasting impression on clear thinking. Pursuing these activities can simultaneously engage the mind, improve focus, and engender creative thoughts.

Curiously, these three activities all employ left-brain, right-brain thinking. Truly, when that duality is activated, an even richer experience follows. (Obviously, other activities would be possible for you to take up, but the three we've chosen have proven benefits that we wanted to specifically point out.)

Sewing

A few years ago, a clinical study revealed that sewing elevates creativity and builds skills in creative problem solving for both males and females. Choices in color selection, fabric and stitch options, and design (right-brain attributes) all help stimulate and focus creative energy. In addition, figuring out proportions, determining measurements, and following patterns (left-brain strengths) work in tandem with that creativity. The result brings clear thinking to critical mass: employing both sides of the brain for creative yet practical accomplishments.

Playing Piano

A number of institutions and organizations—among them Neurological Research, the University of Texas, the Music Educators National Conference—have released an array of studies conducted during the past 15 years that point to the impact of piano playing on clear thinking.

Music composition and performance (right-brain proficiencies) involves ratios, fractions, proportions, and thinking in space in time (left-brain focuses), which fuels general and spatial cognitive development. Those are key faculties for performance in math and engineering, among other intellectual fields.

Among the findings: those taking piano lessons are more confident test takers, are better equipped to comprehend math and science concepts, and score higher on SAT verbal and math sections.

Cooking

According to some sources, cooking a large meal uses nearly 100 percent of your brain. Here's another seemingly creative activity that can fire up your clear thinking. When preparing a difficult recipe or planning a large gathering, you're engaging in a spectrum of creative clear thinking. You plan the dishes and follow recipes for them (left and right brain), measure out ingredients (left brain), schedule the food preparation and have it served accordingly (left brain), and artistically present the meal and table settings (right brain).

Points to Ponder
Who's the most creative person alive? What makes you give that person such a distinction?

Channeling clear thinking into creative pursuits can produce a steady stream of ideas, innovations, inventions, and designs. And that approach also ratchets up those creations' effectiveness as you learn to build upon ideas, think outside the box, and depend on Renaissance thinking to help out.

The Least You Need to Know

- ◆ Clear thinking can be funneled into such creative pursuits as crafting ideas, innovations, inventions, and designs that are boundless in their application areas.

- ◆ Creativity—which is acquired, not inherited—thrives on information, curiosity, challenges, and building on and improving others' ideas.

- ◆ To stimulate imagination, brainstorm, embrace flexibility in thinking, and draw on inspiration from many sources.

- ◆ To create, be clear about what you're trying to improve, formulate options, let ideas incubate, and then evaluate before you implement.

- ◆ Thinking outside of the box means you look at the tried-and-true with blazing new perspectives and fresh twists.

- ◆ Renaissance thinking—drawing on strengths from both sides of the brain—is key to creativity and is often apparent in activities such as sewing and piano playing that engage clear thinking in creative thought.

Part 5

Head Coach

Nurture that noggin! Discover how to give clear thinking the best physical chance to prosper with exercise, plenty of sleep, and a healthful diet. And to maintain clarity today and beyond, follow some directions for detours around Fuzzyland.

Giving Your Focus a Physical

In This Chapter

- Gear your physiology toward optimal clear thinking
- Consider the importance of getting enough sleep
- Delve into the clear mind benefits of yoga, running, and extreme sports
- Determine the best brain foods, as well as herbs, supplements, and vitamins to consider
- Find out about so-called "smart drugs"

Most of our discussion has focused on mental processes concerning clear thinking. But you should also pay attention to the body that houses your focused thoughts. Because when you do, clear thinking naturally follows.

This chapter looks at the physiology that enhances clear thinking, including adequate sleep, physical exercise, and the right foods to promote effective, effervescent concentration.

Mind Games 18

Madge takes a bag of cookies to the office. She gives three to her boss. Then she splits the rest into two even amounts: for the gals on the third floor, and those in the typing pool. The cookies given to the typing pool are divided evenly among the 10 typists; 1 typist gives 1 cookie to Madge, and her other 2 she plans to take home to her kids. How many cookies were in Madge's bag?

(Turn to Appendix D for the answer.)

A Body for Your Thoughts

Do you think you're physically equipped for clear thinking? Do the foods you eat, the vitamins you take, the amount of sleep you get, and the exercises you do boost or deflate your brainpower?

With this quiz, take stock of how you're physically affecting your mental capabilities and acuities. There are no right answers here; with each question, you'll be exploring an area for yourself that we'll be discussing in the chapter. Your answers will help you highlight physiological aspects that might need nurturing to burnish your clear thinking.

♦ Do you think that your physical health could provide a more enlightened mind for clear thinking?

♦ On an average night, how many hours of sleep do you get?

♦ In what two-hour window do you usually get your best thinking done? (In answering this one, consider your thinking, not your moods. When exactly do you do your most accomplished thinking, and how is that channeled toward dynamic productivity?)

♦ How would you describe your eating habits? Do they consist of meals or snacks? Is your diet balanced or weighted to one particular food group?

♦ Do you know which foods are considered "brain foods"? If so, how often are they a part of your diet?

♦ Do you know the types of foods that are considered brain busters?

♦ What is your exercise regimen? Does it ever include mind-centric activities such as yoga or running?

♦ Have you ever taken herbs or supplements that extol memory-boosting virtues?

♦ Do you know what nootropics are?

Ahhhh ... Sleep!

Recent studies have discovered—and it's hardly a surprise—that sleep can be a great stimulus for problem solving. A 2004 study that appeared in the journal *Nature* advances the idea that sleeping brains keep working on a daily dose of obstacles and creative roadblocks. Scientists at the University of Luebeck provided evidence that slumber does just that—particularly the deep-sleep kind that usually occurs during the first four hours of a night's rest. Those findings further validate other biochemical studies that suggest that during sleep, memories are restructured before being stored as the brain processes and consolidates newly minted learning. In so doing, the brain uses that downtime to become a great sort factory, determining locations for recent thoughts and learnings.

Cobweb Buster

Restful nights have brought some significant artistic and scientific contributions. Among those who have credited a good night's sleep for an act of greatness: Samuel Taylor Coleridge for writing his epic poem *Kubla Khan;* Robert Louis Stevenson for memorable sequences in *The Strange Case of Dr. Jekyll and Mr. Hyde;* Elias Howe for the sewing machine; nineteenth-century chemist Dmitri Mendeleev for the periodic table of elements (which literally came to him in a dream); and Keith Richards's inimitable guitar riff in the Rolling Stones' *I Can't Get No Satisfaction.*

So if you're having lapses in concentration or seem perpetually dogged by muddled thoughts, consider your sleeping habits. A longer nightly ritual may give your thinking some needed—and rejuvenating—rest.

Exercises That Elevate

Although the benefits of exercise are routinely touted, a few merit our discussion here as they've been directly linked to clear thinking. In the following sections, we take a closer look at how yoga, running, and extreme sports can promote clear thinking.

Words from the Wise

Concentration is the secret of strength.

—Ralph Waldo Emerson, American poet, author, and philosopher

Yoga

In looking at the way yoga can benefit clear thinking, we turn to Suzanne McGinnis, a yoga instructor whose practice—doled out in daily sessions at her 8Count Wellness Center in suburban Atlanta—has been featured in *Time* magazine. She's the best person we know to turn to in matters of yoga (and she's also our sister). As a family, we began taking yoga when some of us were still in grammar school. We believe we're physical examples of its positive effects on thinking.

Cobweb Buster

The brain uses around 12 percent of the oxygen people inhale. Therefore, bad breathing habits means less oxygen coming into your body (and your brain) which, in turn, causes mental cloudiness.

Yoga incorporates breathing and balance with stretching and strengthening poses. Although not all types of yoga are strenuous—and there are several types—all require concentration and focus ... also known as, according to McGinnis, a "mindful presence." In fact, a popular yoga adage is "flexible body, flexible mind." We asked McGinnis to fill us in on how yoga provides an oasis for clear thinking to flourish.

Q: How does yoga benefit clear thinking?

A: In yoga, the body and mind are connected. Your cardiovascular, physiological, muscular, skeletal, and psychological systems become one. If you take your yoga practice serious, you'll become more alert, more aware, and more present. You will clear the cobwebs (or to-do lists) of the mind and begin to make healthier, more purposeful decisions for yourself, your career, and your family.

Q: Is there a particular exercise that allows and enlightens clear thinking?

A: One sure way to clearer thinking through yoga is through breathing exercises. In yoga, it's specifically called *ujjayi* breathing. This is an audible, rhythmic, steady and soothing breath. It is done by contracting the whispering muscles in your throat to create a long, thin, strawlike flow of air in and out through the nose. This breath is what connects your mind to your body, and you to the present moment.

A steady flow of oxygen to the lungs also means healthier blood to the vital organs, including the "big one"—the brain. Concentrating on breathing keeps one focused and present. Using breath counting will also keep your mind from wandering. Start with inhaling using ujjayi breathing for five slow seconds. And then exhale for five and increase each time as you feel your lung capacity expand. It's best to do breathing specific exercises in either a cross-legged position such as lotus, or lying down on your back. Breathing is also used to cleanse the body of toxins. Less pollution to the organs will improve their function and lead to a healthier lifestyle. When you feel good physically, you will feel better and think clearer.

Q: What regular yoga regimen would you recommend for clear thinking?

A: Of course, before starting any exercise program, consult your physician. What's good for me may not be enough for you, and vice versa. About 30 minutes twice a week for several weeks is a great start to your yoga practice. When you're ready, increase time and intensity. There are more types of yoga than there are ice cream flavors. There is yoga specifically for strength, for relaxation, for cleansing, and for stretching. Hatha Yoga is the most generic type and great for beginners. There are many different poses and exercises that can get you started. Mountain pose, down dog, child's pose, cobra, sun salutations, cat, and tree pose are commonly used, fairly simple, and will give you a solid foundation for starting your practice.

Any pose held for a number of seconds or minutes, especially balancing poses, will require total mental commitment. For instance, try to stand on one leg while thinking about your grocery list and you are sure to lose your balance. To take advantage of the possibilities yoga can bring to your clearer thinking, check out some DVDs, ask your local gym about classes they may offer, or phone a yoga studio in your area to find out what classes they have.

Running

Many people claim that, after exercise—particularly *aerobic exercise*, such as running—they just seem to think more clearly. And certainly, scientific evidence supports the claim that exercise can do just that.

A 2003 study conducted by an exercise scientist at the University of Georgia, Phillip Tomporowski—who's also a triathlete—culled information from 43 papers published during the past 30 years. The papers researched how exercises affect our performance on various mental tasks.

Think Tank

Aerobic exercise refers to fast-paced activities such as running, walking, and swimming that bring increases in respiration and heart rate. As such, they condition your heart and lungs and have proven positive affects on clear thinking.

In a variety of tests that examined everything from focus and concentration to the speed of responding and decision making, it was found that steady-paced aerobic exercise—such as running—improved the brain's ability to solve problems and make decisions quickly and effectively. After that type of exercise, people could jettison irrelevant information and concentrate much better than before on the matter at hand.

Another study by Marriott, Reilly, and Miles had soccer players run on treadmills for two 45-minute periods with a short break in between. On three separate occasions—before the runs and then after each 45-minute session—the players were shown slides depicting real-life game situations. Each situation needed to be figured out and worked through for winning plays. The panel of experts who analyzed the players' choices during each test interval found that—remarkably—the longer the soccer players had been running, the better they were at decision making and problem solving.

Think Tank

Before starting any exercise program, check with your general practitioner to determine the best fit and range of exercises appropriate for you.

Running also is linked to "runner's high," a feeling of well-being and clarity that exercise can bring on. During extended periods of running (and other exercises such as skiing and cycling), the brain releases elevated levels of endorphins and serotonin. Those chemicals allow for the mind to produce a "clean slate" that can wipe out cobwebs and serve as a launch pad for precise, decisive thoughts.

Extreme Sports

Extreme athletic experiences have been associated with supreme cognitive development and intense clarity. In many of these outdoor sports, the participant is so engrossed in the execution that everything else falls away.

Extreme sports such as surfing, hang-gliding, rock climbing, skydiving, and snowboarding feature a combination of speed, height, and sometimes, stunts. That combination brings some degree of difficulty with it and requires an intense focus that—in its near-term goal—can foster clear thinking in bursts of concentration, perception, and judgment. During the best use of these experiences, you ...

- Are focused solely on the skill at hand.
- Are unaware of your own awareness.
- Are completely in control of actions and reactions.

Further, extreme sports put you in the throes of a short-term goal—be it landing safely on the ground, getting to the bottom of the hill, catching a wave, or reaching a mountaintop. To be on task for that, you're engaging your powers of concentration, perception, judgment, and reasoning. And because of the extreme nature of that task, you're actually amplifying your use of those mental skills and processes in the duration.

A Brainiac's Diet

Can you really eat your way to clear thinking? We like to think so. In fact, the same diet that nutritionists and dieticians tout as being healthful for energy, skin, bones, your vital organs, and a youthful appearance also applies to your brain. You could even follow the advice of a phrase we talked about in Chapter 7: GIGO (garbage in, garbage out). For instance, complex carbohydrates are a must for clear thinking; without them you get groggy. They supply a steady dose of glucose that enhances brain function. Ditto high-protein foods for giving memory and concentration a boost.

> **Mind Fogger**
>
> Not sure how your diet rates? Don't just start throwing brain foods into your grocery cart without a plan. Consult your doctor or a registered dietician. They'll guide you to the best thinking-rich foods specifically for you.

In the category of fats, your brain—to function properly and astutely—craves omega-3 fatty acids; they're found in salmon, soybeans, flaxseed oil, scallops, and walnuts, among other foods. Foods rich in omega-3 fatty acids are a boon to concentration and have even been reported to prevent Alzheimer's. These foods help clearer thinking by increasing blood flow to the brain. However, "The World's Healthiest Foods" website whfoods.org—which is the brainchild of Health Valley Foods founder George Mateljan—reports a troubling U.S. statistic. About 99 percent of the U.S. population doesn't get enough of that good stuff.

A good rule of thumb for brain food is that clean-tasting meals are clear for your thoughts. That means—for starters—veering from "junk" foods; hydrogenated fats; and the bad sugars in sodas, candies, and processed sweets. Avoid overeating and artificial ingredients. And have three square meals—especially breakfast. Studies for the first meal of the day have shown that skipping it leads to poorer problem solving and decreased memory.

The best brain foods include avocado, beans, kale and collards, brown rice, eggs, lean beef, poultry, yogurt, peanuts, citrus fruits, oatmeal, and melons.

Herbs and Supplements to Consider

Several vitamins have a positive effect on increasing learning power, and the nutrients from a balanced diet can help the brain process information more efficiently. The discussion in this section pertains to vitamin supplements and herbs that have been associated with memory, speed of information processing, verbal reasoning, and verbal ability.

"B" a Clear Thinker

A diet rich in B group vitamins may improve your capacity to think and remember. They're found in such foods as leafy green vegetables, dairy products, and whole grains. The B vitamin group has been linked to increased mental alertness, concentration, more effective problem solving, and the ability to successfully think about many things simultaneously. The B vitamins are also known as "stress vitamins" because it's believed that their intake successfully reduces stress. Therefore, they can impact cognitive performance by allowing for clearer thinking.

Choline, also available as a supplement, is a fatlike B vitamin found in eggs. Choline feeds the brain's neurotransmitters which, in turn, can boost alertness. In addition, DMAE (also known as 2-dimethylaminoethanol) is found in anchovies and sardines; it helps increase choline production.

Cobweb Buster

Chew on this: A 2003 study in *New Scientist* magazine found that chewing gum can improve memory. In the experiment, a gum-chewing group scored significantly better than control groups on immediate word recall, delayed word recall, and spatial working memory. The findings mirrored a 2000 Japanese study that found activity increases in the hippocampus (a brain area specifically associated with memory) when people chew. Although explanations for the chewing-memory link so far are speculative, one theory is that chewing increases heart rate, which brings more oxygen to the brain, which improves learning.

Boost Your Recall with Herbs

A few years ago gingko biloba surfaced as a choice herb that could greatly, positively affect memory. In fact, the herb—extracted from gingko biloba tree leaves—has been used extensively in Chinese medicine for several hundred years for such a purpose. In the United States, this herb has even become a popular smoothie staple at juice chains if you're looking for a mental pick-me-up or facing a daunting intellectual task.

To a more recent academic point, a 2003 experiment conducted by researchers at the UCLA Neuropsychiatric Institute found significant improvement in verbal recall among a group taking gingko biloba contrasted with those who took a placebo. In Germany, the herb has been used for years to improve memory and treat Alzheimer's. This herb's benefits are associated with increasing oxygen flow to the brain for improved clarity and performance.

Derived from root plants, panax ginseng is another herb to consider for helping out with memory, brain function, and learning stamina. Although it hasn't received as much attention as gingko biloba, it sometimes is, in fact, used in conjunction with it as a treatment to assist memory.

Just Add Water

Sure, water isn't technically a supplement, but you sure should supplement your diet with it. One of Dr. Ric's favorite health tips is to drink more water; dehydration is a handicap for a thinking brain. Who can concentrate when you're sweating and thirsty? It's common knowledge that about 70 percent of the body is water. Well, the brain is nearly 90 percent water, which is more than any other organ, so put that in your cap (and drink to it)!

> **CAUTION**
>
> **Mind Fogger**
>
> In the cases of all vitamin and herb supplements, fully investigate which (if any) are ones you'd want to take, and consult your physician. If you decide to take them, make sure to buy reputable brands from reputable pharmacies or retailers. And also, since some herbs interact with medications, you've got yet another reason to check with your doctor before making them part of your diet!

Medicine on the Cutting Edge

Can a pill really make you smarter? Our discussion wouldn't be complete without giving you the latest scoop on drugs that have been regarded as having an impact on clear thinking. Although we don't believe that any of them can automatically make you a clearer thinker, you need to know about them to keep your clear thinking above this fray.

The Connection to ADHD, Alzheimer's, and Antidepressants

In the treatment of ADHD (attention deficit hyperactivity disorder), ADD (attention deficit disorder), depression, and Alzheimer's, some drugs have been medically linked to improving thinking *if* a patient suffers from one of those ailments. (However, you wouldn't want to take one of these drugs just to be a clear thinker; they're specifically tied in to the treatment of these diseases.)

For ADHD and ADD, drug treatments include stimulants—such as Ritalin, Adderall, and Cylert—that may work to increase mental alertness. Antidepressants—such as Tofranil, Wellbutrin, and Prozac—may work to treat underlying depression that can cause poor concentration. Further, another category of drugs can decrease over-excitement of the brain that can lead to disorganized thinking. These include Catapres, Tenex, and Strattera. Then for Alzheimer's disease, there are drugs—such as Aricept, Reminyl, and Exelon—that increase the availability of acetyl choline (a brain neurotransmitter that's deficient in the illness).

Antidepressant drugs have also been shown to help some patients with Alzheimer's disease perhaps because coexistent depression and its affect on concentration can contribute to cloudy thinking.

But do understand that none of these preceding drugs can provide you—the healthy person seeking clear thoughts—with a magic potion for sudden, sharp thinking.

Nootropics: Just Say No?

"Better thinking through chemistry" seems to be the tagline ushering in a new and pioneering era of medicine. In this arena, scientists are working to provide substantial mental boosts in tiny pills. And, in so doing, these drugs would promote sharpness and memory without stimulant effects. That's been the bane of such previous "thinking aids" as coffee and No-Doz.

For example, Modafinil has been proven to ramp up both memory and attention as has a compound called HT-0712. Although these are still being tested, others on the market, such as Aniracetam and Piracetam, claim to enhance memory and clarity.

All of those pills point to an array of smart drugs that are coming down the pike in a drug category called *nootropics*. Nootropics is derived from the Greek words for mind (*noos*) and changed (*tropos*). With varying degrees of effectiveness, they work to either increase brain metabolism or cerebral circulation, or protect the brain from physical and chemical damage. In most instances, they're trying to mimic—in concentrated doses—the components or benefits you might receive from eating omega-3 fatty acids or choline.

> **Think Tank**
>
> **Nootropics** refer to an array of "smart drugs," which extol the possibilities of sharpening your thinking skills.

The market has also been flooded with smart drinks and snacks that promote their consumption as literal brain food. However, in most cases, their claims to greatness should be considered minimal.

Points to Ponder

Would you rather have a better brain or better body?

Although we all pine for sustained, sharp minds, getting your mental prowess from a pill hasn't exactly commanded widespread allure. But progress in designing them may steadily ignite a fervor. We may only be a short time away from brain bars that dispense quick fixes to foment concentration for an afternoon budget meeting or your kids' next homework session.

Or, for now, you could just eat better, exercise more, and get sleep when you need it.

The Least You Need to Know

◆ Your body can be a temple for clear thinking.

◆ Sleep has been proven to provide an opportunity for the brain to sort thoughts and—in giving your mind a daily reprieve—actually aid in problem solving.

◆ Yoga, aerobic exercises such as running, and even extreme sports bring proven sharpness, alertness, and mental cognition advantages.

◆ Clear thinking benefits from a diet that is rich in complex carbohydrates, protein, and omega-3 fatty acids and avoids junk sugars and processed foods.

◆ Recent studies suggest that some vitamins, supplements, and herbs—long a staple of Chinese medicine—can enhance your capacity to think and remember.

◆ Certain drugs used in the treatment of Alzheimer's disease and other conditions have had positive side effects on clear thinking for patients, while nootropics (smart pills) most likely have a negligible effect.

On a Clear Mind Day

In This Chapter

- ◆ Appreciate your newfound aptitude for clear thinking
- ◆ Learn about gender differences in clear thinking
- ◆ Rise above minutiae
- ◆ Get some tips for steering out of fuzzy territory and staying clear
- ◆ Give some focusing exercises a try
- ◆ Take in some wisdom for de-fogging

In this chapter, we want you to take stock of the attitude and advantages inherent in clear thinking that have become apparent … and how to maintain clarity even when the fog sets in.

In addition, we want to send you onward into future clear thinking with some choice tips and guidelines for avoiding minutiae, looking at the big picture, and using what you've learned on a daily basis.

Mind Games 19

From the word *discovery*, come up with at least 25 words taking up residence within the word. The rules: no proper nouns or verbs, no slang, and no plurals (wherein you just add the *S* to one of the words you've uncovered).

(Turn to Appendix D for some possibilities.)

I Can See the Big Picture Clearly Now!

As you come to this point, you're well on your way to clear thinking being regularly deployed for optimal reasoning; information gathering; decision making; communicating; problem solving; and other business, school, and home routines.

To assess your clear-thinking proficiency, answer the following "fill-in-the-blank" statements from your newly sharpened point of view:

I regard clear thinking as: _____

_____

_____

I'm a _____(left or right)-brain thinker, but I know ways to engage my _____-brain thinking abilities by: _____

_____

_____

Understanding needs: _____

_____

_____

Learning requires: _____

_____

_____

The qualities of an open mind include: _____

_____

_____

Guidelines for knowing information presented as a fact include: _____

_____

_____

I know I've asked a great question when: _____

_____

_____

Information is available in at least these 10 venues: _____

_____

_____

_____

Canvassing a multitude of those resources is: _____

_____

_____

The difference between thinking and knowing is: _____

_____

_____

The difference between the irrational and the rational is: _____

_____

_____

The difference between subjective and objective is: _____

_____

_____

The problems with hoaxes, urban legends, superstitions, and paranormal beliefs are:

_____

_____

You can attain common sense by: _____

_____

_____

The difference between deductive and inductive reasoning is: _____

_____

_____

You can generate alternatives by: _____

_____

_____

You define a problem by: _____

_____

_____

Two methods to make a decision are: _____

_____

_____

A couple of ways to solve a problem include: _____

_____

_____

The advantages to having a better, more extensive vocabulary are: _____

_____

_____

To transform clear thoughts into spoken words, I need to: _____

_____

_____

To transform clear thinking into the written word, I should: _____

_____

_____

Channeling clear thoughts into creative pursuits requires: _____

_____

_____

I'm a victim of fuzzy thinking when: _____

_____

_____

I'm thinking clearly when I: _____

_____

_____

Cobweb Buster _____

Soft drink company 7 Up's "Think Clear" online campaign sports a game that purports to read your mind. In the game, you think of a number that the 7 Up character claims he can identify. The activity actually plays off a mathematical oddity involving the integers one through 9 that, when added up, are divisible by 9. With a little information from you and the numbers you've selected, they can, in fact, guess the number you've picked. The activity—a kind of gamevertisement—bridges the connection between the soda company's advertising slogan ("Think Clear") and the act of "thinking clearly." The game's at www.digicc.com/fido.

Thoughts and Genders

Part of embracing clear thinking in all your daily activities includes understanding that anyone can be a clear thinker if he or she so desires and puts forward the work required. That being the case, we should never think one gender has some edge over the other for making a better argument, stating a better case, or better solving a problem.

Both sexes sometimes can be faulted with jumping to conclusions about how the opposite gender thinks. Based on stereotypes foisted on men and women, you might peg "better communicator" monikers on women, and "better at reading map" labels on men. But don't be lulled into those snap judgments.

As you learned in Chapter 5, stereotypes are always wrong. In actuality, individual men are better at language than the average for women, and many women have better spatial skills than the average for men.

However, evidence does point to a difference in the brains of men and women. In the physical realm, the corpus callosum—the thick band of nerve fibers connecting the brain's left and right hemispheres—is larger in women. In testing, studies following men and women reading or thinking about words have found that men use their left cerebral hemisphere for processing language, and women use both.

Although the studies aren't definitive that men and women think differently, some evidence suggests that the sexes have different mental strengths. Psychological testing consistently shows that men perform better than women on spatial tasks, such as recognizing 3D objects. Conversely, women do better on tests involving reading, writing, and vocabulary. Still, the results are too small to make sweeping conclusions.

Cobweb Buster

In 1994, a Teen Talk Barbie was introduced that spouted the phrase "Math is hard." Upon the product's launch, Barbie manufacturer Mattel was immediately besieged by complaints regarding sexism and the implication that women were incapable of intelligent thoughts. The imbroglio prompted Mattel to pull the dolls from shelves nationwide. In theory, a similar brouhaha faced the esteemed Harvard University in 2005. President Lawrence Summers made controversial comments that some thought unfairly labeled women as inferior to men in the areas of math and science. In the ensuing outcry, he issued a succession of three apologies for his statements.

Mind over Minutiae

Don't let this happen to you:

A vice president for a Fortune 500 company was at work by 7:30 A.M. and didn't leave each night until after 9 P.M. In charge of a wide breadth of advertising, marketing, and publicity for the company's extensive product line-up, she took her job very seriously. She also had trouble doing her job well.

This was because, although she was certainly committed to the job and definitely an intelligent person, she never could rise above the minutiae that consumed her position—because she allowed it to cloud her thinking. Her days were crammed with tasks that had little to do with the job she was actually hired for. She implemented a confusing, circuitous approval route for ads and press materials that caused them to be so waylaid deadlines were routinely missed. She strategized and then attended interviews between studio executives and the press that she could have easily delegated. She even rewrote underlings' e-mails daily ... after they'd already been distributed!

Do you work with someone similar to this executive? Can you tell how she wasn't thinking clearly?

Mind Your Minutiae—The Warning Signs

Take this quiz to ascertain considerations if you're letting *minutiae*—the little things that can sap energy and time that you need for clear thinking—become a too-frequent visitor to your thoughts:

- Do your business phone calls generally veer into lengthy personal conversations?

- Do you constantly check e-mail as a diversion?

- Do you know you and your co-workers' job responsibilities? If yes, do you delegate appropriately and necessarily? (If no, find out so that you don't overlap duties.)

- Is your sense of accomplishment from finishing a big visionary project bigger than your relief from getting lots of little tasks done?

- Do you feel routinely stuck on your to-do lists or jammed-up midstream during projects?

- Have others you respect suggested that you "micro-manage"?

- If you break down your day, is little time actually devoted to responsibilities or duties that have a long-term advantage or impact?

- Are you almost always under the crunch of a deadline?

- Are you a stickler for details that won't matter much in the long run?

- Have you been accused of missing the *big picture*—an ultimate goal—or suffering from *tunnel vision*—the inconsequential details or aspects that can waylay you?

If you answered yes to most of these questions, you might be a slave to minutiae. That being the case, stop letting your thinking be wound up in it by considering the benefits of keeping minutiae sequestered from your clear thoughts. They're just not good at coexisting.

Think Tank

Buzzwords come and go in the business world, but these are three terms that seem bound to continue resonating in the workplace and at home. **Minutiae** refers to the little things that can clog up our thinking and make us lose sight of the **big picture,** the long-term focus or goal that endeavors and efforts should be directed toward. To be its most effective, getting to the big picture needs to be delineated with snapshots, or steps in an action plan. The evil opposite of the big picture is **tunnel vision,** having a narrowly defined scope that directs needed focus toward time- and brain-draining efforts that bear little consequence.

Stop the (Minutiae) Madness

Now that you've learned the benefits of listening, understanding, reasoning well, decision making, and problem solving, you probably realize more than ever that minutiae is a bane to clear thinking. You have to have vision, and concentrate on the matters that matter, or you'll fall prey to focus-depleting tunnel vision.

Don't be mistaken: rising above minutiae is different from ignoring details. Many times, people seem to be attracted to minutiae because it makes them feel like they're accomplishing tasks. But actually, they're usually only ignoring their true responsibilities. Give your clear thinking the challenge it deserves. Move past the minutiae and on to greater achievements that have more scope and longer-lasting, more beneficial results.

Some methods to mitigate minutiae madness:

◆ Prepare a fresh to-do list each day. Analyze it; what can be best delegated to someone else, and what here truly deserves your thinking?

◆ At the end of each day, analyze your activities. Which ones really mattered for long-term potential?

◆ Which of your daily activities were part of a bigger plan?

◆ If you're frequently under the burdens of deadlines, ask "why?"

◆ Ask yourself "How or what could I have used my thinking for to plot, plan, or solve better that would have made the deadline more manageable?" "Or am I just thriving under the crush of deadlines, thinking that ratcheting up pressure enlivens my thoughts and approaches?"

◆ Don't consume your thoughts and your time with fixing other people's problems, situations, or ideas unless you're working together on a common project.

Off Course? Follow This Map from Fuzzyland

No matter how hard you strive to be a consistently clear thinker, undoubtedly you'll find yourself inexplicably pulled off course once in a while. When that happens, realize that you've gleaned the tips and tools you need to put yourself back in a lighted arena of clear thinking. So in that spirit, let these reminders be your guide. Under each point, we've asked another question that will allow you to fine-tune and enlighten yourself further.

On your takeoff from Fuzzyland, consider these questions:

> **Words from the Wise**
>
> Witness the contents of mind, the visions and sounds, the thoughts, as clouds passing through the vast expanse—the sky—like nature of mind. The rootedness of Being is in emptiness, clarity, and awareness: unborn, unspoilt, stainlessly pure.
>
> —Alex Grey, American artist

- Are you thinking with an open mind that is willing to take in as many helpful elements as possible? In so doing, have you banished stereotypes, assumptions, and conclusions in your consideration?

- Do you have enough information? Have you checked into all the possible resources you had time for, even ones that aren't part of the norm?

- Have you fallen for any information masquerading as fact? Is any of that information unsubstantiated or based on fraudulent facts?

- How well are you listening? Are you fully listening or just hearing?

- Do you understand the matters in play? Are you using sound understanding methods such as role playing and case studies and engaging in active learning?

On your approach into Clearville, consider these questions:

- Have you first put the matter to logical and reasoning scrutiny? For instance, have you ensured your use of common sense, and that logical fallacies aren't a culprit?

- Are you exercising enough flexibility in approaching the situation, problem, or decision? Are you staying regimented in considering the matter at hand? Or are you truly, effectively commingling your left- and right-brain thinking modes?

- Are you asking the right questions? Are they well informed and specific enough?

- Are you articulating the components adequately and accurately? In other words, are you relying on precise words and thoughts to, for example, get a message across, define a problem, or explain options?

- Have you given yourself a reprieve from the situation? Have you set up an incubation period, a time-out that will give your thinking a chance to stretch and refocus?

- Are you drawing on creativity to help you out? Are you using it in brainstorming or to spin out possible alternatives that weren't immediately obvious or available?

Working Toward A-Ha Moments

Getting out of Fuzzyland and into Clearville puts you squarely at the arrival gate of "a-ha moments." And couldn't you just live for these? A-ha moments are those times when your mind opens up for a dawning or epiphany—when clear thinking gives way to the perfect solution or a moment of personal awareness. Perhaps it's a situation or problem that you've been grappling with for days or weeks and the light bulb clicks on. Your thinking illuminates with the perfect solution, decision, or reason.

A-ha moments are your reward for clear thinking. You'll find that the more you're thinking clearly, the more you'll have them. And the best part is you'll discover that they multiply.

Still, even as you get better at achieving a-ha moments, it never hurts to examine how others arrive at them, too. To assist your own clear thinking, check out how others make decisions and form opinions that are especially savvy. If you particularly admire how someone has solved a problem, ask that person about his or her technique. Being as specific as possible in the phrasing, consider such general questions as "What considerations did you make?" "What strategies did you employ?" "Was there a turning point?" "How did you set up the matter at hand?"

Similarly, say you read about a plan that's been proposed, a court ruling that's been decided, or a failing business that's succeeded in a turnaround, and you're particularly interested in the details behind the matter. Investigate the situation further. Ascertain how clear thinking is at work, and how it has succeeded. Using your analyzing and reasoning skills in such a way could help you in getting toward an a-ha moment in the future.

Mind Fogger _____

The brain's billions of neurons connect with one another in complex networks. All physical and mental functioning depends on establishing and maintaining these neuron networks. Basically, sparkly neural pathways become literally engraved in your brain with the continuation of habits and skills being played out. When a person stops performing an activity, the neural networks for the activity fall into disuse and eventually may disappear. In other words, when it comes to thinking, use it or lose it.

Exercises to Stay Focused

Chapter 18 discussed some of the ways physical exercise can help concentration. In addition, naturally, mental exercises are required to foster clear thinking. Although you can check out several books and websites that offer up memory games, the list we've compiled here takes advantage of readily available tools and methods. In each of these exercises, you have the opportunity to strengthen concentration skills through a thinking (wo)man's game or simple analysis.

◆ At a party and don't know many people? Take advantage of the unfamiliarity and see how many names of people you meet you can remember after the event. Try alliteration (Tony with the triangles on his tie), matching descriptions (Debbie with the dimples), or rhymes (Mark said he didn't know where to park).

◆ Grab your local newspaper and work the puzzle page. Or perhaps you have some games around that work the brain muscles: crossword puzzles, jumbles, Scrabble, Boggle, and even card games stretch thinking by rearranging, connecting, reasoning, and concluding.

◆ Reading a book? Test your analytical and comprehension skills by periodically pausing to summarize the main plot points you've just read.

◆ Engage in thinking-person's conversations. Next time a conversation verges on gossip or a rehash of the latest pop-culture rage, switch tracks. Try debating a topical issue (with reason and not emotion), or even consider tackling an issue with someone whose opinion differs from yours. Discuss the ramifications of a politician's decision, or—upon a company's reported poor earnings—think of suggestions you'd give the CEO to improve the business's performance.

◆ You can stretch mental muscles even when the TV's on. Game shows such as *Jeopardy!* and *Who Wants to Be a Millionaire?* provide opportunities for chiming in with answers. But even if you're watching sitcoms, dramas, or your kids' favorite shows, you can think of alternative scenarios, advice for the character, or dream up fresh storylines.

◆ Always taking the same routes for work and errands? Try a different one. And if you're headed somewhere new, map out several ways to get there before deciding on the route you'll take.

◆ Next time you get a million-dollar idea, take it to the next step! Sketch out details. Actually sit down and draft what would make it work and what might be a drawback. Include everything you know right now without further research about making the idea a success. If you're further inclined, draw up a diagram that presents a working structure of it.

◆ Read up on great thinkers and their accomplishments. In addition to those outlined in Chapter 2, several superior mental athletes from the past and present who excelled in varied aspects of clear thinking come to mind: Benjamin Franklin, Thomas Jefferson, Carl Sagan, Dr. Jonas Salk, Eleanor Roosevelt, Alexander Graham Bell, George Lucas, Helen Keller. Each of them present cases for revolutionary thought in groundbreaking achievements that could bring you new insights on your own thinking processes.

Wickedly Clear Wisdom

We've compiled a list of clear-thinking advice that we like to follow. Hopefully, it'll be a help for you to refer to it from time to time should you ever have the need for some answers to the question "How can I be a clearer thinker right now?"

◆ Relax.

◆ Be willing to look at your thoughts (as well as problems, decisions, ideas, etc.) from different angles.

◆ When confronted with a complex issue, idea, or problem, approach it in small steps.

◆ To that end, consider analyzing thought and problems from both—and either—ends of the spectrum of possibilities.

◆ When having difficulty, ask yourself "Am I going to die because of this troublesome issue?"—or some other jarring, perspective-provoking question.

◆ Permit yourself to patiently, adequately muck around in your thoughts for a bit.

◆ Sleep on it!

◆ Always ask yourself, "What's the big picture?" and "Why is this important?" Doing so will prevent you from becoming mired in details or minutiae rather than being focused on the end goal.

◆ Be willing—and brave enough—to gather enough information.

◆ Subscribe to psychologist Alfred Adler's idea to have "the courage to be imperfect."

◆ When faced with similar or routine problems or decisions, be systematic in deciding or resolving them in similar ways. Don't sweat thoughts, time, and resources on the inconsequential.

◆ Make a list; prioritize the optimal choices, solutions, thoughts, decisions, etc.

◆ If the issue brings emotional components, consider your response if you weren't involved in it. Try and think about it as an "outsider."

◆ Think thoughts while running; avoid thoughts while practicing yoga.

◆ Talk to your spouse or trusted friend about issues and ideas that require clear thoughts.

◆ Sleep, eat, work, play (in any order).

Cobweb Buster

To the point of analyzing thoughts from ends of the spectrum of possibilities, consider this example. What is the most efficient shape to build a fence by using the least possible materials? Suppose the area needs to be 100 square feet. On one end of the spectrum of possibilities is creating a really long rectangle, or 100 feet long by 1 foot wide (which equals 100 square feet). However, that configuration requires 202 feet of fence. (Two 100-foot sides, plus two 1-foot sides). On the other end of the spectrum is a really short rectangle (a square), which would be 10 feet by 10 feet (to equal 100 square feet). But that solution would only require 40 feet of fence (four 10-foot sides).

Points to Ponder

What's the worst offender to thinking clearly? How can you get rid of it?

Now you're fully equipped and wise for clear thinking. And even prepared should some cloud cover come your way. Be aware that clear thinking begets clear thinking. Don't take a break from it; thinking is such a significant, time-consuming part of our lives that staying focused brings staggeringly positive, effective repercussions. So think, reason, resolve, and engage, and you'll always be ready for clear (mental) skies ahead!

The Least You Need to Know

◆ To stay on course for clear thinking, draw on all you know and have learned about gathering information, asking questions, reasoning, problem solving, and decision making.

◆ One gender is not more predisposed to clear thinking than the other.

◆ Eliminate the drain of minutiae from your thinking by focusing on the big picture.

◆ De-fog your thoughts by relying on such wisdom as being brave enough to investigate further, being flexible in your approaches, and incorporating sleep and exercise into your processes.

Appendix A

Resources

Books

Baggini, Julian, and Jeremy Stangroom, eds. *Great Thinkers A–Z*. London; New York: Continuum, 2004.

Browne, M. Neil, and Stuart M. Keeley. *Asking the Right Questions: A Guide to Critical Thinking*. Upper Saddle River, N.J.: Pearson Education Inc., 2004.

Gelb, Michael J. *How to Think Like Leonardo da Vinci: Seven Steps to Genius Every Day*. New York: Delacorte Press, 1998.

Goldman, Robert, M.D., D.O., Ph.D., with Ronald Klatz, M.D., D.O., and Lisa Berger. *Brain Fitness: Anti-Aging Strategies for Achieving Super Mind Power*. New York: Doubleday, 1999.

Leviton, Richard. *Brain Builders! A Lifelong Guide to Sharper Thinking, Better Memory, and an Age-Proof Mind*. Paramus, N.J.: Prentice Hall, 1995.

Mautner, Thomas, ed. *The Penguin Dictionary of Philosophy*. New York: Penguin, 2000.

Reber, Arthur S., and Emily S. Reber, eds. *The Penguin Dictionary of Psychology*. New York: Penguin, 2001.

Restak, Richard, M.D. *Mozart's Brain and the Fighter Pilot: Unleashing Your Brain's Potential*. New York: Three Rivers Press, 2001.

Stokes, Philip. *Philosophy: 100 Essential Thinkers*. New York: Enchanted Lion, 2003.

Vos Savant, Marilyn. *The Power of Logical Thinking: Easy Lessons in the Art of Reasoning … and Hard Facts About Its Absence in Our Lives.* New York: St. Martin's Press, 1996.

Weston, Anthony. *A Rulebook for Arguments.* Indianapolis: Hackett Pub. Co., 2001.

Websites

www.austhink.org/critical   Tim Van Gelder's Critical Thinking on the Web provides valuable resources, information, and even tutorials in such areas as argument mapping, fallacies, research, logic, hoaxes, and statistics.

www.braingle.com   In the mood for a mental workout? Here you'll find more than 7,500 brain teasers, riddles, logic problems, and mind puzzles.

www.criticalthinking.org   From the Foundation for Critical Thinking, this voluminous compendium of critical thinking topics is geared toward educators. However, it provides insights and information everyone can appreciate and learn from.

www.datanation.com/fallacies   Stephen's Guide to the Logical Fallacies presents more than 70 logical fallacies and extensively highlights criteria and examples for each one.

www.factcheck.org   An exemplary example of clear thinking. In the blur of political spin, Annenburg Political Fact Check—a "nonpartisan, nonprofit, consumer advocate for voters"—sets the record straight daily on U.S. political players' comments, interviews, news releases, and TV ads with thorough research and concise analysis.

www.philosophypages.com   Targeted to students of philosophy, you'll find helpful tools such as a dictionary of terms, history, and study guide.

www.psychology.org   This Encyclopedia of Psychology website allows you to know more about or delve deeper into practically any area of the subject.

www.refdesk.com   Billing itself as "the single best source for facts," this site could be a one-stop shop for your research. You'll find a plethora of resources on virtually any topic with multiple search engines, links to dictionaries, and other information, and even daily diversions, such as word problems.

www.snopes.com   An ever-burgeoning and extremely comprehensive catalog of urban legends reference pages that also includes details on the latest hoaxes and scams.

www.thinkingmanagers.com   A consistent flow of strategic action articles enliven this site, featuring the creative concepts and principles of Edward de Bono, the founder of lateral thinking, and Robert Heller, a best-selling author on business management.

www.wordsmith.org/awad   Clarity relishes a good vocabulary. Improve yours daily by checking out this website.

Appendix B

Glossary

active learning   The practice of insightfully seeking and acquiring knowledge or skills with the intent to understand and apply them.

aerobic exercise   This refers to fast-paced activities such as running, walking, and swimming that bring increases in respiration and heart rate. As such, they condition your heart and lungs and have proven positive affects on clear thinking.

analogy   A found similarity between two things that seem utterly different. With this likeness revealed, a resemblance or relationship between the things becomes apparent.

argument   Reasoning and evidence that supports your position or claim.

assume   Taking something for granted, or supposing something without proof or warrantable claim.

belief   Your acceptance of a fact, opinion, or assertion as real or true, without immediate personal knowledge; your beliefs can also involve the faith or religion you ascribe to and follow.

big picture   The long-term focus or goal that endeavors and efforts should be directed toward. To be its most effective, getting to the big picture needs to be delineated with snapshots, or steps in an action plan.

brain stem   The part of the brain located at the bottom of the brain; the brain stem controls automatic body functions, such as breathing, heartbeat, and regulation of body temperature.

brainstorming The act of suggesting, devising, or generating creative ideas, techniques, or processes that promote new and effective directions.

burden of proof The person taking on a problem has the burden of proof in solving it, or substantiating his or her position. In some cases, that may include making a case for experts or skeptics that his or her belief has the greater probability of being "right." So he or she has the responsibility to justify, to show, and to confirm.

case Your arguments as a whole.

cerebellum Lying below the back part of the cerebrum, this part of the brain controls balance, posture, and coordination of movement.

cerebrum The main part of the brain where thinking, feeling, and remembering take place; speaking, your intellect, personality, sensory interpretations, motor functions, and the ability to plan and organize are all housed here.

cherry-picking The practice of selecting certain statistics because they suit particular needs, not because of their actual merit.

claim The point you're trying to make.

close-ended questions Questions that can be answered with a yes or no.

common sense Beliefs or propositions that seem to most people to be sound and sensible, with no outside need for esoteric knowledge. They are sometimes developed from study, knowledge, research, and experience.

communicating The exchange and interchange of words, thoughts, messages, and opinions, either oral or written.

consequences The results of a decision that are directly determined by your actions (or lack thereof).

conversation An informal dialogue between two or more people. This dialogue—which is usually familiar rather than formal—allows for the oral interchange of sentiments and observations.

corpus callosum A thick band of fibers bridging the right and left hemispheres of the brain, allowing the two sides to communicate with each other.

criteria The standard or measure of judging; the established rules of the game that you're using to test out an alternative for a decision related to your action plan (or lack thereof).

critical thinking This refers to taking a disciplined approach to gathering information that you will determine is true or false, and then employing reason to make decisions based on your findings.

critique An analysis or assessment of a topic, subject, or piece of work, devoted to detailing both good and bad qualities. *See also* review.

debate To argue for or against; to contend for in words and arguments; to maintain a stance by reasoning.

deductive reasoning A thought process that breaks down parts from a whole.

discern To see, identify, and be aware of a difference or differences; to discriminate or distinguish.

double-entendre An expression with two meanings, one of which is humorous or inappropriate.

ego In psychoanalysis, the ego strikes a balance between the id and the superego. *See also* id, superego, and unconscious.

empiricism A branch of philosophy that advocates the pursuit of knowledge by observation and experiment; it basically contends that you need experience to form true ideas.

ethics The branch of philosophy that examines what is "right" and "wrong," "good" and "bad."

evaluate To rate or appraise, with tendencies geared toward determining whether collected information has met, fallen short of, or exceeded its expectations.

experience The act of making practical acquaintance with something, trying it out personally to determine a firsthand account.

fallacy A logical error; incorrect reasoning built on faulty comparisons, information, or language that collapses under closer scrutiny.

free association The ability to spontaneously relate subjects, even if they don't seem to share anything in common.

free will A philosophical doctrine that advocates the power to choose, and that our behavior involved in choosing is under our own control.

hoax A deliberately deceptive trick or story for mockery or mischief. Hoaxes can sometimes disastrously spin out of misconceptions. *See also* misconception.

homograph   One of two or more words that are spelled alike but have different meanings or pronunciation, such as present (gift) and present (make a presentation). *See also* homonym and homophone.

homonym   One of two or more words that are spelled or pronounced alike but have different meanings, such as arms (body parts) and arms (weapons). Homonym has also become the umbrella term to include homographs and homophones. *See also* homograph and homophone.

homophone   One of two or more words that aren't spelled alike but sound alike, such as hoarse and horse. *See also* homonym and homograph.

id   In psychoanalysis, the id deals with basic needs. *See also* ego, superego, and unconscious.

imply   To explain something without directly expressing it. The sender of the message implies it.

inductive reasoning   A thought process that builds up a whole from parts.

infer   To extract meaning out of that explanation. The receiver of the message infers it.

innuendo   A remark or implication that carries a negative or improper connotation.

irrational thinking   This type of thinking is considered bereft of logic, preposterous, or void of reasoning and understanding.

lateral thinking   A concept that prizes a creative approach to solving problems. Rather than tackling a problem head on with preconceived right-and-wrong answers, you approach it from different angles, employing many methods. The concept was invented and pioneered by Maltese physician Edward de Bono.

learning   The process of gaining knowledge or information; ascertaining inquiry, study or investigation; and acquiring the understanding of a skill, topic, or situation.

listening   The ability to receive, interpret, and respond to verbal messages and other clues such as body language.

logic   The science, and sometimes art, of exact reasoning or pure and formal thought, or of the laws according to which the processes of pure thinking should be conducted; the science and formation and applications of found notions.

malapropism   A grotesque misuse of a word, usually to (unintentionally) humorous effect.

metacognition   Thinking about your thinking.

minutiae   The little things that can clog up our thinking and make us lose sight of the big picture. *See also* big picture.

misconception   An erroneous conclusion, a false opinion or wrong understanding.

monkey mind   If you've got a monkey mind, your thoughts swing wildly, preventing you from concentrating on any single topic.

nootropics   An array of "smart drugs," which extol the possibilities of sharpening your thinking skills.

objective   An outward view "uncontaminated" by opinion or intrinsic thought.

observation   The act of seeing and taking notice.

open-ended questions   Questions that allow for answers that are more descriptive, reveal more details, and, in the end, are more productive.

paradox   A situation or phrase that seems too absurdly incompatible to be true.

passing judgment   The act of making a decision that involves comparison and discrimination in the process of using or acquiring knowledge of values, the relationships of things or people, moral qualities, intellectual concepts, logical propositions, or material facts.

philosophy   The branch of knowledge committed to understanding the tenets of truth, existence, and reality.

problems   In psychology, problems are situations in which some of the components require further investigation.

question   As a verb, the act of asking and examining, allowing for more insights in the course of questions followed by answers.

rational thinking   This type of thinking is sensible and reasonable, and endowed with understanding.

reasoning   Systemically combing through thoughts and considerations offered up that support the determination of an opinion, or present just grounds for a conclusion or action.

research   Diligent inquiry or examination in seeking facts or principles; often the best research will also look for "two sides" to the story or problem being addressed.

review   A form of a critique; a critical examination of a piece of work. *See also* critique.

scam   A hoax that involves bilking others out of money. *See also* hoax.

semantics   The interconnectedness of words, phrases, and sentences that can relay clear—or fuzzy—meanings.

statistics   The collection and classification of certain facts from the analysis and interpretation of data.

subjective   A view derived from one's own consciousness and distinguished from external, impartial observation.

superego   In psychoanalysis, the superego conteracts the id by issuing moral and ethical thoughts. *See also* id, ego, and unconscious.

superstition   An irrational but typically strong belief in the magical effects of certain objects, rituals, or actions and their ability to bring good or bad luck.

surface learning   The practice of collecting words rather than uncovering meanings.

syllogism   The regular, logical form of every argument that implies a conclusion to be drawn.

symptoms   From the Greek word for "occurrence," this refers to instances or changes that cause disorder or distress.

think   Using your mind to consider ideas, make judgments and choices, determine beliefs, imagine, understand, and focus on a subject. To be most effective, thinking requires precision, clarity, creativity, and balance.

tunnel vision   The practice of having a narrowly defined scope that directs needed focus toward time- and brain-draining efforts that bear little consequence.

unconscious   In the realm of Freud and psychoanalysis, unconscious refers to repressed id memories that—if called up and dealt with—can ease a person's mental suffering. *See also* id, superego, and ego.

understand   The ability to effectively and definitively detail, explain, or express something.

understanding   To "get it," such that you can take information and knowledge you've learned and expertly apply it to another situation, or to everyday living.

urban legend   A modern-day folktale passed around that, although appearing true, contains bizarre and even sometimes macabre elements. Also sometimes known as an urban myth.

values   The virtues and principles that you hold in high esteem.

Clear Thinking in Action: Three Case Studies

We know that now that you've got clear thoughts, you're just aching to put them to work. Examples of clear thinking are all around you; you just have to be alert to their possibilities. When you uncover a great case study of your own, analyze it. Find out why it shines as an example and what was involved in the thought processes behind it.

Following are three diverse examples of clear thinking. As different as they are, what do you think they all have in common?

Case Study 1: Too Many Pins, Too Little Time

How often have you been given a task that's absolutely mundane but perfectly necessary—and always takes too much time? Often, you can call on clear thinking to approach a problem in such a way that you employ new-found efficiency and make mincemeat out of it.

In the following example, can you see specific uses for—in particular—reasoning, logic, and common sense?

A woman we'll call Pauline was one of the fashion industry's leading talents in the 1960s. She began her career rather inauspiciously as an assistant in the rug and drapery department at a Tampa department store. Whatever her responsibility and no matter how arcane, Pauline liked to use creative, clear thinking. One assignment was to take inventory of thousands of drapery pins, a task that usually took days to complete. But always up for employing efficiency, Pauline accepted the challenge—however time-consuming—with dignity.

Examining the chore—not to mention the piles of pins—before her, Pauline considered a different way than the tried-and-true. She realized that the count could be considered a mathematical problem, one that would require her "weighing in" with a solution.

She grabbed a scale and some pins, adding enough of the pins to the scale's weight to equal one pound. Once a pound was determined, Pauline grabbed up those pins and counted them, assigning x number of pins to each pound. Having assessed the number of pins per weight, she knew she simply had to figure out how many pounds of pins she had—a much less cumbersome task than counting every one. Doing so, Pauline polished off the inventory in no time flat by weighing instead of counting the rest of the pins.

Case Study 2: Diagnosis Dilemma

Health problems are an area prime for clear thinking. To diagnose and overcome them, you have to recognize that many ailments have similar symptoms and, sometimes, the same illness will be cured with different treatments. Further, the market is flooded with advice, and prescription and over-the-counter drugs. And information on health issues and diseases is widely available … but not always trustworthy.

In even an uncommon ailment, such as the one described here, clear thinking can be the healthy conduit to a cure. Notice the information the doctor gathers—then sifts through—to devise a diagnosis that will bring about a resolution.

In the following example, can you see specific uses for—in particular—questioning, reasoning, generating options, decision making, and problem solving?

A 50-year-old patient we'll call Everett is referred to a hematologist for evaluation of a severe anemia requiring blood transfusions. The patient has been seeing numerous other doctors during the past six months for several symptoms and a steady stream of new health problems, but no "cure" has been successful. During the six months, Everett has lost 30 pounds, suffered from fatigue, fevers, and night sweats. He was recently diagnosed with diabetes, jock itch, a rash on his left hand, mouth ulcers, shortness of breath, hives, diarrhea alternating with constipation, and depression. At this point, he has seen an internist, a gastroenterologist, an endocrinologist, an allergist, and a surgeon, but no etiology (the cause or origin of a disease) has been determined.

Seeing Everett for anemia, the hematologist reviews his lengthy list of problems, initially looking for any unifying diagnoses. Potential ailments include infection and cancer.

However, in examining the symptoms, the striking one that makes the case different and begs further evaluation is the severe anemia. So to delve further into that, the hematologist recommends a bone-marrow biopsy, which reveals a condition called myelopdysplastic syndrome (MDS). MDS is a primary bone-marrow disorder characterized by the ineffective production of bone-marrow elements. The treatment would be bone-marrow transplantation.

Yet the patient's platelet count is elevated, which is unusual for MDS. Therefore, other diagnoses must be considered. Surveying those, the hematologist knows that few conditions cause severe anemia with an elevated platelet count, but they include severe infection and lymphomas. Now he must regard those etiology possibilities. To that end, he orders a computed tomography (CT) scan of the abdomen and pelvis, which reveals a few enlarged lymph nodes. A biopsy of those nodes reveals a rare type of lymphoma called angioimmunoblastic peripheral T-cell lymphoma. To treat it, the doctor has Everett begin chemotherapy, resulting in dramatic improvement of his health and resolution of his symptoms.

Case Study 3: Getting a Leg Up on the Competition

We've all been there: trying to find a job, perhaps a coveted one, and not sure how to make a mark. This example regards coming at that problem from a different angle, and relying on some ingenuity to find resolution.

In the following example, can you see specific uses for—in particular—idea generating, creativity, and problem solving?

New to Hollywood and wide eyed with dreams, a Midwestern writer we'll call Brad was aching to write for a prime-time television show. He wasn't choosy, and was eager to cast a wide net, alerting as many producers as possible to his talent, energy, and willingness to launch his career.

Although some would say Brad was naturally creative, his mind was simply always open to new ideas. Having already tried the traditional routes of distributing his resumé and contacting friends of friends who might know someone, he decided to try a new approach. He knew that his target audience—executive producers of series are the ones who do the hiring of writers and writers' assistants—would prize creativity, ingenuity, a way with words, and determination.

Having conducted a few brainstorm sessions, Brad took a break for a walk, and passed by a clothing store that was going out of business. Their windows were full of undressed mannequins. With the store selling all the fixtures—including the mannequins—he bought several of them for a cheap price. Then using a list he had compiled of sitcom producers around town, he sent each one a box that contained a mannequin arm and a leg with the note, "I'd give an arm and a leg to write for your show." If he didn't hear from one of the producers, he'd follow up with another box. This one contained a mannequin foot with the catchy line, "C'mon … I'm just trying to get a foot in the door."

Several interviews followed, and Brad has enjoyed a healthy writing career in Hollywood, with long-running stints on two hit shows.

Mind Games Answer Key

Mind Games 1 (Chapter 1): White; if all the walls face south, the house is at the North Pole. The bear, therefore, is a polar bear.

Mind Games 2 (Chapter 2): Read between the pages … the money can't be found. Because odd-numbered pages are always on the right side, pages 341 and 342 make up a single page, not a spread that money can be sandwiched into.

Mind Games 3 (Chapter 3): From beginning to the end of a year, each is the first letter of a month with 31 days.

Mind Games 4 (Chapter 4): First, the facts: Each of the three guests paid $9, which totals $27. From that, the manager got his $25 and the bellboy has his $2 "tip." Now let's add it up the right way. The bellboy's $2 should now be either added to the manager's $25, or subtracted from—not added to—the guests' $27.

Mind Games 5 (Chapter 5): A coffin.

Mind Games 6 (Chapter 6): These are the numbers—in order—that follow 3 in the number pi.

Mind Games 7 (Chapter 7): The man had the hiccups (scared out of him).

Mind Games 8 (Chapter 8): The West Coaster is in Mountain Time in an Eastern Oregon city (such as La Grande), while the East Coaster is in a Western Florida city (such as Panama City) and it's daylight-savings changeover day at 1:30 in the morning.

Mind Games 9 (Chapter 9): It won't matter; he'll survive if he takes whatever he's mopping his brow with and applies a tourniquet to his wound.

Mind Games 10 (Chapter 10): The answer is B. Because these answer choices are all cowboy "accessories," you have to narrow down the field. Only the Stetson has a second commonality with the tiara; they both go on the head.

Mind Games 11 (Chapter 11): Each of the words pronounces a letter of the alphabet, but "gee" is the only one that starts with the letter it sounds like.

Mind Games 12 (Chapter 12): Because the B.C./A.D. dating system didn't originate until after the birth of Christ, whoever stamped that vase wouldn't have known to give it the B.C. hanger.

Mind Games 13 (Chapter 13): Use two cuts to slice the cake diagonally, making four large pieces. Then, make one cut through the middle of the cake horizontally, turning each of the four wide-and-tall wedges into wide-and-short ones.

Mind Games 14 (Chapter 14): Annie lives in Minneapolis, Katy's in Salt Lake City, which leaves Bette in St. Petersburg.

Mind Games 15 (Chapter 15): Tease, teas, tees; bore, boar, boor; idol, idle, idyll.

Mind Games 16 (Chapter 16): Examples include Polish, Nice, Herb, Job.

Mind Games 17 (Chapter 17): Ideas could include place under hot plates of food, use in a table centerpiece, hang as a wall decoration, put under a potted plant, use as a paperweight.

Mind Games 18 (Chapter 18): 63. To figure this one out, you need to start backward: The lone typist had 3 cookies (who gave 1 to Madge, and kept 2 for her kids), so the typing pool in total got 30 (3 is one tenth of 30). The typing pool and the third-floor staff in total had 60 (60 was split into the 2 groups). Three were given to the boss, so 60 + 3 = 63.

Mind Games 19 (Chapter 19): Words could include: code, core, cove, cover, coy, cry, cried, disc, disco, dive, diver, dove, dry, dye, is, over, red, ride, rove, rye, score, sir, sire, very, vise, vied.

Index